CiTY·SMaRT™
GUIDEBOOK

Kansas City

Second Edition

Michael J. Flynn
Linda Kephart Flynn

John Muir Publications
Santa Fe, New Mexico

Printed in the United States of America.
Second edition. First printing May 1999.

ISBN: 1-56261-426-6
ISSN: 1092-0765

Editors: Sarah Baldwin, Jane Salodof
Graphics Editors: Jill Metzler, Bunny Wong
Production: Rebecca Cook
Design: Janine Lehmann
Cover Design: Suzanne Rush
Typesetter: Kathleen Sparkes
Map Illustration: Julie Felton
Printer: Publishers Press
Front cover photo: Courtesy of the Convention and Visitors Bureau of Greater Kansas City
Back cover photo: © Aneal F. Vohra/Unicorn—Nelson-Atkins Museum of Art

Distributed to the book trade by
Publishers Group West
Berkeley, California

CONTENTS

MAP CONTENTS

See Kansas City the CiTY·SMART™ Way

The Guide for Kansas City Natives, New Residents, and Visitors

In *City•Smart Guidebook: Kansas City*, local authors Michael J. Flynn
and Linda Kephart Flynn tell it like it is. Residents will learn things they
never knew about their city, new residents will get an insider's view of
their new hometown, and visitors will be guided to the very best Kansas
City has to offer—whether they're on a weekend getaway or staying a
week or more.

Opinionated Recommendations Save You Time and Money

From shopping to nightlife to museums, the authors are opinionated
about what they like and dislike. You'll learn the great and the not-so-
great things about Kansas City's sights, restaurants, and accommodations. So you can decide what's worth your time and what's not, which
hotel is worth the splurge and which is the best choice for budget
travelers.

Easy-to-Use Format Makes Planning Your Trip a Cinch

City•Smart Guidebook: Kansas City is user-friendly—you'll quickly find
exactly what you're looking for. Chapters are organized by travelers'
interests or needs, from Where to Stay and Where to Eat, to Sights and
Attractions, Kids' Stuff, Sports and Recreation, Nightlife, and even Day
Trips from Kansas City.

Includes Maps and Quick Location-Finding Features

Every listing in this book is accompanied by a geographic zone designation (see following pages for zone details) that helps you immediately
find each location. Staying in Johnson County and wondering about
nearby sights and restaurants? Look for the Johnson County label at the
end of listings and you'll know that statue or café is not far away. Or
maybe you're looking for the Nelson-Atkins Museum. Flip to the
Museums and Galleries chapter. Along with its address, you'll see a
Plaza/Westport label, so you'll know just where to find it.

All That and Fun to Read, Too!

Every City•Smart chapter includes fun-to-read (and fun-to-use) tips to
help you get more out of Kansas City, city trivia (did you know Teflon
was invented in Kansas City?), and illuminating sidebars (to learn about
Kansas City's sports stadiums, see page 164). And well-known local residents provide their personal "Top Ten" lists, guiding readers to the
city's best barbecue joints, jazz venues, bike rides, and more.

GREATER KANSAS CITY ZONES

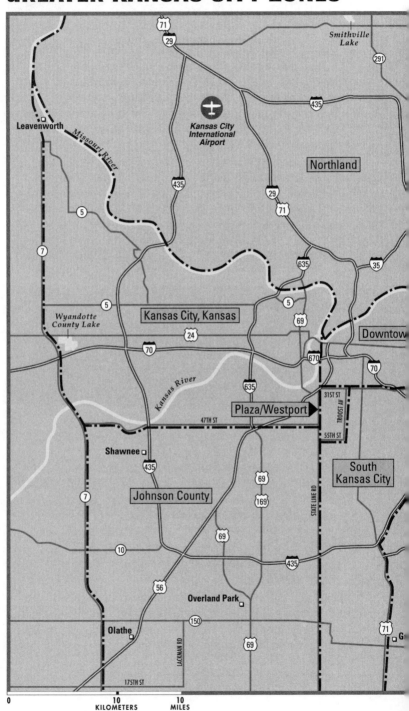

Smithville Lake

Kansas City International Airport

Northland

Leavenworth

Missouri River

Wyandotte County Lake

Kansas City, Kansas

Downtow

Kansas River

Plaza/Westport

31ST ST

TROOST AV

55TH ST

South Kansas City

Shawnee

47TH ST

Johnson County

STATE LINE RD

Overland Park

Olathe

LACKMAN RD

175TH ST

0	10	10
	KILOMETERS	MILES

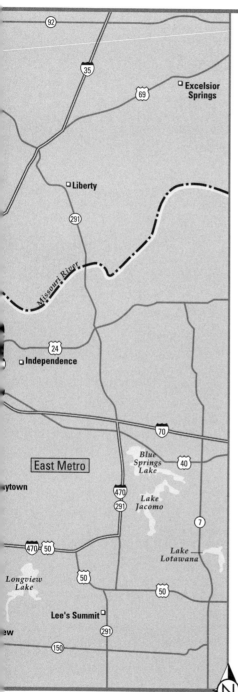

KANSAS CITY ZONES

Downtown (DT)
The area bounded on the north by the Missouri River, on the east by I-435, on the south by 31st Street, and on the west by the Missouri-Kansas state line.

Plaza/Westport (PW)
The area bounded on the north by 31st Street, on the east by Troost Avenue, on the south by 55th Street, and on the west by State Line Road.

South Kansas City (SKC)
The area bounded on the north by 55th Street, on the east by I-435 and 71 Highway, on the south by 175th Street, and on the west by State Line Road.

Johnson County (JC)
The area bounded on the north by County Line Road (47th Street), on the east by State Line Road, on the south by 175th Street, and on the west by K-7.

Kansas City, Kansas (KCK)
The area bounded on the north by the Missouri River, on the east by the Kansas-Missouri state line, on the south by County Line Road (47th Street), and on the west by K-7.

Northland (NL)
The area bounded on the north by Clinton County, on the east by Ray County, on the south by the Missouri River, and on the west by the Missouri River.

East Metro (EM)
The area bounded on the north by the Missouri River, on the east by Ray County, on the south by 175th Street, and on the west by I-435 and 71 Highway (and Troost Avenue from 31st Street to 55th Street).

1

WELCOME TO KANSAS CITY

Who in Europe, or in America for that matter, knows that Kansas City is one of the loveliest cities on earth? And yet it is true. . . . The streets follow the curves of the hills or the winding of streams. Flowering shrubs encircle the houses. The homes themselves, designed in the best of taste, are artfully grouped in an immense park whose trees are unequaled in variety and luxuriance. . . . Few cities have been built with so much regard for beauty.
— André Maurois, *From My Journal,* 1946

A swift current rushes a cottonwood branch downstream, hinting that the river merely sweeps through this broad bend on its hurried way to other places. But this surging, swirling, roiling stream has hugged this precipitous bank longer than humans can remember. The Missouri River is what made Kansas City, and the waters will remain forever entwined in the city's history and its future. Downtown Kansas City rises south of the river. Brick and block, stone and stucco, the modern skyline sits atop bluffs that stand upright as though reaching for a better view of the mighty tide that gave Kansas City life. The city and its sisters spread in all directions, crisscrossing two states in geographical abandon.

Following its waterborne beginnings, the Kansas City metro area has become a sensory delight: boulevards lined with majestic oaks and sweet-smelling sycamores, fountains that sound a welcoming gurgle, and architecture that evokes a sturdy foundation for the ebbs and flows of life. In spring, Kansas Citians emerge to tend their tulips, plant peonies, and transform their city into a multihued garden. Throughout the seasons, the city's boulevards and parks come alive with floral displays, the leaves change tones, and colorful holiday decorations highlight the area's natural beauty.

Ten Best Things About Kansas City, Missouri

by Emanuel Cleaver II, Kansas City mayor 1993–1999

1. **The People:** the friendliest and kindest you'll ever meet.

2. **The Landscape:** rolling hills, tree-shaded parks and boulevards lined with interesting architecture.

3. **The Fountains:** more fountains than any city in the world (except Rome).

4. **The Neighborhoods:** vibrant neighborhoods and neighborhood organizations, such as the Hispanic West Side, the Italian/Asian North End, Hyde Park, Brookside, Blue Hills, Armour Hills, and more.

5. **The Jazz:** America's classic music form grew up in Kansas City and still thrives.

6. **The Food:** more than just the steaks and barbecue for which the city is famous.

7. **The Art:** the Nelson Gallery, Kemper Museum, Art Institute, and a vigorous 1 percent for public art program.

8. **The History:** Harry Truman, Tom Pendergast, Francois Chouteau, Charlie Parker, Count Basie, Jesse and Frank James, Jackie Robinson, Jean Harlow, Buck O'Neil . . .

9. **The Economy:** vibrant and growing, with new corporations such as Harley Davidson and Gateway locating here.

10. **The Future:** a city growing and on the move.

First-time visitors to Kansas City may expect to see a flat prairie, lowing cattle herded through vast stockyards, and dusty roads filled with gangsters. Instead, they're greeted by an unexpectedly craggy topography, a singularly congenial citizenry, and a destination that's filled with surprises aplenty. As a place that's entertained everyone from Hurons to hoodlums, today's Kansas City beckons with a powerful combination of spontaneity and stability, high culture and unpretentious fun.

"Kansas City is one of the best American cities of all," says author David McCullough, who spent 10 years visiting the area to research his Pulitzer Prize–winning book, *Truman*. "It has its own characteristic spirit that's open and friendly and energetic and unpretentious and lively."

Welcome to Kansas City: one of America's best-kept secrets.

Kansas City Landmarks

Late in the last century, civic leaders in Kansas City, Missouri, decided to set their city apart for posterity. A rough and mud-splashed place, Kansas City in its early days was home to dirt streets, boardwalks, and shanty neighborhoods. In the 1890s, visionaries secured more than 2,000 acres throughout the city and set about creating an interlocking park-and-boulevard system.

The planners were so successful that writers often called the area "Paris on the Plains." Partly because of Kansas City's efforts, the City Beautiful movement took hold across the nation in the 1930s. Long after the push had weakened, real estate financier J.C. Nichols kept the philosophy alive by developing additional parkways, importing European fountains, and adding genteel outdoor sculptures. Today Kansas City is often called "the City of Boulevards."

It has also gained a reputation as "the City of Fountains," since more than 200 geysers now decorate the area. There are so many fountains that many assert Kansas City has more spouts than any other metropolis besides Rome (some local boosters claim the Kansas City tally has even surpassed the Italian capital's). Kansas Citians' fondness for sculpture is evident in the countless other pieces that aren't water-related, from gigantic shuttlecocks to majestic lions to a future president on horseback.

No doubt such affinity for public ornamentation led Garrison Keillor (who has staged his popular public radio show, *A Prairie Home Companion*, at the city's Starlight Theatre) to say, "People who think Kansas City is kind of a cow town have not been here, because it's a graceful city, one of the most graceful in America."

Getting to Know the Kansas City Metro Area

Like Kansas City's early settlers, today's visitors can most readily decipher the area by starting at the river's edge. The metro area rests at the confluence of the Missouri and Kansas Rivers, a joining of turbulent and silt-laden currents. Before meeting the Kansas River, the Missouri River forms the Kansas/Missouri state boundary. Shortly after the rivers unite, near downtown, the state line detours southward and the Mighty Mo continues its journey eastward across the state to St. Louis.

One of the Kansas City metro area's greatest challenges comes from that state boundary dividing it. Many American municipalities have experienced urban sprawl, as young families move to newly developing suburbs farther beyond the central core. In Kansas City, that growth often occurs across the Kansas state line, creating competitive groups that argue about lifestyle and municipal priorities—with the ability to keep their tax dollars separate.

As if to highlight a stalwart independence, many neighborhoods in the

Kansas City skyline

past also decided they needed to incorporate. The result is that now you can cross the state line by crossing the street and travel among 11 counties and more than 140 municipalities without leaving the metro area.

North of the Missouri River, the city's rolling, tree-covered landscape eventually settles into prairie, where many neighborhood pockets provide residents with a somewhat more rural way of life. Across the Kansas River, modest Kansas City, Kansas, juts from the bluffs, providing the best—and most under appreciated—views of the grander Kansas City, Missouri, skyline.

Neighborhoods in Kansas City, Missouri

Downtown Kansas City continues to experience a rebirth, as newly renovated lofts and townhouses attract young professionals and others thirsting for the urban scene. In particular, the River Market and Quality Hill neighborhoods have seen a resurgence of interest. In Northeast Kansas City, urban pioneers restoring some of the area's Victorian "painted ladies" mingle with residents who arrived long ago from Italy and more recently from

TRIVIA

Locals usually refer to the Kansas River as the "Kaw." Both names stem from the Kansa Indians, a tribe that formerly inhabited the river region. "Kaw" is said to derive from a Sioux word, *ak'a*, for "south wind."

Vietnam. And in the West Side neighborhood (the area west of downtown), Hispanic culture comes alive in restaurants, shops, and fiestas.

Midtown Kansas City, including the popular Westport area, combines a happening nightclub scene with quaint shops and bistros and some of the area's oldest neighborhoods. New developments throughout the district have regenerated excitement here. Writers and artists have moved into Midtown. African Americans have created a renewal east of Troost. Nearby, the Country Club Plaza was the nation's first shopping district planned for the automobile. Modeled after Seville, Spain, in 1922, the Plaza boasts 12 towers and numerous fountains, statues, and mosaics. Because of the their close proximity, this book combines Westport and the Plaza into one central-city zone.

A number of distinct neighborhoods lie near the Plaza, including Crestwood, Brookside, Armour Hills to the south, and several others adjacent to the Nelson-Atkins Museum of Art. Residents of these vintage 1910 to 1920 homes range from young families to older professionals, from corporate executives to the self-employed. The nearby University of Missouri–Kansas City adds students to the mix as well.

South Kansas City homes are generally newer than their counterparts to the north. Neighborhoods such as Waldo have melded into close communities where residents often hold festivals and gather at local shops and restaurants. Farther south, yards and homes grow larger in neighborhoods such as Red Bridge and Verona Hills. Residents there include families who want to be closer to nearby lakes and shopping malls.

The Northland zone encompasses several smaller towns, such as

A.K.A. Possumtrot, Missouri

Although the first European settlers arrived in Kansas City in the 1820s, the town wouldn't officially bear the name it uses today for another 50 years. Abraham Fonda, a member of the Kansas Town Company—a group of merchants who purchased what is now downtown Kansas City, Missouri, from the Prudhomme family— wanted to name the place "Port Fonda." Others opted for "Possumtrot." Finally they decided to adapt the name of the Kansa Indians, calling their home "the Town of Kansas." Until 1889, however, the town was also referred to as "Westport Landing," "Chouteau's Town," and "Kawsmouth."

Gladstone, Riverside, and Parkville, as well as North Kansas City (a separately incorporated municipality) and Kansas City North (the designation for Kansas City, Missouri, north of the Missouri River). Homes here vary from older dwellings in tree-lined neighborhoods to contemporary designs in upscale developments. The area is convenient for travel: Kansas City International Airport is nearby, 15 miles north of downtown.

East of the city, in the East Metro zone, history-filled Independence is most widely recognized as the home of President Harry S. Truman. A century earlier, Independence was the jumping-off point for the Santa Fe Trail and the destination for Joseph Smith Jr. and his Latter Day Saints movement. Neighborhoods range from the historic to the modern. Residents vary from sixth generation to newly arrived followers of the Reorganized Church of Jesus Christ of Latter Day Saints, whose world headquarters remains in Independence.

Neighborhoods in Kansas

Johnson County comprises at least 15 distinct cities, from Overland Park to Fairway. Mission Hills, one of the oldest, is a neighborhood whose vast yards and lavish homes adorn wooded hills and ravines. Old-money families and corporate chief executives live in this elite environment. Next door, Prairie Village's more modest homes appeal to younger families who want to enroll their children in Shawnee Mission schools. South Johnson County, notably Overland Park, Leawood, and Olathe, has experienced a considerable building boom, as those cities' farms have quickly given way to tony shopping malls and two-story homes.

Kansas City, Kansas, suffers from an unfortunate reputation within the metropolitan area. Aside from the countrified neighborhoods near the Woodlands horse- and dog-racing tracks, much of the city struggles with lower household incomes and higher crime rates. Near downtown KCK, the

Missouri River flood of 1903

Jackson County Historical Society Archives

A Time for Crime

One of Kansas City's most notorious figures, Tom Pendergast parlayed five years on the City Council into a well-oiled machine that controlled local politicians and businesses. For nearly 30 years, Boss Tom reigned over graft, prostitution, gambling, rigged elections, and kickbacks. Pendergast's Riverside Racetrack pulled in millions, his Jefferson Hotel was a den of iniquity, and his Ready-Mix Concrete Company paved the Country Club Plaza's Brush Creek. Some even credit Pendergast with Harry Truman's early political success. Boss Tom was eventually indicted on tax evasion charges; he died days before his probation ended in 1945.

Strawberry Hill neighborhood was settled by Croatian immigrants, whose dedication to church and family has manifested itself in an orderly, if modest, community. Discount stores and salvage resellers abound within KCK's boundaries, evidence of a thriving entrepreneurial spirit. NASCAR promoters plan to build a speedway within city boundaries, which could beef up KCK's economy in years to come.

A Brief History of Kansas City

Long before pioneers arrived with their wagons, dreams, and supplies, the Kansas City area was home to several Native American tribes. The Hopewell Indians occupied a village on what is today called Line Creek, in Platte County, until A.D. 400, when climatic changes forced them to move. Later, between around 800 and 1300, the Mississippian Period Indians built pole houses overlooking the Missouri River in what is now Northeast Kansas City. The region's most widely known Indian tribes—the Kansa, Iowa, Omaha, Osage, and Missouri—all descended from this group.

French explorers were the first Europeans to visit the area, in the early 1700s. Etienne Veniard de Bourgmont, a French soldier of fortune, returned several years after his first visit to establish Fort Orleans in what is now Carroll County. French trappers loved the place's abundance; St. Louis' Chouteau family, in particular, influenced regional settlement by setting up a post for its American Fur Company.

In 1821, William Becknell launched a trading expedition to Santa Fe, New Mexico. The journey proved so successful that the Santa Fe Trail

KANSAS CITY TIME LINE

1670s   The Osage Indians are the predominant tribe in what would become the Kansas City region. By 1825, however, the federal government would forcibly move the tribe to a small area of Kansas, then move it again in 1870 to its present location in Oklahoma.

1713   Etienne Veniard de Bourgmont, the first European to see the Kansas City area, passes it while mapping the Missouri River, believed to be an inland route to the Pacific Ocean.

1804   Meriwether Lewis and William Clark spend three days in the region on their way up the Missouri River to Oregon; they return two years later.

1821   Frenchman Francois Chouteau establishes his American Fur Company trading post on the Missouri River waterfront.

1830   President Andrew Jackson signs the Indian Removal Bill, opening Missouri to mass migration by white settlers.

1838   The Kansas Town Company bids $4,220 for 257 riverfront acres owned by Gabriel Prudhomme, a Canadian killed in a barroom brawl.

1850   Missouri grants a charter to the Town of Kansas. Three years later, it would reincorporate as the City of Kansas.

1869   The Hannibal Bridge is completed, providing the first railroad link to Chicago.

1871   The Kansas City Stockyards open in the West Bottoms.

1880   Newspaper publisher William Rockhill Nelson begins his campaign to revitalize Kansas City.

1893   Kansas City's comprehensive parks-and-boulevard plan is introduced.

1899   The American Royal Livestock Show is founded, furthering Kansas City's growing reputation as an agricultural capital.

1903   The Missouri River floods, leaving more than 20,000 homeless.

1914   Union Station opens to adoring crowds.

1917   Ernest Hemingway gets a job as a reporter for the *Kansas City Star*, but leaves within six months to drive military ambulances in Italy. He would later credit editor Pete Wellington with shaping his trademark writing style.

1921   Liberty Memorial is dedicated to World War I veterans.

1922   J.C. Nichols opens his shopping area, dubbed the Country Club Plaza.

1925   City charter amendments launch the corrupt Pendergast era.

Fifty all-night clubs line 12th Street, offering bootleg whiskey and the beginnings of Kansas City jazz.	**1930**
The Nelson-Atkins Museum of Art opens.	**1933**
Boss Tom Pendergast lands in prison on tax-evasion charges.	**1939**
Aggressive annexation allows the metropolitan area to begin the march outward.	**1940**
Kansas City–based Trans World Airlines shifts from wartime cargo loads to transatlantic passenger service.	**1943**
Harry Truman wins an upset victory for president and announces it at downtown's Hotel Muehlebach.	**1948**
The Missouri River floods again, with devastating results to the lowlands.	**1951**
Chicago businessman Arnold Johnson moves the major league Philadelphia Athletics to Kansas City; they would leave for Oakland in 1967.	**1955**
Streetcars make their last trip. Work begins on the multilaned U.S. Highway 50, which would become Interstate 35.	**1957**
The Dallas Texans professional football team moves to Kansas City, where it becomes the Chiefs. In 1970, the team would win the Super Bowl.	**1963**
Riots erupt after the assassination of Reverend Martin Luther King; six people die.	**1968**
The Royals baseball team arrives in Kansas City as an expansion team.	**1969**
Kansas City International Airport and the twin stadiums of the Harry S. Truman Sports Complex open.	**1972**
The Republican party holds its national convention in Kansas City, nominating Gerald Ford and Bob Dole.	**1976**
The Kansas City Royals win the World Series.	**1985**
The last of Kansas City's stockyards are dismantled.	**1991**
New exhibits at the Kansas City Zoo expand its size and significance; the city enlarges Bartle Hall Convention Center, making it the world's largest contiguous column-free exhibit space.	**1993**
Waterfalls, fountains, and landscaped walkways become part of the Brush Creek Flood Control and Beautification Project near the Plaza; three years later, passenger boats would start cruising the creek.	**1995**

The Standard Theater ca. 1900

became a commercial superhighway. Traders would stock up in Independence, the trail's outfitting headquarters, then embark on 40- to 80-wagon selling ventures. By 1849, Westport, a town founded by John McCoy 10 miles to the west, had become the chief post for equipping Santa Fe Trail expeditions.

Indeed, Westport was initially the area's most desirable development site. But in 1838, 14 businessmen, led by McCoy, formed the Kansas Town Company to bid on riverfront land that rimmed what is now downtown. Taming the limestone cliffs and canyons that carved this area just south of the Missouri River presented massive challenges. Many called the rough settlement "Gully Town."

During the 1860s, Kansas City welcomed countless travelers who arrived by water. In fact, the Missouri River was so popular that some 60 boats regularly made the upriver journey between Kansas City and St. Louis, landing at the Town of Kansas. Passengers then traveled five miles overland to the bustling hub at Westport.

Shortly after the Civil War, cattlemen in the Southwest realized they needed to move their herds closer to the Chicago market for slaughter. Centrally located Kansas City seemed the logical choice for the operation. Businessmen opened the area's stockyards to accommodate the herds. In 1869, town fathers wrested railroad attention from their surrounding competitors by opening the first span across the Missouri River. The Hannibal Bridge cemented Kansas City's importance as a transportation hub.

By 1900, visionaries had transformed Kansas City into a civilized society. Parks and boulevards had been planned and built, and a convention hall opened to host the 1900 Democratic Convention. After the hall burned in April of that year, Kansas Citians determined that they could rebuild it in three months. Their success mobilized the city for future projects and launched what everyone called the "Kansas City Spirit."

During the Twenties and Thirties, Kansas City was home to gangsters and speakeasies, art deco architecture and jazz. With World War II came economic diversification, as manufacturing companies poured into the area. By 1945, Jackson, Wyandotte, and Clay Counties had received 1 percent of every U.S. war dollar.

Through the next two decades, Kansas City began to sprawl in every direction. An ambitious growth plan brought the area north of the river within the city limits. Infrastructure and architectural improvements continued throughout the Sixties and Seventies—and well beyond.

Always proud of their willingness to tear down, build up, and charge ahead, Kansas Citians continue to look for inventive ways to make their town more livable. An expanded convention center that promises to bring new groups to the area, a renewed appreciation for what a vibrant downtown could mean to the city, and a concerted effort to attract new corporate citizens all hold promise for Kansas City's future. Still, the area must resolve its identity confusion, the riverfront remains largely ignored, and the various independent entities will have to forge a unified whole if the city's full potential is to be realized.

Kansas City is well equipped to journey into the twenty-first century. The only question is how far it will go.

The People of Kansas City

As a group, the residents of Kansas City are extraordinarily philanthropic. Volunteering their time, energy, and money ranks high on their lists of

---

Famous Kansas Citians

Oleta Adams	*Jean Harlow*
Robert Altman	*Leroy "Satchel" Paige*
Ed Asner	*Charlie "Yardbird" Parker*
Count Basie	*Ginger Rogers*
Wallace Beery	*Russell and Clara Stover*
Thomas Hart Benton	*Calvin Trillin*
Joan Crawford	*Harry S. Truman*
Walt Disney	*Dee Wallace*

---

priorities. This may stem from an inherently friendly Midwestern ethic, but it also signals residents' long-term commitment to their hometown. Although Kansas Citians heartily welcome newcomers, much of the population was born and remains in the area.

The Kansas City area's population totals about 1.6 million people, 450,000 of them living in Kansas City, Missouri. Ethnic groups are numerous and long entrenched. Kansas City's Latino community, for example, originated during the opening of the Santa Fe Trail. A large Irish contingent arose when laborers came to build a Catholic church in 1857. Croatians, Serbians, Russians, Greeks, and Slovakians followed in the late 1800s to work in the growing meat-packing industry.

African Americans represent the area's largest minority. Two weekly newspapers, the *Kansas City Globe* and *Kansas City Call*, are produced for the black community, and KPRS-FM and KPRT-AM are highly respected black-owned radio stations. African Americans live throughout greater Kansas City, although a large percentage reside east of Troost Avenue and in Kansas City, Kansas.

The Hispanic population also has its own newspaper, *Dos Mundos*, and is increasingly active in restoring neighborhoods and supporting small businesses. Many Latino residents live in the West Side community near downtown and in Kansas City, Kansas. Businesses owned by Hispanics and African Americans often belong to their respective chambers of commerce.

In addition, the metro area has a sizable Jewish population. The *Kansas City Jewish Chronicle* delivers weekly news to the community, and the Jewish Community Center actively promotes metrowide programs, fes-

Neptune fountain, one of over 200 fountains in Kansas City

Convention and Visitors Bureau of Greater Kansas City

tivals, and civic awards. Like other ethnic groups, Jews reside throughout the metro area, though a majority live in Johnson County.

When to Visit

Like many other places that boast four distinct seasons, Kansas City attracts more attention during the year's warmer months. Spring through fall, a host of events tempt people outdoors to celebrate together.

Every municipality and community group devises its own methods of revelry. The Lenexa Spinach Festival, for example, culminates in building the world's largest spinach salad; the 18th & Vine Heritage Festival features a weekend of free concerts; and Fiesta Hispaña celebrates Kansas City's Latino culture. Even neighborhoods get into the act with historic-homes tours and subdivision open houses that welcome the town. Weekends are packed with options throughout the greater metro area.

Spring is particularly enchanting in Kansas City. Trees and flowers wake from their winter's nap. Fountains gurgle to life. It's a time when walkers stroll their favorite parks, runners gear up for weekly races, and spring showers prepare the city for summer.

Anyone with the good fortune to be in Kansas City during autumn will find a resplendent scene at every turn. The area's oaks, maples, and elms put on a foliage show that rivals those to the east. Before the air turns crisp, the Kansas City Chiefs kick off their National Football League season, while major-league baseball's Kansas City Royals wrap theirs up. In fall, the area's two sports stadiums become a metrowide magnet, luring crowds of 80,000 to the games. Kansas City's other sports teams—playing soccer, hockey, and team tennis—also draw sizable crowds throughout their respective seasons.

Winter arrives in December—or is it November, or January? In Kansas City, it's sometimes difficult to determine. Many residents consider the Plaza Lighting Ceremony the official transition, since the Thanksgiving-night event heralds the holiday season. Throughout December, historic homes welcome visitors for candlelit tours, tree-lighting rituals lure thousands, and oratorios enthrall music lovers. Winter also offers opportunities to enjoy opera, chamber music, ballet, and repertory theater.

Calendar of Events

JANUARY
Kansas City Blades professional ice hockey, Kemper Arena

FEBRUARY
Flower, Lawn & Garden Show, Bartle Hall, downtown Kansas City
Ice Carving Competition, Country Club Plaza

MARCH
St. Patrick's Day Parade, downtown Kansas City
Annual Gem & Mineral Show, North Kansas City

APRIL
Kansas City Royals' opening day, Kansas City
Michael Forbes Trolley Run, Country Club Plaza

MAY
Southwest Boulevard Cinco de Mayo Celebration, Kansas City
Truman Week, Independence

JUNE
Heart of America Shakespeare Festival, Southmoreland Park
Kansas City International Jazz Festival, Crown Center

JULY
Kansas City Blues & Jazz Festival, Penn Valley Park
Wyandotte County Fair

AUGUST
Taste the World Ethnic Enrichment Festival, Swope Park
Kansas City Spirit Festival, Penn Valley Park
Santa-Cali-Gon Days Festival, Independence

Kansas City Weather

	Average Daily High Temps (°F)	Average Daily Low Temps (°F)	Average Monthly Precipitation (inches)
January	34.7	16.7	1.1
February	40.6	21.8	1.2
March	52.8	32.6	2.8
April	65.1	43.8	3.0
May	74.3	53.9	5.5
June	83.3	63.1	4.1
July	88.7	68.2	3.8
August	86.4	65.7	4.1
September	78.1	56.9	4.9
October	67.5	45.7	3.6
November	53.2	33.6	1.9
December	38.8	21.9	1.6

Best Views in Kansas City

Lewis & Clark Point *(8th and Jefferson). Views of the Missouri and Kansas Rivers; Kansas City Downtown Airport; Kansas City, Kansas; and North Kansas City.*

City Hall Observation Deck *(414 E. 12th St.). Thirty-story views of downtown in all directions from this 1930s-era art deco building.*

Liberty Memorial *(Penn Valley Park). Although the World War I tower is closed for renovation, the lookout nearby provides encompassing downtown views.*

Skies Restaurant *(Hyatt Regency Crown Center). Downtown views from the 42nd floor's revolving restaurant.*

Ritz-Carlton Kansas City Elevator *(401 Ward Pkwy.). A glass-enclosed elevator ride provides views of the Country Club Plaza.*

SEPTEMBER
Renaissance Festival, Bonner Springs
Plaza Art Fair, Country Club Plaza
Spirit Festival, Liberty Memorial
The NFL's Kansas City Chiefs season begins, Arrowhead Stadium

OCTOBER
American Royal Barbecue Contest, Parade, and Rodeo
Octoberfest, Lee's Summit; Kansas City Marathon, Country Club Plaza

NOVEMBER
Plaza Lighting Ceremony, Thanksgiving night
Presentation of Handel's *Messiah*, RLDS Auditorium, Independence

DECEMBER
A Christmas Carol, Missouri Repertory Theatre

About the Weather

Weather is a constant topic of conversation in Kansas City, partly because of its mercurial nature. A day might bring sunshine, rain, snow, or all three.

TRIVIA

What was invented in Kansas City? Teflon, McDonald's Happy Meals, Eskimo Pies, Rival Crock Pots, the melt-in-your-mouth-not-in-your-hands M&M candy coating, the jazz jam session, Wishbone salad dressing, the multiscreen theater concept, wax-coated ice cream containers, and the swing sound in jazz music.

Weeks of sweltering heat convince residents it's going to be a long, hot summer, until the morning they awake to a 60-degree rain. Winters bring piles of snow—or mild temperatures perfect for prolonged walks outdoors.

Dressing in Kansas City

Overall, Kansas City is a fairly casual town that allows plenty of leeway for individual expression. While men might feel more comfortable wearing suits and ties to many evening functions—and women, cocktail dresses—no one would look askance if the outfit varied. Jeans are becoming increasingly common even at once-dressy affairs such as the opera and the symphony. Business attire generally means jackets and ties for men, except on Fridays, when most companies embrace casual days.

Winter visitors should plan on bringing coats, hats, and boots; even spring and fall can sometimes turn chilly. In the summer, plan on short sleeves and sandals.

Business and Economy

People sometimes call Kansas City a cow town, perhaps a vestige of its prolific beef-producing past. Throughout its history, however, the region has been buffered from economic swings by a fairly diverse industrial base. Manufacturers, transportation companies, banks, health-care operators, and service providers call Kansas City home. Greater Kansas City is the second-largest rail center in the country, the top inland foreign-trade-zone space, and the largest frozen-food storage and distribution location. And Kansas City hasn't forgotten its agricultural heritage: The area still headquarters the nation's largest farm cooperative, Farmland Industries.

In addition, the area has initiated an aggressive strategy for doing business electronically. Perhaps inspired by hometown Sprint Corporation, the city has installed state-of-the-art communication systems downtown and north of the river. The efforts have lured high-profile companies that include Gateway, Citicorp Credit Services, and EDS Global Travel Services.

Sprint also represents one of Kansas City's largest employers. Others include Ford Motor Company, AT&T, Trans World Airlines, Health Midwest, Hallmark Cards, University of Kansas Medical Center, Southwestern Bell Telephone, and the federal and state governments.

As Johnson County's resident population has grown, so have its corporate players multiplied. Overland Park, in particular, has launched energetic efforts to attract companies. Organizations such as Yellow Corporation, La Petite Academy, American Teleconferencing Services, and International Tours and Cruises are headquartered in Johnson County.

Taxes

Comparing taxes from town to city and state to state can be a confusing proposition. In general terms, Kansas residents pay a maximum individual income tax rate of 6.45 percent, while Missouri residents pay 6 percent maximum. The city of Kansas City, Missouri, however, imposes a 1 percent tax on salaries, wages, and commissions earned by anyone who lives or works within its limits. Kansas residential real estate is taxed at 11.5 percent of appraised market value, while Missouri assesses real estate at 19 percent of true value. Of course, each community can assess its own levies for street improvements, public parks, and so on. Various temporary sales taxes are used to fund civic projects such as the renovation of Liberty Memorial.

Cost of Living

Kansas City is an affordable place to live. Homes are priced well below the national average, while staples such as bread and milk cost less, too. In a survey of 18 comparably sized cities, conducted by the American Chamber of Commerce Researchers Association, Kansas City's costs ranked lowest in groceries and health care. Prices for housing, utilities, transportation, and miscellaneous goods and services were also all below the national

---

Major Companies Based in Kansas City

AMC Entertainment

American Century Mutual Funds

Andrews McMeel Universal

Applebee's

Black & Veatch

Cerner Corp.

H&R Block

Hallmark

Lee Apparel Company

Russell Stover Candies

Sprint Corp.

Yellow Freight

---

average. For comparison, here's a list of prices for a random selection of goods and services in the Kansas City area:

Five-mile taxi ride: $7.50
Average dinner for two: $20
Daily newspaper: 50 cents
Hotel, double room: $71
Standard movie admission: $5.75
Gallon of gas: 85 cents
Gallon of milk: $2.25

Housing

Because the Kansas City area is so diverse, home prices range from $25,000 for a ragged-but-livable two-story house near downtown to $4 million or more for a Mission Hills mansion with acreage and a swimming pool.

The median price for the area in 1997, however, was $106,800, according to the National Association of Realtors. This compares with a national median of $124,100. In fact, the area is consistently rated among the most affordable large metro-area housing markets.

Kansas City Schools

New residents often target neighborhoods according to available schools. But it's daunting research considering that the metropolitan area contains 72 school districts, with more than 20,000 faculty members in 600 schools serving nearly 300,000 students.

In Johnson County, the Shawnee Mission and Blue Valley school districts represent a move-in magnet for many inbound. Others prefer the districts in small-town communities such as Parkville or Independence.

Until recently, the metro area's largest district was involved in one of the country's greatest desegregation endeavors. Starting in 1986, the Kansas City, Missouri, school district spent $1.8 billion trying to improve urban education, including the construction of 15 new schools. With the withdrawal of the massive federal spending that supported desegregation, the KCMO district is working hard to improve the system.

Some parents elect to have their children attend one of the many private schools available. Many are affiliated with religious institutions; others are nonsectarian. Among the most prestigious secondary schools are Pembroke Hill School, Rockhurst High School (for boys), and St. Theresa's Academy (for girls).

Higher-education options abound. The University of Missouri at Kansas City and the University of Kansas Medical Center, the Keller Graduate School of Management, four-year colleges such as Avila College and the Kansas City Art Institute, and five community colleges provide a range of degrees. In addition, professional schools in chiropractic, osteopathy, and dentistry give students further educational options.

Convention and Visitors Bureau of Greater Kansas City

2

GETTING AROUND KANSAS CITY

When calculating the size of Kansas City's metropolitan area, city officials differ on just what to include. Some claim the territory covers more than 6,000 square miles in 13 counties. Others say it's closer to 4,500 square miles in 11 counties. Still others focus on much narrower parameters, considering cities isolated by significant stretches of countryside as distant suburbs or neighboring towns, not part of the metropolitan whole.

It's little wonder: On maps, the Kansas City area resembles Swiss cheese. Raytown, for example, lies surrounded by Kansas City, Missouri. Above the Missouri River, Gladstone cuts a similar doughnut hole in the Northland. Bits and pieces of municipal management pop up throughout the area, creating a hodgepodge of "local" civic pride.

Practically speaking, the sheer size of the greater metropolitan area makes it a challenge to travel extensively in anything other than an automobile. No bus system covers the entire region, which means that riders who want to travel from one side of the metropolis to the other often must negotiate transfers both in routes and transportation companies.

Kansas City Layout

Streets

In Kansas City, Missouri, and much of Johnson County, streets follow a fairly predictable grid system. Numbered streets, which travel east to west, start at the Missouri River and are numbered successively both north and south, going as high as about 100th Street to the north and 175th Street to the south. Often, numbered streets are followed by the same-numbered terrace immediately adjacent (one street to the south below the

State Line Monikers

Kansas City residents often find it frustrating to live in a city divided by a state line. Occasionally they even discuss changing the boundary name—State Line Road—to make the division less noticeable. Among the "most creative" ideas:

Interstate Avenue	*United Cities Road*
MoKan Road	*Hands Across the Border Street*
Harmony Lane	*Rancor Road*
Our Road	*Bitterness Boulevard*
Date Line Road	*Eat Dirt Street*

river, to the north above). For example, 55th Terrace is one street south of 55th Street when you're south of the river.

Main Street is the major east-west divider south of the Missouri River; addresses begin with 0 at Main and ascend in both easterly and westerly directions (1400 E. 44th Street, for example, lies 14 blocks east of Main). Blocks for north-south streets correspond to the numbered cross streets. For example, 5806 Main lies between 58th and 59th Streets. North of the Missouri River, streets follow the same basic format, with the addition of an "N." following the number. Therefore, 5800 NW 86th Street indicates the address is north of the river and west of Main Street.

Of course, exceptions exist throughout the area. Starting with J.C. Nichols, many local developers favored roadways that follow the irregular contours of the land. Streets in Mission Hills, for example, wander with conspicuous abandon. Many areas throughout Johnson County and the Northland, in particular, were developed as cul-de-sac havens to promote neighborliness and to reduce pass-through traffic. Independence streets tend to follow a pattern of their own, although several numbered east-west Kansas City streets extend through the area and can provide reference points.

Major Arteries
A booming development era took place in the decades following World War II, creating an explosive expansion of Kansas City's borders. At the same time, city fathers lobbied for—and received—massive federal funds to build the highways that would support a growing population and the region's increasing role as a transportation hub. Today Kansas City has more highway miles per capita than any other major American city.

When telephoning the Kansas side of Kansas City's metro area, including Kansas City, Kansas, and all Johnson County communities, the area code is 913. On the Missouri side, including north of the Missouri River and Independence, it's 816. When you're in the region, however, it's not necessary to use an area code.

Three interstate freeways serve the area: I-70 traveling east-west; I-35, northeast-southwest; and I-29, which heads north from Kansas City. Interstate 435 circles the region, then connects with I-470 and Highway 291 to pass through Lee's Summit and Independence. In addition, two more interstate linkages serve the area, and 10 federal highways provide easy access around greater Kansas City.

Public Transportation

Bus Systems

Kansas City, Missouri's bus service, the Metro, serves Jackson County and parts of Kansas City, Kansas, with a fleet of full-size buses. Several routes start as early as 4 a.m., with the last scheduled run completed soon after midnight. The Metro offers an array of route maps and service information, obtainable aboard buses, in public libraries, within hotels, and from the Metro's main terminal at 1200 E. 18th Street.

Fares depend on the routes and zones traveled. Generally, routes within Jackson County cost 90 cents. Travel in Kansas City, Kansas, costs $1 and Independence routes, $1.20. Seniors 65 and older, children to age 18, and disabled riders pay half. Monthly passes are available. Bus patrons can request free transfers within a zone; intraroute transfers require payment of the fare balance. For example, those traveling in Jackson County pay 90 cents upon boarding, then another 30 cents to complete a ride that ends in Independence. Exact change is required.

Call the Metro Information Center for routes, map, and service details, Monday through Friday 6 a.m. to 7 p.m., Saturday 7:30 to 6:15, at 816/221-0660.

Johnson County Transit offers a Monday through Friday commuter service between Johnson County and downtown Kansas City, Missouri. Hours are from 6 to 9 a.m. and 2:30 to 7 p.m. Riders may get off the buses at intermediate stops along the route. Short feeder-route fares within the system cost $1, regular routes are $1.25, and the full trip to downtown, $1.75. Discounts are available for seniors, students, and those with disabilities. Call Johnson County Transit at 913/541-8450 for information; the Metro Information Center for Kansas City's bus line also can provide most information about this service. Johnson Country Transit offers bicycle racks on its buses—it's the only metropolitan bus service to do so.

Kansas City, Kansas, and other portions of Wyandotte County are served Monday through Friday by The Bus. This regular service travels nine routes starting intermittently from 5:30 to 6:30 a.m. and ending by 7:30 p.m. The flat fare is $1; seniors, youths 12 to 18, and those with disabilities ride for 50 cents. The Metro's monthly passes and transfers are accepted; bus tokens are not. Route information is available from The Bus' main office in the Kansas City, Kansas, City Hall, 701 N. 7th St., Room 504, 913/551-0480, or on any Bus.

Taxicab Service

Taking a taxi in the greater Kansas City area is simple—if you call in advance. Telephone requests provide fast, efficient driver response from a large number of competing companies, which offer everything from standard cabs to limousines.

Kansas City regulates fares for standard routes by city ordinance. The flat fee between Kansas City International Airport (KCI) and downtown is $26. From KCI to the Country Club Plaza the fare is $32. A typical driver starts off with $1.50 on the meter and charges $1.20 for each mile thereafter. Up to five passengers ride for the same price; luggage is free.

Among the area's largest taxicab services are Yellow Cab Company, 816/471-5000; Kaycee Cab Inc., 913/677-0444; and KCI Airport Limousine & Livery, 816/454-1500.

Kansas City Trolley

Anyone who believes the fun of arriving is getting there in style will want to try the Kansas City Trolley. This fleet of turn-of-the-century-styled trolleys provides one of the area's unique conveyances. The 35-passenger, open-sided trolleys, with brass handrails and varnished woodwork, travel a 90-minute loop between the River Market and the Country Club Plaza, stopping at 20 locations including Crown Center, Westport, hotels, and cultural attractions. Removable rain curtains keep the colorful carriages running in inclement weather. Drivers narrate the trip, pointing out sites and mentioning local events of interest.

Trolley tickets are $9 for adults, $6 for children 6 to 12, and free for kids   under 6. Fares include the option to reboard the trolleys up to three times on the day of purchase. Trolleys pick up at major stops about every 30 minutes, Monday through Saturday from 10 to 6 and Sunday noon to 6. Route brochures and tickets are available at most hotels, attractions, and merchant associations. Call 816/221-3399 for information.

Plaza Carriages

In New York, travelers ride horse-drawn carriages around Central Park. In Kansas City, they can take equestrian-powered spins through the Country Club Plaza. These leisurely rides treat passengers to views of Spanish architecture, public sculpture, and splashing fountains. The one-horsepower rigs move at a genteel pace that seems to stretch the 25-minute tour. No one is sure just how many nervous suitors have proposed marriage from the rolling carriages, but romance seems hitched to this means of transport.

Several companies offer carriage rides. Hours vary with the season but are generally between early evening and 10 or 11 p.m. Lap robes and narrated tours, if requested, are available from the drivers. Fares start at about $25 for two adults, or $10 for adults and $5 for children younger than 10 in larger parties. One operator, Pride of Kansas City Carriages, on the Plaza, can accommodate from 2 to 15 passengers per trip. Tours longer than 25 minutes may be arranged. Call Pride of Kansas City at 816/531-1999.

That's Heartland, Not Heart Attack

Built in the late 1870s, Kansas City's original train station, Union Depot, was situated at the foot of steep cliffs below downtown. Known as the West Bottoms, the neighborhood was notorious for its gambling halls, pawnshops, tacky hotels, and saloons.

Train passengers exited the area via the 9th Street Incline, an elevated track built in 1885 by streetcar owner Robert Gillham, who wanted to bring a piece of San Francisco to the Heartland. Gillham's ride was breathtaking, both because the supports looked so rattletrap and because the trip occurred at a rapid, exceedingly sharp angle. In addition, the cable car brakes were none too reliable, sometimes causing the cars to jump the track.

Driving in Kansas City

Kansas Citians have a local reputation as notoriously bad drivers, although many would apply the designation to everyone on the road but themselves. Residents forget to signal, speed up when approaching a yellow light, and honk when someone violates their space. Put them behind the wheel of a car and, most residents will admit, their generally friendly natures take a hike.

So here are some tips when driving in this otherwise pleasant hamlet: Remain alert for drivers who may not be paying attention. At intersections, don't punch the accelerator at the first sign of a green light. Never believe that an oncoming driver won't make a left turn in front of you just because his signal isn't on. Honking occurs most often when you've decided to enter a street and an approaching driver thinks you've come too close.

Parking Tips

Downtown Kansas City parking is at a premium. In mid-1998, the City Council raised the street parking rate to 75 cents an hour—the first raise since the 1980s. Parking garages charge about $2.75 a day. The largest lots

---

Cruising the Muddy Mo

In the 1850s, the Missouri River was the Route 66 of the steamboat era. Waterborne traffic proved so frenetic that boats often lined the banks waiting to unload at local landings. Passenger service was widespread; those in first-class accommodations paid $25 for the three-day voyage from St. Louis.

Aboard these luxurious paddlewheelers, travelers enjoyed elegant dining rooms, ornate bars, and exquisite cuisine. Cabins were richly furnished and carpeted. Often a house orchestra entertained. Residents in each port flocked to the docks when a steamboat arrived, and greeting parties were a common occurrence.

The Mighty Mo was a treacherous waterway, however, and many steamboats failed to reach port. Numerous vessels sank in the Missouri's dangerous bends, several near Kansas City. Although loss of life was minimal in these disasters, cargo was rarely recovered.

The Kansas City Trolley gets you around town in style.

are at the Municipal Auditorium and Bartle Hall. The River Market has several ample lots, which are most crowded on weekends.

The Country Club Plaza boasts free parking throughout the area. The only trick is to find the lots, which are often underground or on rooftops. Look for signs. Street parking is also free.

Throughout the rest of the metro area, except for the free parking at major shopping malls and residential streets, meters rule. Always carry quarters.

Biking in Kansas City

Kansas City is a wonderful biking town, with wide streets, plenty of traffic-free side streets, and a wealth of fellow cyclists from whom to seek advice. The problem is a distinct scarcity of designated bicycle lanes for a metropolitan area of this size. City planners and taxpayers, it seems, have yet to embrace two-wheel travel with the same enthusiasm as their counterparts in, say, Denver or Seattle.

Nevertheless, biking provides a satisfying way of seeing more of the region than can commonly be caught from a car seat. Kansas City drivers, despite the challenges they present to their fellow four-wheelers (see above), are generally friendly and accepting of cyclists. Exceptions exist, however, and every local rider has a favorite near-miss story. Successful city riders follow all motor traffic rules and precautions, give way when prudent, and ride as though they're invisible to drivers.

Biking advice and companionship abound in Kansas City. In partic-

Ten Favorite Bike Rides in the Kansas City Metro Area

by Bill Crawford, past president and board member of the Johnson County Bicycle Club

1. **Eye Care to Ride to the Lake Ride**—a 40-mile moderately paced scenic ride from the Eye Care parking lot on the southeast corner of 117th and Roe to Longview Lake.

2. **Mike Olin's LETTUCE (Lower Exurbia Tour to Unveil Country Estates) Ride**—a 38-mile moderate ride from Heritage Park marina at 160th and Pflumm.

3. **Les' Fat Tire Ride**—a 40-mile easy-paced ride on mostly gravel roads from the Shawnee Mission Park observation tower to DeSoto.

4. **Andy's Weston Ride**—a monthly 57-mile fast and hilly ride from the Wyandotte County Lake Park ranger station through Leavenworth to Weston for breakfast.

5. **Margretta's Fire Station Ride**—a 40-mile moderate ride during which you can count five fire stations, starting behind the Hy-Vee at Shawnee Mission Parkway and Pflumm.

6. **Stone Canyon Pizza Ride**—a 10- to 40-mile moderate monthly tour of Platte County; begins at the Parkville City Market parking lot and finishes with a full meal at Stone Canyon Pizza.

7. **JCBC Pedal & Pizza Welcome Ride**—a 12.5-mile weekly, easy-paced ride, especially for new riders (guaranteed not to be left behind) from behind the QuikTrip at College and Pflumm, with pizza to follow.

8. **JCBC Spring Classic**—33-, 48-, or 72-mile annual April tour of Bonner Springs, DeSoto, and Gardner starting from the southwest corner of 95th and Loiret (just east of I-435); sag support included.

9. **JCBC Lone Star Century**—30-, 50-, or 100-mile annual late May supported ride from Olathe's Oregon Trails Park (west of Parker on Dennis) to Clinton and Lone Star Lakes southwest of Lawrence.

10. **Waid's Ride**—All speeds Saturday Show & Go from Waid's Restaurant in the Prairie Village Shopping Center (7 a.m. June–Aug; 8 a.m. Sept–Nov and Mar–May; 9 a.m. Dec–Feb), with regular 25- to 60-mile rides to brunch in Olathe and Greenwood via Grandview and Lee's Summit or DeSoto.

For more information, call the ride lines of bike clubs listed in this chapter.

ular, new riders are welcomed by the Greater Kansas City Bicycle Club, 816/436-5641, and the Johnson County Bicycle Club, 913/871-5150.

Air Travel

Kansas City International Airport

It seemed like folly back in the Sixties, when civic leaders chose a 4,700-acre site in Platte County—15 miles north of downtown—to build a new international airport. But the Municipal Airport, just across the Missouri River from the central business district, had outgrown its space, and airport backers believed a modern facility would carry them into the next century. At the time, the area's population seemed to be growing northward, and promoters promised that one day the airport would again be close to town.

Although it's still a fair distance from the major population centers, Kansas City International Airport (KCI) has stood the test of time. When it opened in 1972, its innovative design was called a "drive to your gate" system, a classification that still holds true. Leaving and arriving at an airport doesn't get any simpler than this.

KCI's scheme places check-in, gates, baggage retrieval, and parking areas within easy walking distance.

Getting to KCI

About a 20-minute drive from downtown, KCI is easily reached via I-29 or I-435. From downtown, take I-35 or Highway 169 (over the Broadway Bridge) and get on I-29 north. Exit signs are well marked. From south

Kansas City International's terminals are easy to navigate.

Convention and Visitors Bureau of Greater Kansas City

Major Airlines Serving KCI

Air Canada, Terminal C, 800/776-3000

America West, Terminal A, 800/235-9292

American Airlines, Terminal A, 800/433-7300

Continental, Terminal C, 800/523-3273

Delta, Terminal B, 800/221-1212

Midwest Express, Terminal C, 800/452-2022

Northwest Airlines, Terminal C, 800/225-2525

Southwest Airlines, Terminal B, 800/435-9792

Trans World Airlines, Terminal B, 800/221-2000

United Airlines, Terminal C, 800/241-6522

USAirways, Terminal A, 800/428-4322

Johnson County, I-435 north is often the fastest route—it has less traffic and higher speed limits than I-635. Again, airport exits are clearly noted.

The KCI Shuttle, among other competitors, offers round-the-clock service between the airport and hotels in the downtown, Crown Center Plaza, Westport, Overland Park, Mission, and Lenexa areas. Tickets cost $12 to $20 one way. Arriving passengers should look for KCI Shuttle ticket carts for assistance. To obtain a schedule with exact departure times, call 816/243-5000 or 800/243-6383.

Getting Around KCI
As travelers approach KCI, signs identify terminals that house the different departing airlines. If you want American Airlines, for example, head for Terminal A and park in the lot there. For Southwest, go to Terminal B. If you need to change terminals and don't want to move your car—or don't have a car—complimentary shuttles run between the terminals.

Other Airports
Kansas City International handles all scheduled commercial flights in the area, but several smaller fields support private pilots flying through the region. Kansas City's old Municipal Airport, for example, is now called Kansas City Downtown Airport and serves arriving and departing corporate jets, charter flights, and cargo services. For more information, call 816/471-4946.

Other area airfields include the New Century AirCenter, 913/782-5335, Independence Memorial Airport, 816/795-8774, and Lee's Summit Municipal Airport, 816/251-2492.

Train Service

Although Kansas City's reputation as a passenger-rail mecca has dwindled with the popularity of train service, Amtrak's Southwest Chief continues to roll through the area on its regular Chicago–Los Angeles run. Residents of Kansas City and St. Louis also are fond of the daily rail service between their cities. A one-way ticket from Kansas City to St. Louis ranges from $25 to $49, depending on how early you book. Call Amtrak at 800/872-7245.

Kansas City's Amtrak station sits directly northeast of the old Union Station, jutting from the modern office building called Two Pershing Square. The actual address is 2200 Main Street, and a circular drive allows passengers to pull in to drop off baggage. Parking is available beneath Union Station, entered via Pershing Road. As of mid-1998, space had been allocated in the refurbished Union Station for Amtrak passenger service, awaiting congressional funding approval.

Interstate and Regional Bus Service

Both Greyhound and Jefferson bus lines serve the greater Kansas City area, with routes throughout the country. These two major transporters share terminals at 1101 Troost Avenue, Kansas City, Missouri, and at 730 State Street, Kansas City, Kansas. In addition, a terminal in Grandview serves passengers of the two bus companies. Call 800/231-2222 for fare and schedule information. Both lines may move to Union Station in the future.

3

WHERE TO STAY

Kansas City lodges visitors in style. Whether it's world-class suites and uniformed doormen or a handmade quilt and a relaxed morning sipping coffee, travelers can find what they're looking for here.

One-of-a-kind accommodations are scattered throughout the metropolitan area, complemented by numerous regional and national hotel and motel chains. This selection ensures that everyone can find a home away from home at an affordable rate. Beyond the lodgings suggested here, consider contacting your favorite national hotel chain. Nearly all are represented in Kansas City or, given the hotel-building boom underway, soon will be.

And thanks to Kansas City's miles of urban highways and major thoroughfares—and light traffic compared to similarly sized cities—you can stay virtually anywhere in the area and still be within easy reach of what you came for. Reservations, however, are always recommended. When a large convention (drawing 40,000 members of the American Dental Association, for example) or combined weekend events (such as a Chiefs game and the Plaza Art Fair) roll into town, the area's nearly 22,000 rooms quickly disappear behind "No Vacancy" signs.

Price rating symbols:
$ **$50 and under**
$$ **$51 to $75**
$$$ **$76 to $125**
$$$$ **$126 and up**

DOWNTOWN

Hotels and Motels

DOUBLETREE HOTEL
1301 Wyandotte St.
Kansas City
816/474-6664 or 800/843-6664
$$$–$$$$
Once known as the Americana, this 1970s-era property had languished before finally closing its doors in 1994. Following a $26-million refurbishment, the hotel reopened in 1997 as the Omni, adding new life to the area. Recently it experienced an exciting rebirth as the 28-floor DoubleTree. Throughout the hotel, rich wood detailing and mission-style furnishings with colorful touches in maroon, green, and taupe create a regal Old World/New World look. The decor's triangle and diamond motif mirrors the design of the art deco–style artwork atop nearby Bartle Hall. ஃ (Downtown)

HISTORIC SUITES OF AMERICA
612 Central St.

Hyatt Regency Crown Center

© Hallmark Cards, Inc.

Kansas City
816/842-6544 or 800/733-0612
$$$–$$$$
The former Builders and Traders Exchange building and Barton Brothers Shoe Factory have been transformed into the beautifully appointed Historic Suites. Within walking distance of the River Market, downtown, restaurants, and clubs, this all-suite hotel features a complimentary breakfast buffet and evening reception, exercise rooms, whirlpool tub, and an outdoor pool. Historic Suites offers 100 kitchen-equipped suites that are configured in 32 different floor plans. ஃ (Downtown)

HOLIDAY INN–CITY CENTER
1215 Wyandotte St.
Kansas City
816/471-1333 or 800/354-0986
$$$
Built in 1925, the Holiday Inn–Citi Centre lies just across the street from Kansas City's Municipal Auditorium and Barney Allis Plaza. Inside, Italian marble, mahogany, and bronze highlight the public spaces, while the hotel's 189 rooms are decorated in florals. The Holiday Inn's mezzanine lounge, Reflections, is a favorite meeting spot for folks who work downtown; Aladdin's Restaurant is an on-site dining option. ஃ (Downtown)

HYATT REGENCY CROWN CENTER
2345 McGee St.
Kansas City
816/421-1234 or 800/233-1234
$$$–$$$$
Steps from Crown Center, the Hyatt sports sweeping views of the downtown skyline, especially from its revolving rooftop restaurant, Skies. The Hyatt's 731 rooms and suites reflect the company's customary attention to detail and come with 24-hour room

DOWNTOWN KANSAS CITY

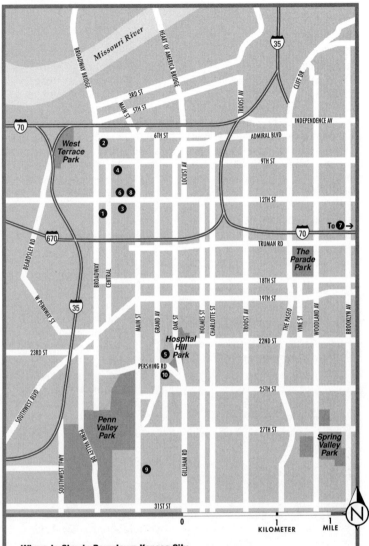

Where to Stay in Downtown Kansas City

1 DoubleTree Hotel
2 Historic Suites of America
3 Holiday Inn–City Center
4 Hotel Savoy
5 Hyatt Regency Crown Center
6 Kansas City Marriott–Downtown
7 Park Place Hotel
8 Radisson Suite Hotel
9 Residence Inn by Marriott–Union Hill
10 Westin Crown Center

Commercial Success

Although its 100 suites boast all the modern conveniences, Historic Suites began with three unique, turn-of-the-century structures. Built in 1887, the Builders and Traders Exchange was designed to house locally distinguished and nationally recognized contractors and architects. The Exchange members themselves provided nearly all of the building's planning and construction. At the time the Kansas City Star *called craftsman T.T. Moore's work "undoubtedly the finest piece of carpentry in Kansas City today."*

Complementing the Exchange is the adjacent Burnham-Munger building, a five-story red brick structure designed by architect Walter C. Root. Built in 1892, the Neo Romanesque–style facility was home to the Burnham-Hanna-Munger Dry Goods Company before the McPike Drug Company, a prominent pharmaceutical concern, moved there in 1904.

Historic Suites' third portion lies within the Barton Brothers Shoe Company Building, an 1895 five-story brick structure designed by Shepard & Farrar in the Second Renaissance Revival Style. Like many companies in the area, Barton Brothers used the space for storage, a showroom, and sales. The building was later occupied by the Morrin-Powers Wholesale Liquor Company.

Converting these commercially oriented buildings into suites presented a challenge, but Historic Suites redevelopers prevailed, creating 32 unique floor plans within the three structures.

service, minibars, and movie channels. Hotel amenities also include a complimentary health club, an all-weather pool, tennis courts, and two other restaurants. ♿ (Downtown)

**KANSAS CITY
MARRIOTT DOWNTOWN**
200 W. 12th St.
Kansas City
816/421-6800 or 800/228-9290
$$$$
Its 983 rooms and suites within steps

of Bartle Hall, the Marriott is a prime convention facility. The hotel also has 23 meeting rooms of its own. The Marriott's lobby, bars, and restaurants attract many downtown workers, who duck in for a meal or after-work cocktail. In 1997, the Marriott opened an additional 420 rooms in the renovated Muehlebach Hotel. The 1914 Kansas City classic, now known as the Muehlebach-Marriott, is joined with the hotel's newer portions by an elevated skywalk. The

Lodged in the Past

Downtown's coffee smell comes from the Folger Coffee Company, at 7th and Broadway, as it pumps the roasted beans through its plant. But coffee has long been featured in Kansas City.

In 1888, the owners of the Arbuckle Coffee Company built the opulent Hotel Savoy on the corner of 9th and Central. Conveniently located, the hotel was the first lodging travelers saw as they came up the slope from the old Union Depot. The Savoy was an architectural wonder, featuring a rooftop garden, Italian tile floors, and a lavish ballroom. In its early years, the property welcomed guests such as Teddy Roosevelt, W.C. Fields, and Lillian Russell.

By 1903, the hotel owners opened the Savoy Grill exclusively for men, although women were soon admitted. After dinner, guests would push aside their tables to dance.

When the nation's post–World War II suburban boom began, downtown started to wane—as did the fortunes of the Hotel Savoy. In 1960, restaurateur Don Lee bought the Grill, then purchased the hotel five years later. For 20 years, Lee operated the hotel as a residential property, even after it was placed on the National Register of Historic Places. In 1985, he renovated the Hotel Savoy and now operates it as an all-suite bed-and-breakfast.

beloved Pam Pam, a legendary upscale coffee shop, also reopened in the Muehlebach to popular acclaim (open from 6 a.m.–midnight). Special weekend rates. ♿ (Downtown)

PARK PLACE HOTEL
1601 N. Universal Ave.
Kansas City
816/483-9900
$$–$$$
"Industrial/Office" could precede this hotel name and accurately describe its setting, just off I-435 at

Front Street. Nevertheless, this 327-room lodging offers quality accommodations and amenities such as an indoor swimming pool and health club. The location, two miles from Worlds of Fun, minutes from Station Casino and five miles from Truman Sports Complex, is also hard to beat. ♿ (Downtown)

RADISSON SUITE HOTEL
106 W. 12th St.
Kansas City
816/221-7000 or 800/333-3333

$$$–$$$$

The Radisson opened in 1931 as the Phillips House, on the original site of the Haberdashery, a men's clothing store co-owned by Harry Truman. The hotel set a standard for European-style elegance with its art deco decor, grand dining room, and classic suites. Today the hotel attracts business travelers and those looking for a historic setting in a central location. Rooms come with computer hook-ups, HBO, and a complimentary breakfast buffet. ᴳ (Downtown)

WESTIN CROWN CENTER
1 Pershing Rd.
Kansas City
816/474-4400 or 800/228-3000
$$$$

Like much of Kansas City, Crown Center's site was a hill of limestone that had to be excavated for development. The five-story waterfall in the Westin's lobby cascades over some of that remaining outcropping. Connected to Crown Center's shops, theaters, and restaurants, the popular hotel has 725 rooms. Guests can further enjoy the skyline view from Benton's rooftop steakhouse. The Westin completed an $11-million renovation in April 1998, which included new furnishings in the rooms and suites, plus installation of extra in-room phone lines, desk/work areas, and improved lighting. ᴳ (Downtown)

Bed-and-Breakfasts

HOTEL SAVOY
219 W. 9th St.
Kansas City
816/842-3575 or 800/SAVOY-BB
$$$

More than a dozen years ago, Don Lee renovated the Hotel Savoy, changing it from a residential hotel into a luxurious B&B. He furnished 22 suites in a turn-of-the-century style, enhancing the original stained glass windows and Corinthian columns. Now Lee markets the lodging with his Savoy Grill and hopes to expand the hotel by remodeling all the rooms and meeting spaces. It's near downtown's Garment District and within walking distance of major businesses. (Downtown)

Extended Stay

RESIDENCE INN BY
MARRIOTT–UNION HILL
2975 Main St.
Kansas City
816/561-3000 or 800/331-3131
$$$–$$$$

The Residence Inn resembles a cozy enclave of brick and gray-clapboard townhouses. Overlooking Crown Center from the gentrifying Union Hill neighborhood, the inn provides equipped kitchens with grocery service, complimentary breakfast, fireplaces, and manager's hospitality

Westin Crown Center

PLAZA/WESTPORT

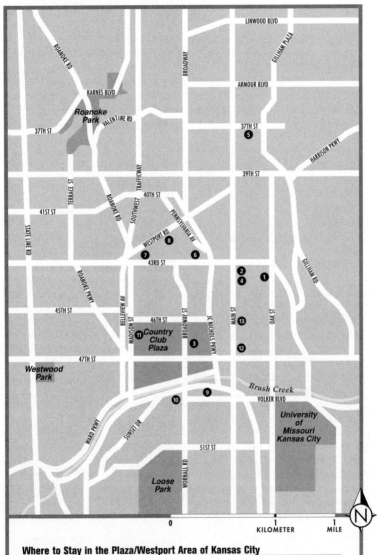

Where to Stay in the Plaza/Westport Area of Kansas City

1 Behm's Plaza Carriage House
2 Best Western Seville Plaza Hotel
3 Broadway Plaza Suites
4 Crowne Plaza Hotel
5 Doanleigh Inn
6 Embassy Suites Country Club Plaza
7 Holiday Inn Express–Westport

8 The Quarterage Hotel–Westport
9 Raphael Hotel
10 The Ritz-Carlton
11 Sheraton Suites Country Club Plaza
12 Southmoreland on the Plaza
13 Wyndham Garden Hotel

hours. Outdoors, guests find a barbecue area, swimming pool, and hot tub. Discounts are available for stays longer than a week. ♿ (Downtown)

PLAZA/WESTPORT

Hotels and Motels

**BEST WESTERN
SEVILLE PLAZA HOTEL**
4309 Main St.
Kansas City
816/561-9600 or 800/825-0197
$$$
Located right on busy Main Street, the Best Western Seville is only four blocks from the Country Club Plaza and three blocks from Westport. The Spanish-style hotel features 77 spacious rooms, with complimentary continental breakfast, local phone calls, and movie channels. An indoor whirlpool spa gives guests respite after exploring the area. ♿ (Plaza/ Westport)

CROWNE PLAZA HOTEL
4445 Main St.
Kansas City
816/531-3000 or 800/227-6963
$$$–$$$$
The Country Club Plaza, Westport, and the Nelson-Atkins Museum of Art are just minutes away from this hotel. All 296 rooms feature two telephones with voice mail, individual climate control, and cable television. A health club and indoor swimming pool are also available. The hotel serves lunch and dinner in the Main Street Grill and drinks in its Lobby Bar. ♿ (Plaza/Westport)

**EMBASSY SUITES COUNTRY
CLUB PLAZA**
220 W. 43rd St.

Kansas City
816/756-1720 or 800/EMBASSY
$$$–$$$$
Midway between Westport and the Country Club Plaza, Embassy Suites is a Spanish-style property that features suites with living rooms and bedrooms as well as microwave ovens, coffeemakers, refrigerators, and wet bars. Rates include a complimentary breakfast and evening beverages at the manager's reception. ♿ (Plaza/ Westport)

**HOLIDAY INN EXPRESS–
WESTPORT**
801 Westport Rd.
Kansas City
816/931-1000 or 800/HOLIDAY
$$
The Holiday Inn celebrates its historic location on the original Santa Fe Trail with a plaque above the door. Inside, a trail map details the importance of the roads heading westward. The hotel's decor also contains a Western focus, with Southwest fabrics and a Frederic Remington sculpture. Exec-

The Quarterage Hotel, p. 38

The Quarterage Hotel

TRIVIA

The cascading waterfall that greets visitors at The Ritz-Carlton Kansas City provides a backdrop for *Diana*, goddess of the hunt, attended by three cherubs. Commissioned by Plaza developer J.C. Nichols in 1970, the fountain sculpture is a copy of a 1912 artwork made for the Moreton estate in Warwickshire, England.

utive king rooms have work stations, dataport phones, coffeemakers, welcome baskets, ironing boards, hair dryers, and sofas in their separate sitting areas. A complimentary continental breakfast comes with every room; other Westport restaurants and nightclubs lie nearby. ᴄ (Plaza/Westport)

THE QUARTERAGE HOTEL–WESTPORT
560 Westport Rd.
Kansas City
816/931-0001 or 800/942-4233
$$$
From the outside the Quarterage seems contemporary. Inside, however, the oak, brass, and marble lobby—with a roaring wintertime fireplace—looks downright nineteenth century. Still, the Quarterage Hotel provides modern amenities, such as a health club, complimentary breakfast, and an evening cocktail hour. It also offers free local calls and complimentary HBO. Nearby, Westport's nightlife and shopping beckon. ᴄ (Plaza/ Westport)

RAPHAEL HOTEL
325 Ward Pkwy.
Kansas City
816/756-3800 or 800/821-5343
$$$–$$$$
Built in 1927, the Raphael once was an apartment building with a commanding view of the Country Club Plaza. It was converted into 123 hotel rooms—72 of which are spacious suites—and opened as the Raphael in 1975. The lobby is intimate, with two Raphael prints lending a European flair. The hotel operates a fine-dining restaurant, which also provides in-room continental breakfast daily. ᴄ (Plaza/Westport)

THE RITZ-CARLTON KANSAS CITY
401 Ward Pkwy.
Kansas City
816/756-1500 or 800/241-3333
$$$$
The Ritz-Carlton, an AAA Four Diamond and Mobil Four Star property, lies just across Brush Creek from the Country Club Plaza. Between Thanksgiving and Christmas, rooms facing the shops are usually sold out months in advance to Plaza Lights aficionados. European art, crystal chandeliers, and rich fabrics create an Old World feel. Rooms include amenities such as bathroom telephones, hair dryers, and terry robes. ᴄ (Plaza/ Westport)

SHERATON SUITES COUNTRY CLUB PLAZA
770 W. 47th St.
Kansas City
816/931-4400 or 800/325-3535
$$$–$$$$
This hotel is right in the thick of the Plaza. Starting with its marble-decked lobby, the lodging provides an oasis within an oasis. Each of the

Ritz-Carlton Kansas City, p. 38

hotel's 257 suites comes with a living room, bedroom, refrigerator, and coffeemaker, among other amenities. The hotel contains an indoor-outdoor swimming pool, whirlpool, and exercise room, as well as the Gallery Art Restaurant & Bar. &. (Plaza/Westport)

WYNDHAM GARDEN HOTEL
1 E. 45th St.
Kansas City
816/753-7400 or 800/WYNDHAM
$$$
Perched on a hill just east of the Country Club Plaza, this property was formerly called the Hilton Plaza Inn. In its new incarnation, the 240-room property boasts marble floors, antiques, and murals in the public areas, plus a restaurant, lounge, and library, offering plenty of chances for relaxation. An outdoor swimming pool and health club round things out. &. (Plaza/Westport)

Bed-and-Breakfasts

BEHM'S PLAZA CARRIAGE HOUSE
4320 Oak St.

Kansas City
816/753-4434
$$$
Established by Del and Shirley Behm, this 1910 Georgian Colonial home recently changed hands. New owners Rick Winegar and Lionel Martin may change the name by late 1999, but the bed-and-breakfast inn—listed on Missouri's Register of Historic Places—should continue to provide relaxing hospitality. Set on a quiet street among the Nelson-Atkins Museum of Art, the Country Club Plaza, and Westport, the stately brick residence has five bedrooms, each with private bath; guests enjoy a full breakfast and complimentary wine and hors d'oeuvres. (Plaza/Westport)

DOANLEIGH INN
217 E. 37th St.
Kansas City
816/753-2667
$$$–$$$$
This 1907 home features five luxuriously decorated guest rooms —two include fireplaces, and four have hot tubs—that come with their own direct telephone, bath, and cable TV. The Doanleigh offers a full breakfast, homemade cookies, and nightly hors d'oeuvre service. The antique-filled mansion, owned by Cynthia Brogdon and Terry Maturo, provides a convenient setting between downtown and the Country Club Plaza. (Plaza/Westport)

SOUTHMORELAND
ON THE PLAZA
116 E. 46th St.
Kansas City
816/531-7979
$$$–$$$$
The inn keepers here make certain their guests find time to relax on the verandah, enjoy a roaring fire, or get

Southmoreland on the Plaza, p. 39

to know each other. The Southmoreland's 12 rooms are named after prominent Kansas Citians—such as artist Thomas Hart Benton, baseball legend Leroy "Satchel" Paige, and candy barons Clara and Russell Stover—and are decorated with a nod to their namesakes. Each room has a special touch such as a private deck, fireplace, or hot tub, and comes with a full breakfast and late-afternoon wine and hors d'oeuvres. ♿ (Plaza/Westport)

Extended Stay

BROADWAY PLAZA SUITES
4615 Broadway Blvd.
Kansas City
816/753-1044
$$
Talk about location, location, location. These 46 studio and one-bedroom suites sit about a block from the action on the Plaza. Ivy-covered, ocher-brick buildings, the Broadway Plaza Suites were built in the 1940s as

apartments and were transformed into fully furnished executive suites in 1996. Because they were apartments, the one-bedroom suites have full kitchens, ideal if you can resist the abundance of dining options right around the corner. Seven-night minimum stay. ♿ (Plaza/Westport)

JOHNSON COUNTY

Hotels and Motels

DAYS INN–LENEXA
9630 Rosehill Rd.
Lenexa
913/492-7200 or 800/DAYS-INN
$–$$
"Follow the Sun" says the Days Inn logo, and this south Kansas City motel provides the cheery and relaxing setting, especially for those traveling along adjacent I-35 just west of this property. The three-story lodging underwent an extensive renovation in late 1996, providing guests with improved facilities and services ranging from guest rooms to a swimming pool to its continental breakfast. ♿ (Johnson County)

DOUBLETREE HOTEL–KANSAS CITY CORPORATE WOODS
10100 College Blvd.
Overland Park
913/451-6100 or 800/222-TREE
$$–$$$$
A pillar of the College Boulevard business and residential corridor, the DoubleTree provides convenient access to the offices within adjacent Corporate Woods. Walking and running trails of 1.5 to nearly 4 miles thread from the hotel through the office-park-within-a-park. The hotel's 356 rooms and suites also provide access to racquetball, indoor swim-

JOHNSON CO./KANSAS CITY, KS

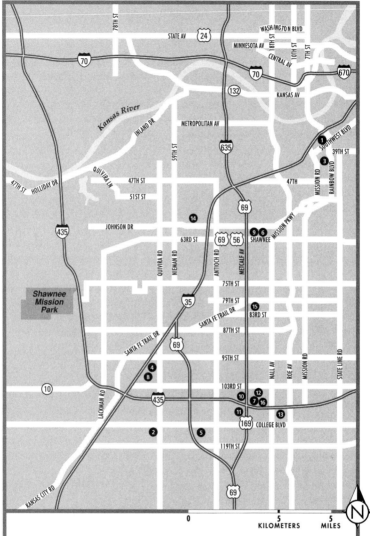

Where to Stay in Johnson County and Kansas City, Kansas

1 Best Western Inn & Conference Center (KCK)
2 Candlewood Studio Hotel (JC)
3 Days Inn–KU Med Center (KCK)
4 Days Inn–Lenexa (JC)
5 DoubleTree Hotel–Kansas City Corporate Woods (JC)
6 Econolodge of Overland Park (JC)
7 Embassy Suites Overland Park (JC)
8 Guesthouse Suite Hotel (JC)
9 Holiday Inn Mission–Overland Park (JC)

10 Homewood Suites (JC)
11 Overland Park Marriott (JC)
12 Red Roof Inn (JC)
13 Residence Inn by Marriott–Overland Park (JC)
14 Walnut Grove RV Park (JC)
15 White Haven Motor Lodge (JC)
16 Wyndham Garden Hotel–Overland Park (JC)

ming, saunas, whirlpool, and the Rotisserie Restaurant. & (Johnson County)

ECONOLODGE OF OVERLAND PARK
7508 Shawnee Mission Pkwy.
Overland Park
913/262-9600
$

This centrally located, 86-room motel lies only five miles west of the Country Club Plaza and even closer to Johnson County's malls, restaurants, and attractions. Free airport bus service provides access from Kansas City International, doughnuts and coffee are free each morning, and a Budget Rent-A-Car facility sits directly across Shawnee Mission Parkway from the motel. & (Johnson County)

EMBASSY SUITES OVERLAND PARK
10601 Metcalf Ave.
Overland Park
913/649-7060 or 800/362-2779
$$$

East of Metcalf near I-435, this property boasts an atrium rising through the hotel's seven levels. Terraces overlook a bar, floral-print market umbrellas, and tropical vegetation. All rooms include a breakfast buffet and evening reception. From the hotel, restaurants can be found in every direction—and two malls are within three miles. & (Johnson County)

HOLIDAY INN MISSION– OVERLAND PARK
7240 Shawnee Mission Pkwy.
Overland Park
913/262-3010 or 800/465-4329
$$–$$$

One of three Holidome lodgings in the metro area, this hotel has a swim-

ming pool beneath a large atrium. Kids also throng to its video arcade, table tennis, and indoor Nerf tennis court. While kids play, parents and other guests at this 195-room hotel can enjoy the whirlpool, exercise area, and in-house restaurant and lounge. & (Johnson County)

OVERLAND PARK MARRIOTT
10800 Metcalf Ave.
Overland Park
913/451-8000 or 800/228-9290
$$–$$$

The College Boulevard corridor has become a southern-central business district, and the Marriott sits dead center in the action. This 397-room property has myriad roles, providing meeting space, restaurants, and amenities ranging from indoor/outdoor swimming pools to in-room movies. Such offerings mean the Marriott stays busy, hosting everything from visiting softball teams to ballroom-based purebred cattle auctions. & (Johnson County)

RED ROOF INN
6800 W. 108th St.
Overland Park
913/341-0100
$–$$

This hotel, one of three Red Roofs in the metropolitan area, provides some of the least-expensive accommodations near College Boulevard. Offering function not frills, the inn allows easy access to nearby businesses, shops, and restaurants, such as Dick Clark's American Bandstand Grill. The lodging's guest rooms include ESPN, Showtime, and CNN, morning coffee, and *USA Today*. & (Johnson County)

WHITE HAVEN MOTOR LODGE
8039 Metcalf Ave.
Overland Park

913/649-8200 or 800/752-2892
$–$$

Operated by the White family since 1957, the cozy White Haven is one of Johnson County's oldest lodgings— and one of its most respected. "Value and comfort" remain the driving forces behind its success. Guests park outside the rooms of the two-story building, which wraps around a statue-bedecked swimming pool. The helpful staff provides new and faithful customers with everything from microwave ovens to morning doughnuts. ♿ (Johnson County)

WYNDHAM GARDEN HOTEL–OVERLAND PARK
7000 W. 108th St.
Overland Park
913/383-2550 or 800/WYNDHAM
$$$

After a $7-million renovation, this former Best Western Hallmark Inn was transformed into one of Johnson County's premier hotel properties. Marbled entryways lead to the Garden Cafe restaurant, a full health club, ample on-site meeting space, and tastefully appointed guest rooms. Near the intersection of I-435 and Metcalf, the Wyndham provides easy access to Overland Park and attractions throughout the metropolitan area. ♿ (Johnson County)

Extended Stay

CANDLEWOOD STUDIO HOTEL
11001 Oakmont St.
Overland Park
913/469-5557 or 800/946-6200
$$–$$$

There aren't many places in town where you can get a can of soda for a quarter. But at the Candlewood, that's only one of the amenities. Newly built, across College Boulevard from Johnson County Community College, the Candlewood also offers an exercise room, free laundry facilities, fully equipped kitchens, two phone lines in every room with free local phone calls, and 25-inch TVs with HBO and 21 other premium channels. Boasting 122 studios and one-bedroom suites, Candlewood attracts corporate clients, many of whom are relocating to the area. ♿ (Johnson County)

GUESTHOUSE SUITE HOTEL
9775 Lenexa Dr.
Lenexa
913/541-4000 or 800/EXT-STAY
$$

Living room, full kitchen, oversized bed, health club membership—you could be at home. That's exactly the idea behind this all-suite property directed at extended-stay business travelers and others who appreciate its location near I-35, Oak Park Mall, and numerous restaurants. Guests can even access a library of books and family games. It's home—except for your pets, who are not welcome. ♿ (Johnson County)

HOMEWOOD SUITES
10556 Marty Ave.
Overland Park
913/341-5576 or 800/225-5466
$$–$$$

All-suite hotel customers look for more than a single room, and this property delivers. From apartment-style accommodations with full kitchens—some with fireplaces—to an executive business center, Homewood lets both overnight and long-term guests settle in comfort. The lodging even offers an on-site, 24-hour convenience store with video rentals. ♿ (Johnson County)

RESIDENCE INN BY MARRIOTT–OVERLAND PARK
6300 W. 110th St.
Overland Park
913/491-3333 or 800/331-3131
$$$–$$$$

This property is so expertly built and landscaped that you could forget it's right by the freeway. Low-rise with a chalet feel, this Residence Inn features studios and penthouse suites, which include living space on two floors. Rooms come with working fireplaces and full kitchens, as well as laundry and exercise facilities and complimentary newspapers and grocery shopping. In addition, guests can enjoy a complimentary breakfast buffet every morning and, Monday through Thursday, a hospitality hour with drinks and a light supper. ♿ (Johnson County)

Country Club Plaza Merchants Association

Sheraton Suites, Country Club Plaza, p. 38

Campgrounds

WALNUT GROVE RV PARK
10218 Johnson Dr.
Merriam
913/262-3023
$

Pull up and plug in. What could be simpler? This RV park, nestled in a residential area with convenient access to I-35, could be just the place for those tired of unpacking, hauling luggage, and eating coffee shop meals. The facility offers showers, coin laundry service, pay telephone, and long-term rates for those who wish to stay a while. Reservations are highly recommended. ♿ (Johnson County)

KANSAS CITY, KANSAS

Hotels and Motels

BEST WESTERN INN & CONFERENCE CENTER

I-35 and Hwy. 169
Kansas City, KS
913/677-3060 or 800/368-1741
$$
Two blocks from the University of Kansas Medical Center, the refined Best Western Inn & Conference Center also hosts small meetings and folks in town for the American Royal festivities each fall. Rooms come with refrigerators and coffeemakers, complimentary continental breakfast, and free local phone calls. The property includes a heated outdoor pool, an indoor whirlpool, and restaurants on three sides. ♿ (Kansas City, Kansas)

DAY'S INN–KU MED CENTER
3930 Rainbow Blvd.
Kansas City, KS
913/236-6880 or 800/766-6521
$$
Under new management, this 80-room Day's Inn has been fully renovated in mauves and greens, with its woodwork transformed from dark to light. Set across the street from the University of Kansas Medical Center and within walking distance of 39th Street's many restaurants, the two-story brick property offers a refurbished outdoor swimming pool (open only during summer months) and complimentary coffee, juices, and doughnuts each morning. ♿ (Kansas City, Kansas)

NORTHLAND

Hotels and Motels
BEST WESTERN COUNTRY
INN–KCI AIRPORT
11900 Plaza Circle
Kansas City
816/464-2002 or 800/528-1234

$$
Whether you're staying in Kansas City or making it your hopping-off point, this 43-room hotel could be your ticket. The park-and-fly program allows those who stay at least one night to leave their cars for up to seven days. The convenient hotel features free airport shuttle, complimentary continental breakfast, and air-conditioned rooms. ♿ (Northland)

BEST WESTERN COUNTRY
INN–WORLDS OF FUN
7100 NE Parvin Rd.
Kansas City
816/453-3355 or 800/528-1234
$$–$$$
For families intent on getting maximum roller coaster time at Worlds of Fun or a full wash of waves at Oceans of Fun, this motel couldn't be more convenient. Handy to I-435 travelers and casino buffs, the Country Inn's 86 rooms come with daily continental breakfast service and summertime use of an outdoor swimming pool. ♿ (Northland)

COURTYARD BY MARRIOTT
KCI AIRPORT
7901 NW Tiffany Springs Pkwy.
Kansas City
816/891-7500 or 800/321-2211
$$–$$$
It's a free shuttle ride from the airport to the Courtyard, with only 3.5 miles to cover. That leaves plenty of time to enjoy this 149-room hotel's amenities, ranging from an indoor swimming pool and exercise room to the Courtyard restaurant, serving breakfast and dinner. All rooms feature telephones, televisions, and in-room coffee. ♿ (Northland)

EMBASSY SUITES–
KCI AIRPORT

NORTHLAND

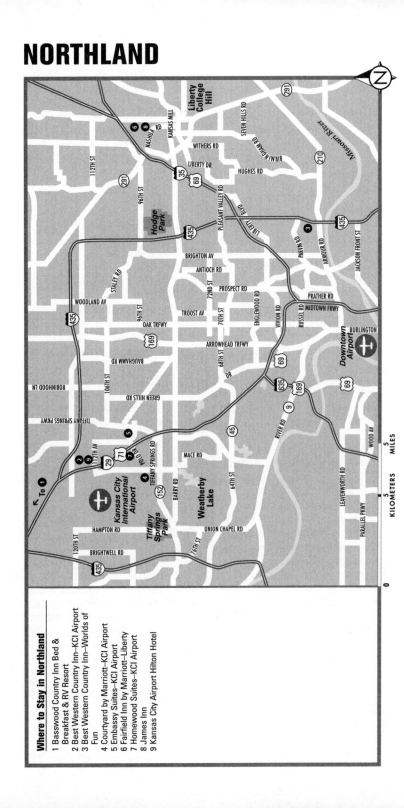

Where to Stay in Northland

1 Basswood Country Inn Bed & Breakfast & RV Resort
2 Best Western Country Inn–KCI Airport
3 Best Western Country Inn–Worlds of Fun
4 Courtyard by Marriott–KCI Airport
5 Embassy Suites–KCI Airport
6 Fairfield Inn by Marriott–Liberty
7 Homewood Suites–KCI Airport
8 James Inn
9 Kansas City Airport Hilton Hotel

Many Kansas City hotels offer special packages—combining Chiefs tickets, admission to Worlds of Fun, or casino shuttles with their nightly room rates. Whether you're planning a honeymoon, romantic getaway, or shopping excursion, be sure to ask about rate breaks. Some hotels even package rental cars with their rooms, which can make a vacation downright affordable.

7640 NW Tiffany Springs Pkwy.
Kansas City
816/891-7788 or 800/EMBASSY
$$$–$$$$
An eight-foot waterfall highlights the atrium courtyard of this airport hotel. The tropical setting could place you nearly anywhere, but you'd probably never think you were four short miles from KCI. Like all Embassy Suites, this one includes a full breakfast buffet, and the manager throws in nightly cocktails to boot. & (Northland)

FAIRFIELD INN BY
MARRIOTT–LIBERTY
8101 N. Church Rd.
Kansas City
816/792-4000
$$
Located only five minutes from Liberty's town center and 15 minutes north of downtown Kansas City, Missouri, this 104-room hotel is at the budget end of Marriott's accommodations spectrum. But guests are not shorted on amenities and services, which include an outdoor swimming pool, free local phone calls, and daily continental breakfast. & (Northland)

KANSAS CITY AIRPORT
HILTON HOTEL
8801 NW 112th St.

Kansas City
816/891-8900 or 800/525-6322
$$–$$$$
Talk about convenience: This lodging's 347 rooms lie less than a mile from KCI's runways. Rest assured, however, that all is calm within the Hilton confines, where indoor and outdoor swimming pools, whirlpool, saunas, and a lobby bar keep guests' jet-age cares at bay. Weatherby's restaurant, on the lobby level, serves up some memorable café-style meals. & (Northland)

Bed-and-Breakfasts

JAMES INN
342 N. Water St.
Liberty
816/781-3677
$$$
Lodged in a former church, this B&B maintains its peaceful atmosphere. The check-in area, once the sanctuary, lies beneath a St. James crucifixion mural painted by a German artist in 1918. Guest rooms off the lobby boast queen beds and unusual bathrooms, placed in overhead lofts in the old choir station. The basement serves as an exercise room, with an outdoor deck and hot tub. Full breakfast served. & (Northland)

Ten Largest Hotels in the Kansas City Area

1. Hyatt Regency Crown Center, 731 rooms
2. The Westin Crown Center, 725 rooms
3. Kansas City Marriott Downtown, 573 rooms
4. Overland Park Marriott, 397 rooms
5. Doubletree Hotel, 390 rooms
6. KCI Airport Marriott, 382 rooms
7. Adam's Mark, 374 rooms
8. The Ritz-Carlton Kansas City, 373 rooms
9. DoubleTree Hotel at Corporate Woods, 357 rooms
10. Kansas City Airport Hilton Hotel, 348 rooms

Source: Convention and Visitors Bureau of Greater Kansas City

Extended Stay

HOMEWOOD SUITES KCI
7312 N. Polo Dr.
Kansas City
816/880-9880 or 800/225-5466
$$–$$$
Located across Interstate 29 from the Kansas City airport, Homewood Suites has become a popular destination for travelers who need a home base. Homewood's standard suites include two sleeping areas; the deluxe units come with fireplaces. Two-bedroom suites also provide double bathrooms. Guests enjoy a complimentary breakfast every morning and evening receptions Mon–Thu. ⅋ (Northland)

Campgrounds

BASSWOOD COUNTRY INN BED
& BREAKFAST & RV RESORT
15875 Interurban Rd.
Platte City

816/858-5556
$–$$$
This former fish hatchery offers something for everyone. The owners spent eight years converting the lakes and surrounding 73 acres into a resort that combines bed-and-breakfast suites, RV and tent sites, a country store, activities, and four spring-fed fishing lakes. Since the park lies 25 miles from downtown Kansas City, visitors looking for a summertime getaway from the city often opt for Basswood. ⅋ (Northland)

SOUTH KANSAS CITY

Bed-and-Breakfasts

BROOKSIDE HOUSE
6315 Walnut St.
Kansas City
816/491-8950

$$$

Industrial trainer Brenda Otte and veterinarian Vern Otte operate this Brookside residence as a no-host bed-and-breakfast, but they make certain the occupants of their Dutch Colonial are well cared for. Singles, couples, families, or groups—one party at a time—can rent the three-bedroom, no-smoking home and have full run of its living, dining, and family rooms, along with a fireplace. The Ottes stock continental breakfast items before your arrival. (South Kansas City)

Extended Stay

WINDSONG CORPORATE APARTMENTS
114 W. 103rd St.
Kansas City
816/942-5997 or 800/692-2468
$

Formerly an apartment building, the Windsong offers guest lodgings for 30 days or more at an affordable price. Apartments come with one, two, or three bedrooms, as well as separate living rooms, dining rooms, kitchens, and baths. Guests can enjoy an outdoor swimming pool, HBO, wake-up calls, and 24-hour message service; maid service, however, comes but once a week. (South Kansas City)

EAST METRO

Hotels and Motels

ADAM'S MARK KANSAS CITY
9103 E. 39th St.
Kansas City
816/737-0200
$$–$$$

The Adam's Mark overlooks I-70 and the Truman Sports Complex, which makes it a great hotel for sports-minded visitors in town for a professional football or baseball game. The lodging features the well-regarded Remington's Steak & Seafood Grill and one of the best party nightclubs in the East Metro area, Quincy's. An indoor pool and exercise room round out the amenities. & (East Metro)

AMERICAN INN EAST
4141 S. Noland Rd.
Independence
816/795-1192 or 800/905-6343
$

One of the first motels as you enter town from the east, American Inn sits right on the southern edge of I-70. In addition to 123 comfortably furnished rooms, this property also provides an outdoor pool for the kids and a cocktail lounge for road-weary adults. Although the American Inn doesn't have a restaurant, ample choices are within easy walking distance. & (East Metro)

BENJAMIN HOTEL & SUITES
6101 E. 87th St.
Kansas City
816/765-4331 or 800/228-2828
$$–$$$

Yeeee-haw! This hotel property caters to folks interested in the adjacent Benjamin Ranch, a working spread that rustles up barn parties, hayrides, and horseback rides. The Benjamin Hotel resembles a Swiss chalet on the outside, but inside is an all-western motif. Within the hotel, the H.B. Steakhouse specializes in huge steaks and prime rib. & (East Metro)

BUDGETEL INN
8601 Hillcrest Rd.
Kansas City

SOUTH KANSAS CITY/EAST METRO

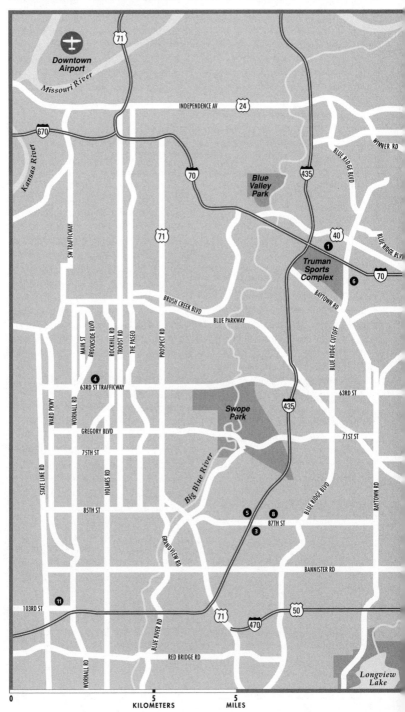

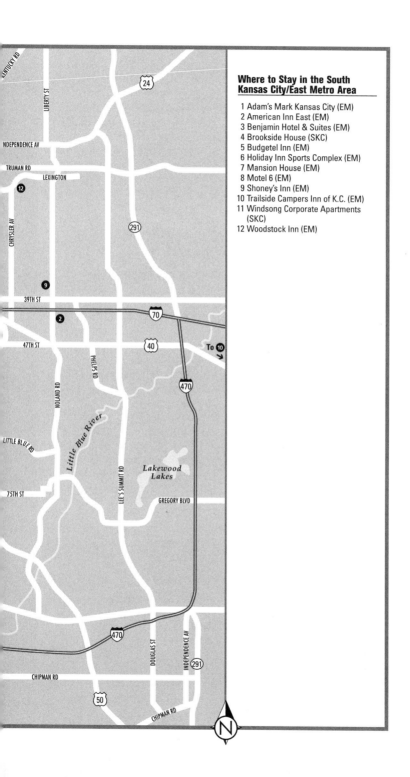

Where to Stay in the South Kansas City/East Metro Area

1 Adam's Mark Kansas City (EM)
2 American Inn East (EM)
3 Benjamin Hotel & Suites (EM)
4 Brookside House (SKC)
5 Budgetel Inn (EM)
6 Holiday Inn Sports Complex (EM)
7 Mansion House (EM)
8 Motel 6 (EM)
9 Shoney's Inn (EM)
10 Trailside Campers Inn of K.C. (EM)
11 Windsong Corporate Apartments
   (SKC)
12 Woodstock Inn (EM)

816/822-7000
$$

Technically in the South Kansas City zone, this hotel sits just across I-435 from Benjamin Ranch and the other attractions in the East Metro zone. The Budgetel's beige and green exterior blend well with the surrounding landscaping, its comfortable rooms providing a pleasant stop for those traveling north and south. Nearby Bannister Mall offers a variety of restaurants, from Luby's to the Olive Garden. & (East Metro)

HOLIDAY INN SPORTS COMPLEX
4011 Blue Ridge Cut-off
Kansas City
816/353-5300 or 800/465-4329
$$$

Just across the street from Kansas City's two professional stadiums, the Holiday Inn is a prime spot for sports lovers. Recently renovated, the hotel features 163 guest rooms with private balconies, many of which face the sports complex. There's an on-site restaurant and lounge, as well as a business center with a wide range of professional office equipment. An indoor pool, sauna, and whirlpool tempt the post-game crowd. & (East Metro)

MOTEL 6
6400 E. 87th St.
Kansas City
816/333-4468
$

This modern Motel 6 commands a hill a half-mile north of Bannister Mall and across the street from Benjamin Ranch. Rooms are simple and clean, and coffee's available at the front desk until 10 a.m. Right next door, a Denny's restaurant is open from 6 a.m. 'til midnight. & (East Metro)

SHONEY'S INN
4048 S. Lynn Court Dr.
Independence
816/254-0100 or 800/222-2222
$–$$

Anyone who's bellied up to one of Shoney's famous "all you can eat" breakfast bars can appreciate the proximity of this hotel to the company's restaurant. Shoney's Inn boasts a convenient I-70 location, a few miles from the attractions in Independence. The hotel offers a pool, cable TV, and free local calls. & (East Metro)

Bed-and-Breakfasts

MANSION HOUSE
2121 S. Sterling Ave.
Independence
816/254-5416
$$$

Dave and Paula Swayne purchased this historic home, its carriage house, and two surrounding acres, then spent a year renovating it. Now the elegant pre–Civil War mansion boasts four guest rooms, a Jacuzzi, meeting and event facilities, and a ballroom, all decorated in Victorian splendor. Once the residence of some of Independence's most illustrious citizens—the Ralstons, Winners, Nolands, and Colburns, for example—the Mansion House maintains its upscale origins. A full breakfast is served every morning in the formal dining room. (East Metro)

WOODSTOCK INN
1212 W. Lexington Ave.
Independence
816/833-2233
$$

Although it's in the Independence historic district, the Woodstock Inn has a decidedly more contemporary ambiance. Set across the street from the RLDS Temple and Auditorium, this B&B features nine guest rooms and two suites, all with private baths, telephones, and tasteful furnishings. Each morning, owners Todd and Patty Justice lay out a gourmet breakfast that includes delicacies ranging from thick Belgian waffles to crepes to quiche. & (East Metro)

Campgrounds

TRAILSIDE CAMPERS INN OF K.C.
1000 R.D. Mize Rd.
Grain Valley
816/229-2267 or 800/748-7729
$
Open since 1969, Trailside provides 90 trailer and tent sites within 20 to 30 minutes of Independence and the Truman Sports Complex. Besides water, electric, and sewer hookups, the complex includes a seasonal swimming pool and hot tub, and year-round shower and laundry facilities. Take I-70 Exit 24. & (East Metro)

Convention and Visitors Bureau of Greater Kansas City

4

WHERE TO EAT

In the early days, Kansas City cuisine gained acclaim largely for its beef. From sirloins to strips, steak in all its incarnations was usually the Heartland's meal du jour. And why not? The stockyards that bustled down in the West Bottoms gave local restaurateurs a tailor-made way to develop their gastronomical talents.

But times have changed in Kansas City. Latinos have introduced chile rellenos and chalupas; Japanese, soba noodles and shark fin. Vegetarians have opened restaurants featuring meatless delicacies. Fresh fish—from albacore to mahimahi—is flown in daily and appears regularly on Kansas City menus.

Still, in all fairness, many people visit here hankering for barbecue. One of the nation's great barbecue capitals, Kansas City boasts nearly 100 different barbecue restaurants, from hole-in-the-wall joints to renovated roadhouses to cloth-napkin-and-silver cafés. You could make it your mission to sample every barbecue bistro in the area and spend a pleasant year in the effort, hitting one every third day.

Whether you want a baby-back rib or a baby artichoke heart, you can find it in this Midwestern enclave. Although trends hit Kansas City a little later than on the coasts, the metro area catches on quickly. From coffeehouses to brew pubs, the greater Kansas City area offers stylish options to diners of all ages.

This chapter begins with a list of restaurants organized by the type of food each offers. Each name is followed by a zone abbreviation and the page number where you can find a full description. Restaurant descriptions are organized alphabetically within each geographic zone. Dollar-sign symbols indicate how much you can expect to spend per person for a typical entrée.

Price rating symbols:
$	$10 and under
$$	$11 to $20
$$$	$21 and up

RESTAURANTS BY FOOD TYPE

American/Casual
Chappell's Restaurant
& Lounge (NL), p. 77
Cheesecake Factory (PW), p. 64
Timberline Steakhouse
& Grill (EM), p. 84

Barbecue
Arthur Bryant's Barbeque (DT), p. 56
BB's Lawnside Barbecue (SKC), p. 80
Fiorella's Jack Stack
Barbeque (SKC, JC), p. 71, 80
Gates Bar-B-Q (DT, PW, JC, EM,
KCK), p. 65
Hayward's Pit Bar-B-Que (JC), p. 71
K.C. Masterpiece Barbeque
& Grill (PW, JC), p. 67, 71, 72
L.C.'s Bar-B-Q (EM), p. 81
Ricky's Pit Bar-B-Que (NL), p. 79
Rosedale Barbeque (KCK), p. 75
Smokehouse Bar-B-Que (NL), p. 79
Winslow's City Market
Smokehouse (DT), p. 62

Breakfast
Cascone's Grill (DT), p. 58
Corner Restaurant (PW), p. 64
First Watch (PW, JC, NL), p. 65

Brew Pubs
River Market Brewing
Company (DT), p. 61
75th Street Brewery (SKC), p. 80

Burgers and More
Dick Clark's American
Bandstand Grill (JC), p. 71
Otto's Malt Shop (PW), p. 68
Paradise Grill (NL), p. 77

Cajun, Etc.
Copeland's of New
Orleans (JC), p. 71
Kiki's Bon Ton Maison (PW), p. 68
Mardi Gras Café (NL), p. 77

Chinese
Bo Ling's Chinese
Restaurant (PW, JC), p. 62, 69
Genghis Khan Mongolian
Grill (PW), p. 65

Contemporary
Café Allegro (PW), p. 62
Californos Westport (PW), p. 62
Club 427 (DT), p. 58
Harry's Bar & Tables (PW), p. 65
Japengo (PW), p. 66
Stolen Grill (PW), p. 69
Yahooz (JC), p. 74

Delis
d'Bronx on Bell Street (PW), p. 64
Einstein Bros. Bagels
(DT, PW, JC, EM, NL), p. 64
New York Bakery
& Delicatessen (SKC), p. 81

Down Home
Mrs. Peter's Chicken
Dinners (KCK), p. 75
Stephenson's Old Apple Farm
(EM), p. 84
Stroud's (SKC, NL), p. 80, 81

Fine Dining
The American Restaurant
(DT), p. 56
EBT Restaurant (SKC), p. 80
JJ's (PW), p. 66
Rembrandt's Restaurant (NL), p. 79
Savoy Grill (DT), p. 61

French
La Méditerranée (JC), p. 72
Le Fou Frog (DT), p. 60
Tatsu's French Restaurant
(JC), p. 74

Greek
Mr. Gyro's Greek Food
& Pastries (JC), p. 73
Tasso's Greek Restaurant
(SKC), p. 81

Italian
Cascone's Restaurant
  & Lounge (NL), p. 77
Garozzo's Ristorante
  (DT, JC, EM), p. 58
Il Trullo (JC), p. 71
Lidia's Cucina (DT), p. 60

Japanese
Hibachi Japanese
  Steak House (PW), p. 66
Kabuki Japanese
  Restaurant (DT), p. 59

Light Lunch
Andre's Confiserie Suisse (PW), p. 62
La Dolce Vita (JC), p. 72

Mediterranean
Iliki Café (NL), p. 77
Jerusalem Café (PW), p. 66
Shiraz Restaurant (DT), p. 61
Tribal Grill (PW), p. 69

Mexican
Acapulco Mexican
  Restaurant (NL), p. 75
Guadalajara Café (SKC), p. 80
La Cocina del Puerco (JC), p. 72
Los Amigos Mexican Restaurant
  (KCK), p. 75
Manny's Restaurante Mexicano
  (DT), p. 60
Margarita's (DT), p. 60
Panzon's (JC), p. 74

Pizza
Minsky's (PW), p. 68
Wood Roasted Pizza (EM), p. 84

Seafood
The Bristol Bar & Grill (JC), p. 69
Mad Jack's Fresh Fish (KCK), p. 75
Marina Grog & Galley (EM), p. 84

Soul Food
Madry's Dash of Flavor (PW), p. 68
Maxine's Fine Foods (DT), p. 60

Steak
Hereford House (DT, JC), p. 59
Jess & Jim's Steak House
  (SKC), p. 81
Plaza III–The Steakhouse (PW), p. 69

Vegetarian
Bluebird Café (DT), p. 58
Eden Alley (PW), p. 64

Vietnamese
May Vietnamese Restaurant
  (JC), p. 72
Saigon 39 (PW), p. 69

DOWNTOWN

THE AMERICAN RESTAURANT
Crown Center
2450 Grand Ave.
Kansas City
816/426-1133
$$$
One of Kansas City's most revered
fine-dining restaurants, the American
boasts a generous view of down-
town. The cuisine, designed by
husband-and-wife chef team Michael
Smith and Debbie Gold, features lo-
cally grown meats and produce
blended into artistic dishes featuring
seafood, game, and veal. An elegant
spot for a quiet dinner, and the place
to be seen power lunching. Reserva-
tions recommended. Lunch Mon–Fri;
dinner Mon–Sat. & (Downtown)

ARTHUR BRYANT'S BARBEQUE
1727 Brooklyn Ave.
Kansas City
816/231-1123
$–$$
More than any other Kansas City
restaurant, Arthur Bryant's is a legend. Despite its seedy neighborhood,
the restaurant packs in everyone
from downtown executives to K.C.

DOWNTOWN KANSAS CITY

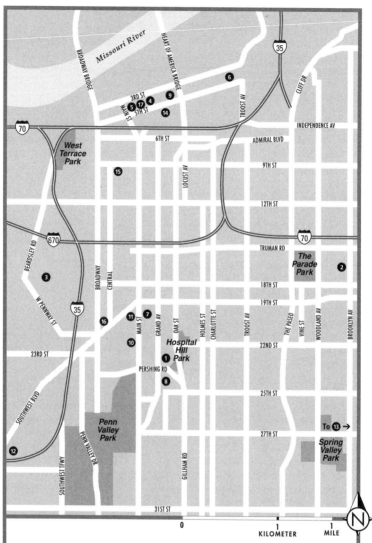

Where to Eat in Downtown Kansas City

1 The American Restaurant
2 Arthur Bryant's Barbeque
3 Bluebird Café
4 Cascone's Grill
5 Club 427
6 Garozzo's Ristorante
7 Hereford House
8 Kabuki Japanese Restaurant
9 Le Fou Frog

10 Lidia's Cucina
11 Manny's Restaurante Mexicano
12 Margarita's
13 Maxine's Fine Foods
14 River Market Brewing Company
15 Savoy Grill
16 Shiraz Restaurant
17 Winslow's City Market Smokehouse

visitors. Eager diners line up at the counter, while a sweaty crew labors before the blackened oven to load plates with beef brisket or ribs and unpeeled fries that will be sure to shoot cholesterol-counters into the stratosphere. Lunch and dinner. Also, look for Arthur Bryant's at Station Casino. & (Downtown)

BLUEBIRD CAFÉ
1700 Summit Dr.
Kansas City
816/221-7559
$
One of the area's few vegetarian restaurants, the Bluebird Café provides tasty selections in a cozy spot near downtown. Highlights include daily soup and pizza specials, basil *bruschetta*, curried vegetable pastries, and desserts. Owner Kathy Marchant harvests the restaurant's fresh produce from a garden across the street. Dinner reservations recommended. Lunch Mon–Fri; dinner Thu–Sat; brunch Sat and Sun. & (Downtown)

CASCONE'S GRILL
20 E. 5th St.
Kansas City
816/471-1018
$
Eating breakfast here on a Saturday morning is like dining in a Brooklyn boxcar. A counter, two long rows of booths set next to sweaty griddle-flipping cooks, and a line snaking out the door create a memorable atmosphere. Served with fried potatoes and Italian toast, the Italian omelet stuffed with peppers and onions starts a morning off with decadence. Lunch, Cascone's only other meal, is also good and less hectic. No credit cards; no reservations. Closed Mon. & (Downtown)

CLUB 427
427 Main St.
Kansas City
816/421-2582
$$
You'd never know this nightly jazz venue was created by the owner of Winslow's City Market Smokehouse next door. Club 427 is strictly uptown, with balcony tables overlooking the main floor and a tasteful gray and mauve decor. Dishes are innovative, ranging from grilled Kansas City filet mignon to Tuscan chicken served atop fresh orzo. Live jazz in a sophisticated environment creates a stunning atmosphere. Reservations recommended. Lunch Tue–Fri; dinner Tue–Sat. & (Downtown)

GAROZZO'S RISTORANTE
526 Harrison St.
Kansas City
816/221-2455
$$
Sinatra tunes provide the backdrop at this cozy bistro, a gem of a restaurant in an erstwhile Italian neighborhood. Old World specialties range from veal

Arthur Bryant's Barbeque, p. 56

Convention and Visitors Bureau of Greater Kansas City

Barbecue Beginnings

Kansas City's barbecue fame was unassumingly launched in the late 1920s by Henry Perry. The black entrepreneur dug a pit outside an abandoned streetcar barn to cook the meat that he sold wrapped in newspaper. In fact, barbecue was the domain of Kansas City's African American community until the late 1940s.

Today, African Americans own and operate many of the area's barbecue restaurants: Ollie Gates, who runs Gates Bar-B-Q, Kansas City's largest barbecue enterprise; Hayward Spears, who caters to the suburban lunch-time crowd; Ricky Smith, who claims a direct barbecue line to President Clinton with his Ricky's Pit Bar-B-Que; and Grace Harris, who offers her special barecue at the Grand Emporium blues club. All add definitive touches to Kansas City's barbecue culture, their individualistic interpretations giving variety to a joyous local cuisine.

to chicken to pasta, from most regions of Italy. Tables are set close in this intimate spot, while old family photos look down from the walls. Every dish on Mike Garozzo's menu is *molto bene*. Lunch Mon–Fri; dinner Mon–Sat. Closed Sun. Additional locations in Johnson County and East Metro. ♿ (Downtown)

HEREFORD HOUSE
2 E. 20th St.
Kansas City
816/842-1080
$$–$$$
A local institution since 1957, the Hereford House cooks its T-bone, prime rib, and K.C. Strip dinners over a hickory-fueled fire. Diners enjoy the clubby atmosphere, filled with dark woods and soft lighting. Desserts, especially peach cobbler, top off many meals. In 1996, *Wine Spectator* gave the restaurant an "Award of Excellence" for having one of the world's outstanding restaurant wine lists. Reservations recommended. Lunch Mon–Fri; dinner nightly. Additional location in Johnson County. ♿ (Downtown)

KABUKI JAPANESE RESTAURANT
Crown Center
2450 Grand Ave.
Kansas City
816/472-1717
$$
Lending an Asian flair to Crown Center, the Kabuki serves Japanese specialties such as tempura and sukiyaki. An authentic sushi bar gives diners a chance to try everything from *onaga* to *tako* to the venerable California roll. At the sushi bar you can watch the edible works of art unfold. Reservations recommended. Lunch Mon–Sat; dinner nightly. ♿ (Downtown)

LE FOU FROG
400 E. 5th St.
Kansas City
816/474-6060
$$–$$$

A Marseilles native, chef Mano Rafael opened his first restaurant in New York City to rave reviews. Later he married Kansas Citian Barbara Bayer, and the couple relocated to the Heartland, where they opened Le Fou Frog in the River Market area. The cozy dining room sets the stage for "The Crazy Frenchman" (Rafael's translation of Le Fou Frog) and his delectable dishes, such as *gambas grilles et panisse* (marinated and grilled prawns) and *carre d'agneau panne au jus* (rack of lamb). Fresh ingredients, an inspired chef, and a sophisticated setting create a charming dining experience. Reservations recommended. Lunch Wed–Fri; dinner Wed–Sun. & (Downtown)

LIDIA'S KANSAS CITY
101 W. 22nd St.
Kansas City
816/221-3722
$$–$$$

In their first restaurant venture outside New York City, mother-and-son duo Lidia and Joseph Bastianich opened Lidia's in the emerging Freight District. Known for Manhattan bistros Felidia and Becco, this pair has won rave reviews for their Northern Italian cuisine, such as *cozze alla Triestina* (braised mussels) and *osso buco alla giardiniera* (veal with spinach tagliatelle). Any of the three pastas of the day could become a favorite meal. Decor includes a two-story stone fireplace and three enormous chandeliers made of blown-glass grappa bottles. Reservations suggested. Lunch Mon–Fri; dinner nightly. & (Downtown)

MANNY'S RESTAURANTE MEXICANO
207 Southwest Blvd.
Kansas City
816/474-7696
$

A fire closed Manny's for months in 1998, but the restaurant reopened to a packed house. Its Southwest-style building has an impressive gold-topped tower; inside, the restaurant features two kinds of salsa, generous portions at reasonable prices, and an ongoing fiesta atmosphere. Dining rooms flow from one to the next, some at different levels. A popular spot for Mexican-food aficionados. Lunch and dinner. Closed Sun. Additional location in Johnson County. & (Downtown)

MARGARITA'S
2829 Southwest Blvd.
Kansas City
816/931-4849
$

Voted Kansas City's best Mexican restaurant for nine years, Margarita's boasts a loud and fun *ambiente*, especially during Friday happy hours. Expect a wait, but the abundant portions and tasty namesake concoctions make the delay worthwhile. Lunch and dinner. Additional locations in Gladstone, Shawnee Mission, and Martin City. & (Downtown)

MAXINE'S FINE FOODS
3041 Benton Blvd.
Kansas City
816/924-2004
$–$$

Maxine Byrd opened her place more than 35 years ago. Same restaurant, same place, same great soul-food menu. Breakfast is big—consider link, Polish, beef, or Italian sausage for starters. Lunch always includes

The Savoy Grill

baked chicken with dressing and black-eyed peas, then runs to pig hocks, oxtails, and neck bones. Photographs of prominent African American athletes, musicians, and others line the walls. Breakfast and lunch Tue–Fri; breakfast only Sat and Sun. No credit cards. & (Downtown)

RIVER MARKET
BREWING COMPANY
500 Walnut St.
Kansas City
816/471-6300
$$

Before the River Market Brewing Company moved in, every restaurant in recent memory had failed at 500 Walnut. But this brew pub packs them in, serving pizzas, sandwiches, and American-style specialties in addition to its own signature brews. A billiard parlor and live music on Friday nights round out the entertainment. Lunch and dinner. & (Downtown)

SAVOY GRILL
9th and Central Sts.
Kansas City

816/842-3890
$$$

Open since 1903, the Savoy is a K.C. classic. In the movie *Mr. and Mrs. Bridge*, the characters played by Paul Newman and Joanne Woodward favored the elegant restaurant for its timeless appeal. From the revolving glass doors to the white-jacketed waiters to the steak and seafood menu, the Savoy remains a traditional fine-dining favorite. Reservations required. Lunch Mon–Sat; dinner nightly. & (Downtown)

SHIRAZ RESTAURANT
320 Southwest Blvd.
Kansas City
816/472-0015
$–$$

The chef/owner at Shiraz blends some of his favorite flavors into an eclectic menu that combines Asian with American, Middle Eastern with continental. The result is a tasty ensemble of innovative dishes, such as Curry of Chicken & Seafood and Eggplant Marrakesh. A courtyard provides pleasant seating in warmer weather, while monthly exhibitions featuring local artists create a decorative dining experience. Reservations recommended. Lunch Mon–Fri; dinner Tue–Sat. Closed Sun and Mon. ♿ (Downtown)

WINSLOW'S CITY MARKET SMOKEHOUSE
20 E. 5th St.
Kansas City
816/471-7427
$–$$

From the River Market, follow the fragrant fumes to Winslow's City Market Smokehouse, where you'll discover the Famous Smokie (a chopped burnt-ends sandwich) and rib platters to tempt big eaters. Everything's fresh, bought right from the farmer's market just outside. Proprietor Dave Winslow regularly offers live Kansas City blues—and now packages the restaurant's spice rubs and sauces for use at home. Lunch daily; dinner Wed–Sun. ♿ (Downtown)

PLAZA/WESTPORT

ANDRE'S CONFISERIE SUISSE
5018 Main St.
Kansas City
816/561-3440
$

They make it simple at Andre's. Each day the chef prepares three lunch entrées; at least one is always the most delicious quiche you've ever tasted. A crispy vegetable and a dressed salad accompany the main course, followed by dessert—choose one of several from the cart or anything from the amply stocked cases up front. Diners appreciate the Swiss chalet atmosphere, the appetizingly simple fare, and the one-price-gets-all format. No reservations. Open Tue–Sat for lunch only. ♿ (Plaza/Westport)

BO LING'S CHINESE RESTAURANT
4800 Main St.
Kansas City
816/753-1718
$$

Bo Ling's original location commands the Board of Trade building's first floor, serving as a refined gathering spot for local Chinese families. In addition to traditional Asian main dishes, such as Seafood in Bird's Nest and Famous Bei Jing Roast Duck, the menu includes treats such as steamed buns, four-happiness rolls, and dim sum. Lunch and dinner daily. Two locations in Johnson County offer the same flavorful food with a slightly different ambiance. ♿ (Plaza/Westport)

CAFÉ ALLEGRO
1815 W. 39th St.
Kansas City
816/561-3663
$$–$$$

When founding chef/owner Steve Cole opened Café Allegro in the 1980s, it started 39th Street's restaurant revival. Within this sophisticated café, Cole has devised an eclectic menu featuring veal, fish, and pasta artfully combined with exceptional sauces and accompaniments. The restaurant specializes in seasonal produce, so you know everything's fresh. Reservations recommended. Lunch weekdays; dinner Mon–Sat. ♿ (Plaza/Westport)

CALIFORNOS WESTPORT
4124 Pennsylvania St.
Kansas City
816/531-7878
$$

In the spring and fall, Californos boasts one of the most pleasant outdoor dining spots. Patrons can sit streetside or out back on the expan-

PLAZA/WESTPORT

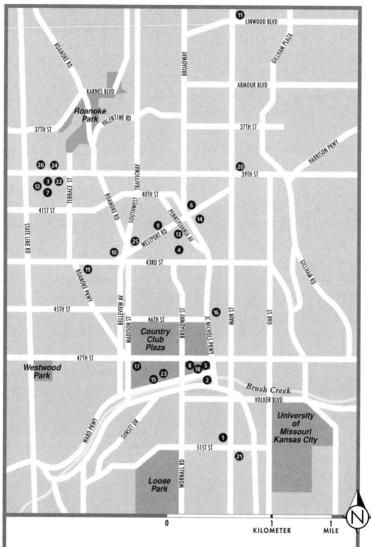

Where to Eat in the Plaza/Westport Area

1 Andre's Confiserie Suisse
2 Bo Ling's Chinese Restaurant
3 Café Allegro
4 Californos Westport
5 Cheesecake Factory
6 Corner Restaurant
7 D'Bronx on Bell Street
8 Eden Alley
9 Einstein Bros. Bagels
10 First Watch
11 Gates Bar-B-Q
12 Genghis Khan Mongolian Grill
13 Harry's Bar & Tables
14 Hibachi Japanese Steak House
15 Japengo
16 Jerusalem Café
17 JJ's
18 K.C. Masterpiece Barbeque & Grill
19 Kiki's Bon Ton Maison
20 Madry's Dash of Flavor
21 Minsky's
22 Otto's Malt Shop
23 Plaza III—The Steakhouse
24 Saigon 39
25 The Stolen Grill
26 Tribal Grill

sive redwood deck. Indoors, the ambiance becomes more sophisticated, with intimate tables covered in white cloths. The lunch menu ranges from sumptuous sandwiches to fresh salads; dinners concentrate on beef, chicken, and seafood. Owner/chef Barbara Burns has created a lovely spot in Westport. Dinner reservations recommended. Lunch and dinner. &
(Plaza/Westport)

CHEESECAKE FACTORY
4701 Wyandotte St.
Kansas City
816/960-1919
$$
From the minute it opened, the Cheesecake Factory has been packed. That's partly because the food at this Plaza eatery comes in gigantic portions. From Cajun jambalaya pasta to Baja fish tacos—with ample samples in the steak, salad, and sandwich departments—this place piles food so high that doggy bags are a common occurrence. Even the restaurant's namesake, the cheesecake, is doled out in pieces that will amaze you. No reservations. Lunch and dinner. &
(Plaza/Westport)

CORNER RESTAURANT
4059 Broadway Blvd.
Kansas City
816/931-6630
$
The Corner is an authentic neighborhood coffee shop that serves hearty omelets, pan-fried potatoes, pancakes, and sandwiches. Once a vegetarian hangout for Westport's hippie crowd, the Corner now attracts residents from all over town who value a good breakfast or lunch at a reasonable price. Expect a weekend wait on the sidewalk. No reserva-

tions; no credit cards. Breakfast and lunch daily; no lunch on Sun. &
(Plaza/Westport)

D'BRONX ON BELL STREET
3904 Bell St.
Kansas City
816/531-0550
$
Despite the name, here's a deli that will make you think you're in the heart of Manhattan—in fact, national rankings often list this emporium up there with Carnegie Deli and the like. The food—ranging from piled-high pizzas to massive deli sandwiches—fills you up, while the intellectually hip atmosphere of the 39th Street area feeds your "cool" quotient. No reservations. Lunch and dinner Mon–Sat. Closed Sun. & (Plaza/Westport)

EDEN ALLEY
707 W. 47th St.
Kansas City
816/561-5415
$–$$
The basement of Unity Temple on the Plaza provides an unconventional setting for Monica Jones and Sandi Corder's unconventional restaurant, but the quirky combination works. Vegetarian victuals—from a veggie burger to a falafel platter, Moroccan pizza to a quesadilla—prevail among the hand-painted tables and local artwork. Lunch and dinner Mon–Fri. Closed first Tue of each month. No credit cards. & (Plaza/Westport)

EINSTEIN BROS. BAGELS
556 Westport Rd.
Kansas City
816/561-2080
$
Einstein Bros.' Brookside location (6322 Brookside Plaza) was the first in Kansas City to take the round rolls

mainstream (as Bagel & Bagel), but the company's Westport spot is its largest and most accessible. Einstein Bros. features all kinds of bagel sandwiches as well as salads, soups, and beverages. Bagels flavored with onion, cinnamon raisin, and a whole lot more are available to go, too. Breakfast, lunch, and dinner. Closes at 5 p.m. Sat and Sun. Many additional locations throughout the metro area. & (Plaza/Westport)

FIRST WATCH
1022 Westport Rd.
Kansas City
816/931-1054
$
A national chain with a local feel, First Watch has at least six restaurants in the Kansas City area, which is a good indication of its popularity in these parts. Fluffy pancakes, flavorful omelets, and nonstop coffee guarantee a heavy repeat clientele. The Westport location attracts an urban crowd and is the place for professionals who meet for power breakfasts. The other locations tend to bring in more families. All enjoy

this restaurant's "breakfast anytime" attitude. Breakfast and lunch. Additional locations in the Johnson County and Northland zones. & (Plaza/Westport)

GATES BAR-B-Q
3205 Main St.
Kansas City
816/753-0828
$
The first time you enter a Gates restaurant, the shouts of "*Hi! May I help you?*" knock you back. Get used to it, though, because this is an important selling point that proprietor Ollie Gates instills in his staff at his legendary Rib Tech. Another important element at Kansas City's five Gates locations is the barbecue itself: succulent, spicy beef and pork that keep 'em coming back. No reservations. Lunch and dinner. Additional locations in all zones except Northland. & (Plaza/Westport)

GENGHIS KHAN
MONGOLIAN GRILL
3906 Bell St.
Kansas City
816/753-3600
$$
This quiet Westport restaurant lays out a splendid buffet of raw meats, vegetables, and condiments that diners pile onto their plates, then take to the chef at the expansive grill. It's one price for all you can pack away. There's a menu, too, featuring specialties like Clay Pot Chicken and Shanghai Wonton Main. Weekend reservations recommended. Lunch and dinner; closed Sun. & (Plaza/Westport)

HARRY'S BAR & TABLES
501 Westport Rd.
Kansas City

816/561-3950
$$

Harry's occupies a prime corner in Westport, with large windows that look out on the passing crowd. Plenty of interest takes place inside, however, starting with Harry's 58 brands of single-malt Scotch and 30 cigar varieties. It's definitely a smoke-and-Scotch setting, but the place offers everything from tapas to steak, from seafood à la carte to a fixed-price menu. In warm weather, Harry's opens its converted-caboose patio. Lunch and dinner. Call ahead if you require wheelchair assistance. (Plaza/ Westport)

HIBACHI JAPANESE STEAK HOUSE
4745 Wyandotte St.
Kansas City
816/753-0707
$$

Need a meal *and* entertainment? Head to Hibachi, where knife-wielding chefs command your attention at the *teppanyaki* grill. At this restaurant, more than a dozen of these grills invite diners to pull up a seat and watch the chefs work their cutting-edge magic. The team is ready to cook just about any Japanese-style grilled food imaginable. Lunch Mon–Fri; dinner nightly. Because it is located up one flight of stairs, Hibachi has limited wheelchair access. (Plaza/Westport)

JAPENGO
600 Ward Pkwy.
Kansas City
816/931-6600
$$–$$$

One of the most exciting new restaurants in town, Japengo bills itself as a Pacific café. That means it's inspired by flavors from the Pa-

cific Rim, such as ginger, mango, coconut, curry, wasabi, lemon grass, basmati rice, and so on. Set in a delightful spot on the Plaza and sporting its own courtyard, Japengo attracts diners eager for steamed lobster tails with a sweet soy–red curry sauce; Hawaiian ahi tuna with marinated *somen* noodles; and swordfish pan-seared in green chile. Reservations recommended. Lunch and dinner. ♿ (Plaza/Westport)

JERUSALEM CAFÉ
431 Westport Rd.
Kansas City
816/756-2770
$

Look for a blend of Greek, Middle Eastern, and other Mediterranean foods in this Midtown favorite. Located in Westport between the arty Tivoli Theatre and Natural Wear's organic apparel, Jerusalem recently doubled its space to accommodate the crowds. The moussaka rates especially high, as do the falafel and hummus. Lunch and dinner. Limited wheelchair access. (Plaza/Westport)

JJ'S
910 W. 48th St.
Kansas City
816/561-7136
$$$

An intimate restaurant just west of the Country Club Plaza, JJ's boasts one of the city's most acclaimed international wine lists. The American/continental menu features seafood, pasta, and steak in a romantic, artistic setting. Waiters are attentive, and the food is divine. Reservations recommended. Lunch weekdays; dinner nightly. ♿ (Plaza/Westport)

Ten Favorite Kansas City Restaurants

by Charles "Chomp" Ferruzza, restaurant critic for Sun Newspapers

1. **Stroud's** (1015 E. 85th St., Kansas City). You'll wait for a table, but the crispy fried chicken and cinnamon rolls are worth it all. Diet be damned!

2. **Cascone's Grill** (20 E. 5th St., Kansas City). Best place to see and be seen on a Saturday morning; superb fluffy pancakes with Italian sausage and marinara.

3. **L.C.'s Bar-B-Q** (5800 Blue Pkwy., Kansas City). The tender barbecue in this joint is good, but the french fries are the best on the planet, Janet.

4. **Rozelle Court** (Nelson-Atkins Museum of Art, Kansas City). The food is overpriced but tasty enough. It's the gorgeous ambiance that satisfies hunger here. The most romantic spot in town.

5. **Café Allegro** (1815 W. 39th St., Kansas City). The city's most glam boîte. It's the place to go when someone else picks up the tab.

6. **Skies** (Hyatt Regency, Kansas City). Revolving restaurants are back in style, and this one has a fab view, great food, and divine service.

7. **Grand Street Café** (4740 Grand St., Kansas City). Even the hamburgers are stylish at this elegant and hip Plaza eatery.

8. **Japengo** (600 Ward Pkwy., Kansas City). Pacific grill cuisine in an elegant, colorful setting that's pure Fellini!

9. **Three Friends Barbecue** (2461 Prospect, Kansas City). Delicious pork chops, catfish, chicken, and the finest peach cobbler a la mode.

10. **The Savoy Grill** (219 W. 9th St., Kansas City). Big ol' lobsters and steaks, and the fin de siècle decor hasn't changed since the Taft administration.

**K.C. MASTERPIECE
BARBECUE & GRILL**
4747 Wyandotte Rd.
Kansas City
816/531-3332
$–$$
The barbecue at K.C. Masterpiece will probably seem familiar to visitors, since the signature sauce is sold nationwide. Kansas City's two Masterpiece locations (the other's in Overland Park) serve everything from burnt ends to baby-back ribs to brisket; the K.C. Combo is a good way

to sample several hickory-smoked favorites, while Ribs, Ribs, Ribs provides enough, you guessed it, for two. Onion straws—mounded on a platter—have become a popular pre-dinner warm-up. Lunch and dinner. & (Plaza/Westport)

KIKI'S BON TON MAISON
1515 Westport Rd.
Kansas City
816/931-9417
$–$$

When you're in the mood for a festive atmosphere and exceptional Cajun cuisine, head to Kiki's Bon Ton Maison. Here, you'll find hearty food from Louisiana, such as red beans and rice with Creole smoked sausage, jambalaya, and an array of po'boys. Live music often features the enthusiastic and entertaining Bon Ton Soul Accordion Band, led by Kiki's husband, Richard Lucente. Lunch and dinner. & (Plaza/Westport)

MADRY'S DASH OF FLAVOR
26 E. 39th St.
Kansas City

Plaza III–The Steakhouse

Haddad Restaurant Group, Inc.

816/753-3274
$–$$

For Dorothy Madry, meals come hale and hearty. With her husband, James Madry Sr., this restaurateur serves up a bountiful soul food buffet of chicken, beef brisket, ham, and meatloaf, as well as all the trimmings, from mashed potatoes and gravy to bread pudding, white rolls, green beans, and pie. Lunch and dinner. & (Plaza/Westport)

MINSKY'S
5105 Main St.
Kansas City
816/561-5100
$

A trusty neighborhood joint, Minsky's lures diners who love pizza. Especially noteworthy are Nature's Choice–a veggie pizza on a honey whole-wheat crust–and the Tostada Pizza, stacked high with chicken, beans, cheese, tomatoes, and salsa. Minsky's also serves pasta and sandwiches in its publike setting. Lunch and dinner. Six additional locations. & (Plaza/ Westport)

OTTO'S MALT SHOP
3903 Wyoming St.
Kansas City
816/756-1010
$

Owner Kathleen McSweeny brings the Fifties-style diner back to life, complete with burgers, blue plate specials, shakes, and malts. The big-eyed brave go for "bucket-size" malts—a whopping 32 ounces—and Fat Boys, a 6-ounce patty beneath four cheeses, bacon, and a fried egg. Lunch and dinner daily. No credit cards. & (Plaza/Westport)

PLAZA III–THE STEAKHOUSE
4749 Pennsylvania Ave.

Kansas City
816/753-0000
$$$

Resembling a dark-paneled men's club of the Forties, the Plaza III reigns as one of Kansas City's favorite up-scale steakhouses. Specialties include prime cuts of Midwestern beef, as well as fresh fish and lobster. At lunch, look for lighter fare, including sandwiches, salads, and the signature Steak Soup. Plaza III has been noted for its extensive wine list. Reservations recommended. Lunch Mon–Sat; dinner nightly. ♿ (Plaza/Westport)

SAIGON 39
1806½ W. 39th St.
Kansas City
816/531-4447
$$

Vietnamese specialties at this bustling Westport restaurant include stir-fried meats, fish, and vegetables served over a variety of noodles and fried rice. You can choose mild or spicy; it's all flavorful and authentic. Occasionally, owner/chef Mimi Perkins ventures into the dining area to make sure you're happy with what she's cooked. Lunch and dinner; closed Sun. No credit cards. ♿ (Plaza/ Westport)

THE STOLEN GRILL
904 Westport Rd.
Kansas City
816/960-1450
$$$

This sophisticated spot in Westport has been a foodie's dream since it opened in mid-1997. The cuisine— created by a young, inventive chef named Patrick Weber—has lured a hip and urbane crowd with dishes such as grilled swordfish with summer squash, foie gras–stuffed breast

of Campo Lindo Farms range hen with portobello mushrooms, and roast garlic stuffed Hereford beef filet. The menu changes often here, and Weber emphasizes fresh dishes that boast an impressive combination of flavor, aroma, and presentation. Reservations recommended. Dinner only Mon–Sat. ♿ (Plaza/Westport)

TRIBAL GRILL
1808½ W. 39th St.
Kansas City
816/756-5566
$–$$

One of the most popular new restaurants in the 39th Street enclave, Tribal Grill serves Mediterranean food with style and flair. Fans flock here for the hummus, *balila*, *muhammara*, and *batata kisbara*, all served for the entire table to sample. Owner Marwan Chebara creates a peaceful atmosphere, making dining a pleasant and savory experience. Reservations recommended on weekends. Lunch and dinner Mon–Sat. ♿ (Plaza/Westport)

JOHNSON COUNTY

BO LING'S
CHINESE RESTAURANT
9055 Metcalf Ave.
Overland Park
913/341-1718
$$

See Plaza/Westport section.

THE BRISTOL BAR & GRILL
5400 W. 119th St.
Leawood
913/663-5777
$$–$$$

Long a staple on the Country Club Plaza, the Bristol was unceremoniously bounced a few years ago by

JOHNSON CO./KANSAS CITY, KS

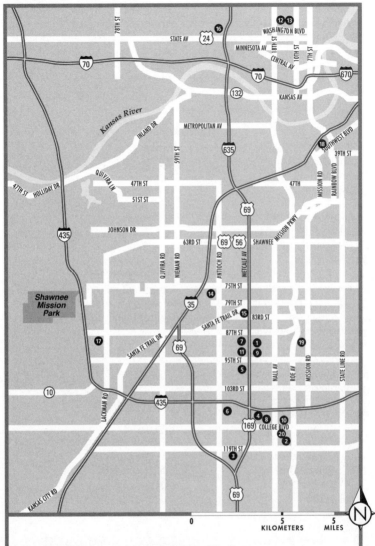

Where to Eat in Johnson County and Kansas City, Kansas

1 Bo Ling's Chinese Resturant (JC)
2 The Bristol Bar & Grill (JC)
3 Copeland's of New Orleans (JC)
4 Dick Clark's American Bandstand Grill (JC)
5 Fiorella's Jack Stack Barbeque (JC)
6 Hayward's Pit Bar-B-Que (JC)

7 Il Trullo (JC)
8 K.C. Masterpiece Barbeque & Grill (JC)
9 La Cocina Del Puerco (JC)
10 La Dolce Vita (JC)
11 La Méditerranée (JC)
12 Los Amigos Mexican Restaurant (KCK)
13 Mad Jack's Fresh Fish (KCK)
14 May Vietnamese Restaurant (JC)

15 Mr. Gyro's Greek Food & Pastry (JC)
16 Mrs. Peter's Chicken Dinners (KCK)
17 Panzon's (JC)
18 Rosedale Barbeque (KCK)
19 Tatsu's French Restaurant (JC)
20 Yahooz (JC)

Plaza owners who wanted some new blood. But it rebounded in a south Johnson County location, boasting bigger crowds than ever. Known for its classy seafood dishes—from seared yellowfin tuna to mesquite-grilled mahimahi—the Bristol also offers nonstop buttermilk biscuits and an impressive wine list. Reservations recommended. Lunch, dinner, and Sunday brunch. ᕯ (Johnson County)

COPELAND'S OF NEW ORLEANS
11920 Metcalf Ave.
Overland Park
913/663-5290
$$

Beloved former Chiefs player Neil Smith opened this Cajun-American café before he defected to Denver—but the business keeps pulling him back to Kansas City. It's easy to see why. This delightful restaurant features Cajun and Creole specialties, such as crawfish *étouffée*, shrimp and redfish creole, and chicken *fais do do*, as well as prime rib and pasta. On Sunday, Copeland's lays out a lavish brunch buffet, complete with live jazz. Reservations recommended. Lunch, dinner, and Sunday brunch. ᕯ (Johnson County)

DICK CLARK'S AMERICAN BANDSTAND GRILL
10975 Metcalf Ave.
Overland Park
913/451-1600
$$

Dick Clark entertained millions with his weekly TV show. Now you can enjoy his restaurant and dance club, which serves burgers, pasta, seafood, chicken, steaks, and ribs. At Dick Clark's Walk of Fame, celebrity hounds can see mementos from stars such as Elton John, Madonna, and Michael Jackson.

Dessert specials such as the 45 RPM Chocolate Orgy (chocolate ice cream, chocolate chip cookie, dark chocolate sauce) continue the theme. Lunch and dinner. ᕯ (Johnson County)

FIORELLA'S JACK STACK BARBEQUE
9520 Metcalf Ave.
Overland Park
913/385-7427
$$–$$$

See South Kansas City section.

HAYWARD'S PIT BAR-B-QUE
11051 Antioch Rd.
Overland Park
913/451-8080
$

Barbecue master Hayward Spears dishes up succulent ribs, smoky brisket, and delicious sauces at this eatery in the College Boulevard neighborhood. Johnson Countians naturally line up here for lunch, but the rest of the city heads over, too, for Hayward's chicken, smoked sausage, and beef sandwiches on plump buns. Lunch and dinner. ᕯ (Johnson County)

IL TRULLO
9056 Metcalf Ave.
Overland Park
913/341-3773
$$

Joe Avelluto's upscale restaurant features food from the Adriatic coast's Apulia region, often described as the heel of Italy's boot. The cozy, candlelit atmosphere only enhances the food, which includes everything from pizza with homemade ingredients to *zuppa di mare* (soup of the sea). Weekend reservations recommended. Lunch Mon–Fri; dinner nightly. ᕯ (Johnson County)

Bob Green Photography

Copeland's of New Orleans, p. 71

K.C. MASTERPIECE BARBEQUE & GRILL
10985 Metcalf Ave.
Overland Park
913/345-8646
$–$$
See Plaza/Westport section.

LA COCINA DEL PUERCO
9097 Metcalf Ave.
Overland Park
913/341-2800
$
In the summer, La Cocina del Puerco's outdoor patio resembles a colorful Mexican fiesta. But throughout the rest of the year, this diner features hearty food in an authentic cantina setting. Served cafeteria style, the food at La Cocina includes everything from enchiladas to *carne asada* to burritos. A salsa bar gives patrons the chance to try several varieties: red to green, chunky to smooth, mild to hot. Folding chairs, simple tables, and piñatas accompany the Mexican tunes. Lunch and dinner. ♿ (Johnson County)

LA DOLCE VITA
4821 W. 117th St.
Leawood
913/498-8785
$–$$
Located in Leawood's Town Center Plaza, La Dolce Vita radiates a quiet appreciation for the good life. Specializing in *panini*, this eatery serves up sandwiches such as the Firenze—provolone, fresh spinach, artichoke hearts, sweet basil, roasted red pepper, and sun-dried tomatoes on focaccia. Breakfast, lunch, and dinner. ♿ (Johnson County)

LA MÉDITERRANÉE
9058 Metcalf Ave.
Overland Park
913/341-9595
$$–$$$
Once a Plaza institution, La Méditerranée has continued serving its classic French menu to adoring fans who followed it to Johnson County. The formal setting provides a stunning backdrop to dishes such as salmon with wasabi sauce, seasonal wild boar, and chateaubriand. Reservations suggested. Lunch Mon–Fri; dinner Mon–Sat. Closed Sun. ♿ (Johnson County)

MAY VIETNAMESE RESTAURANT
8841 W. 75th St.
Overland Park
913/648-1688
$–$$
"May" is old-growth bamboo. For this family-run operation, it symbolizes flexibility for customers and the hope for a long business history. They're on the right track. Serving Vietnamese dishes from sautéed vegetables to meal-size soups and Vietnamese-influenced Chinese, the restaurant keeps patrons returning for more. A waterfall, pond, and fountain add to

Ten Best Places to Drink Wine

by Doug Frost, author of *Uncorking Wine* and one of only two people in the world to hold both the Master of Wine and Master Sommelier designations

Kansas City is a happy accident of very good restaurants and excellent wine lists. The wine offerings at many establishments are surprisingly serious. Best of all, food is just as serious at the places listed below:

1. **Classic Cup Café** (4130 Pennsylvania). This multi-personalitied Plaza eatery boasts a massive list and the best prices in the city.

2. **The American Restaurant** (Crown Center). This wine list is a wine-lover's dream. Though prices can be high, there are many bargains to be hunted down.

3. **JJ's Bar & Grill** (910 W. 48th St.). A Plaza bistro that owns a *Wine Spectator* Grand Award for its bigger-than-massive list and excellent pricing, JJ's has enough champagne and port to drown yourself in.

4. **Starker's Private Reserve** (200 Nichols Rd.). Once a private club, this elegant room is open to the public, has an even longer list than before, and sports its own *Wine Spectator* Grand Award.

5. **Joe D's Winebar** (6227 Brookside Plaza). The friendliest waitresses in town serve a wine-by-the-glass selection of more than 50 offerings here. Its list is revamped every few months.

6. **Café Allegro** (1815 W. 39th St.). This restaurant's great food is complemented by a rich, selective, and exciting list and by equally serious wine-by-the-glass offerings.

7. **Il Trullo** (9056 Metcalf, Overland Park). It's fun to drink wine here because the food is as straightforward and delightful, as the proprietor.

8. **Plaza III–The Steakhouse** (4749 Pennsylvania). Here you'll find a long list of reds and some great rarities.

9. **The Majestic Steakhouse** (931 Broadway). This restaurant offers another huge red wine collection with constantly changing features.

10. **The Stolen Grill** (904 Westport Rd.). Aside from being one of the finest restaurants in the Midwest, the Stolen Grill's list is short and well chosen, with more deliciousness per selection than any other list in town.

the serene surroundings. Lunch and dinner. ♿ (Johnson County)

MR. GYRO'S GREEK FOOD & PASTRY

**8234 Metcalf Ave.
Overland Park
913/381-4218
$**

Mr. Gyro's is an auspicious amalgam

of fast food and palate-pleasing Greek comestibles. As the name implies, the restaurant specializes in gyro sandwiches, but you can also find delicious souvlaki, moussaka, and *tzatsiki* with generous portions of pita bread. A great place to get a quick Greek fix. Lunch and dinner. Closed Sun. & (Johnson County)

PANZON'S
8710 Lackman Rd.
Lenexa
913/492-9555
$

Widely regarded as the best place in town for guacamole, Panzon's also boasts a variety of vegetarian and black-bean Mexican specialties. While there's often a dinner wait, Panzon's makes it worth your while, delivering fresh and spicy enchiladas, tacos, and tamales in gigantic portions. Reservations for parties of six or more. Lunch Mon–Sat; dinner nightly. & (Johnson County)

TATSU'S FRENCH RESTAURANT
4603 W. 90th St.
Prairie Village
913/383-9801
$$$

Tatsu's Japanese owner/chef—who lent his own name to his exquisite restaurant—has created a nearly hidden gem in a tiny Johnson County commercial development. Combining elegant French cuisine with stylish surroundings, Tatsu counts fresh seafood, beef tenderloin, and veal among his specialties, all impeccably presented at your table. Fresh flowers and French decor await as well. Reservations are recommended. Lunch Mon–Fri; dinner Mon–Sat. Closed Sun. & (Johnson County)

YAHOOZ
4701 Town Center Dr.
(117th St. and Nall)
Leawood
913/451-8888
$$–$$$

"Upscale cowboy" sounds like a contradiction in terms, but that's ex-

Dick Clark's American Bandstand Grill, p. 71

Dick Clark's American Bandstand Grill

actly what you'll find at Yahooz, a newer restaurant at the Town Center Plaza that has the feel of a Rocky Mountain lodge. Massive beams, large Western murals, and lots of leather create a comfy setting for dishes that range from prime ribeye to wood-fired rainbow trout to enchiladas. Side dishes, salads, and desserts are robust and flavorful. Reservations recommended. Lunch and dinner. & (Johnson County)

KANSAS CITY, KANSAS

LOS AMIGOS
MEXICAN RESTAURANT
2808 State Ave.
Kansas City, Kansas
913/281-4547
$
Charlie Moretina guarantees you won't leave his casual, family-run restaurant hungry—that's because he serves feasts such as the Ultimate Burrito Spread, a beef, chicken, or pork wonder with chili, cheese, cheese sauce, and sour cream. Conservative weight estimate: one-and-a-half to two pounds of food. Lunch and dinner Mon–Sat. Closed Sun. Limited wheelchair access. (Kansas City, Kansas)

MAD JACK'S FRESH FISH
1318 State Ave.
Kansas City, Kansas
913/371-8862
$
Proprietor John Reed renamed the long-time State Avenue Fish Market after its former owner, a commercial fisherman who hauled hoop nets from Missouri River backwaters. The fish no longer come from the Muddy Mo, but Reed serves some of the best fried fish in Kansas City, from catfish

to shark to bluegill (no kidding). It's all delivered in a funky structure that still features a fresh-fish counter. Lunch and dinner. Closed Sun. & (Kansas City, Kansas)

MRS. PETER'S CHICKEN DINNERS
4960 State Ave.
Kansas City, Kansas
913/287-7711
$
The local newspaper calls Mrs. Peter's "an icon," and the publication's truly got it right. Fried chicken served family style with all the fixings—mashed potatoes, vegetables, salads, and biscuits—keep both the faithful and new converts coming back for more. Pork chops and catfish also have their followings here. Lunch and dinner. Closed Mon. & (Kansas City, Kansas)

ROSEDALE BARBEQUE
600 Southwest Blvd.
Kansas City, Kansas
913/262-0343
$
Down among the railroad tracks and warehouses, Rosedale continues its long-standing tradition: dishing out high-quality barbecue. A modest setting that attracts a veritable cross-section of the population, Rosedale presents substantial servings of smoked ribs, sandwiches piled high, and tasty accompaniments. Some in town will let no other sauce touch their lips. Lunch and dinner. & (Kansas City, Kansas)

NORTHLAND

ACAPULCO MEXICAN
RESTAURANT
1041 Burlington Rd.
North Kansas City

Ten Favorite Kansas City Barbecue Joints

by Carolyn Wells, publisher of *The K.C. Bullsheet*, the official publication of the Kansas City Barbeque Society (motto: "Barbecue: It's not just for breakfast anymore")

1. **Arthur Bryant's.** "Beef and fries" is the order of the day—brisket piled high between slices of white bread, complemented by fries, fresh cut and fried in pure lard. Be adventuresome: Try the vinegar/paprika sauce for which Bryant's is famous.

2. **K.C. Masterpiece Barbeque & Grill.** Upscale "que" here, covered with the famous K.C. Masterpiece Barbecue Sauce. The only place in town to get a "Carolina" pork sandwich—my personal favorite.

3. **Lil' Jake's Eat It and Beat It.** This tiny, 18-seat establishment has a big following. Best bets are the brisket sandwich, followed closely by the grilled chicken breast.

4. **BB's Lawnside Bar-B-Q.** Blues and barbecue aficionado Lindsay Shannon serves up hickory-smoked ribs and rib tips. The fries are a house specialty.

5. **Grand Emporium.** "Amazing Grace" Harris, head pitmaster, rules her barbecue kingdom at this wildly eclectic blues, booze, and barbecue palace. She offers a full complement of barbecue meats, seasoned with her secret sauces and rubs.

6. **Gates Bar-B-Q.** Local "living legend" Ollie Gates has the closest thing to a chain of barbecue restaurants in K.C. Servers enthusiastically call, "HI! MAY I HELP YOU?" as you enter. Gates' regionally popular sauces complement the array of barbecued meats.

7. **Winslow's City Market Smokehouse.** The perfect ending to a morning of heavy-duty City Market shopping. The beef sandwich is the best bet.

8. **Marty's Bar-B-Q.** All the standard barbecued fare, plus Memphis-style pork and Texas-style beef. Grilled chicken breast and great Italian sausage offer additional variety in this Northland eatery.

9. **Rosedale Barbeque.** From the oldest continually operated barbecue place in the Kansas City area, Anthony Riecke serves loyal rib aficionados. Offerings are topped with his signature sauce.

10. **L.C.'s Bar-B-Q.** With a smoker chained to a utility pole in front of this modest establishment, L.C.'s is the pit stop of choice for sports fans on the way to Arrowhead and Kauffman Stadiums.

816/472-8689
$

After 30 years downtown, restaurant owner Rafael Jimenez moved his Acapulco Mexican Restaurant to a larger location north of the river. The food—made from recipes the Guadalajara native learned from his mother—stayed the same, however, as did the trademark palm-tree sign out front. Spicy tamales, cheesy enchiladas, and bean tacos each have their enthusiastic following. The Acapulco has a full bar, serving tasty margaritas. Lunch and dinner. Closed Sun. & (Northland)

CASCONE'S RESTAURANT & LOUNGE
3733 N. Oak Trafficway
Kansas City
816/454-7977
$$–$$$

Italian food lovers head to Cascone's for chicken, seafood, and *fantastico* pasta dishes such as baked lasagna and fettucini Alfredo. Cascone's covers Italy from north to south in a friendly, family-owned setting. Lunch Mon–Sat; dinner nightly. Additional location in Johnson County. & (Northland)

CHAPPELL'S RESTAURANT & LOUNGE
323 Armour Rd.
North Kansas City
816/421-0002
$–$$

Owner Jim Chappell has amassed a championship collection of sports memorabilia, including World Series trophies, vintage uniforms, and thousands of photos. They're all on display at this all-American restaurant. Specialties range from stuffed jalapeños to juicy burgers to succulent prime rib. Don't miss the football hel-

met collection hanging from the rafters. Lunch and dinner. Closed Sun. & (Northland)

ILIKI CAFÉ
6427 N. Cosby Ave.
Kansas City
816/587-0009
$

When you want to replicate a trip to the Middle East, head to the Iliki Café. This small eatery specializes in hot and cold *mezze*, which are appetizer-sized portions meant to be shared. The cold *mezze* sampler, for example, combines *baba ganouj*, a classic eggplant and tahini dip; tangy tabbouleh and herbs stuffed in grape leaves; and *muhammara*, a sweet red-pepper dip. Entrées are available, too, at a slightly higher price. Lunch and dinner. Closed Sun. & (Northland)

MARDI GRAS CAFÉ
420 NW Englewood Rd.
Kansas City
816/452-5252
$–$$

Anyone who dreams of Bourbon Street will want to head north to this Cajun-Creole café for everything from jambalaya, *shrimp étouffée*, and po' boy sandwiches—most of it four-alarm hot. A vibrant and colorful atmosphere is embellished by live music several nights a week and the occasional services of a chiromancer ($10 per reading). Boiled crawfish have become a local favorite. Lunch and dinner. & (Northland)

PARADISE GRILL
5225 NW 64th St.
Kansas City
816/587-9888
$$

"High-tech Fifties" is the way this

NORTHLAND

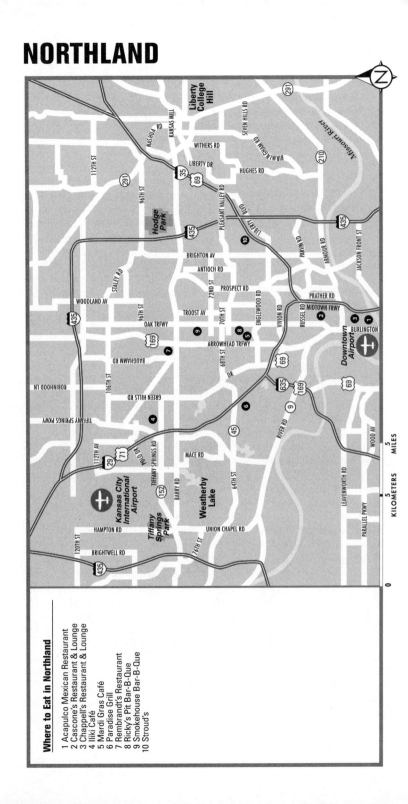

Where to Eat in Northland

1 Acapulco Mexican Restaurant
2 Cascone's Restaurant & Lounge
3 Chappell's Restaurant & Lounge
4 Iliki Café
5 Mardi Gras Café
6 Paradise Grill
7 Rembrandt's Restaurant
8 Ricky's Pit Bar-B-Que
9 Smokehouse Bar-B-Que
10 Stroud's

restaurant explains its bright colors and local artwork design. "Fun" is the word most regular patrons use to describe both the food and the experience here. Consider the Squawking Nachos, Kickin' Chicken, or Vodka Chive Pasta, just a few of the wacky menu winners at this eatery eight miles south of KCI airport, off I-29. Reservations recommended. Lunch and dinner. & (Northland)

REMBRANDT'S RESTAURANT
2820 NW Barry Rd.
Kansas City
816/436-8700
$$–$$$

A genteel restaurant set on a 15-acre estate, Rembrandt's features four dining rooms and a European-style menu. Entrées include prime rib,

smoked Missouri ham, and rack of lamb. Every Sunday, Rembrandt's lays out an enormous brunch. The estate is also a favorite spot for weddings, receptions, and other parties. Reservations recommended. Dinner nightly. & (Northland)

RICKY'S PIT BAR-B-QUE
311 NE Englewood Rd.
Kansas City
816/413-0800
$

He's moved from KCK to north of the river, but Ricky Smith still serves up the barbecue that put his name in lights. Crowds flock here for the restaurant's signature sandwiches: the RickBo, a triple-decker of beef, ham, and turkey; and Ricky's Melt, sliced meat with sauce and hot-pepper cheese, steamed on rye. Unlike his competitors, Ricky mixes cherry and hickory woods together for a unique smoking blend. Ricky's is one of Bill Clinton's favorite barbecue joints. Lunch and dinner. & (Northland)

SMOKEHOUSE BAR-B-QUE
6304 N. Oak Trafficway
Gladstone
816/454-4500
$–$$

This is a full-service restaurant, but it's the hickory-smoked ribs, fish, and chicken that have earned its reputation. Burnt ends also continue to be a favorite. The not-so-barbecue-enamored can try steak, catfish, and trout for variety. The Smokehouse's stained-glass and wood decor make everyone feel right at home. Lunch and dinner. & (Northland)

STROUD'S
5410 NE Oak Ridge Dr.

Kansas City
816/454-9600
$$
For a description, see listing in the
South Kansas City section, page 71

SOUTH KANSAS CITY

75TH STREET BREWERY
520 W. 75th St.
Kansas City
816/523-4677
$$
Set on a busy street in the Waldo
neighborhood, the 75th Street Brewery draws a yuppie crowd for happy
hour. Handcrafted beer, made in a
glass-walled room in the brew pub's
center, varies from Cowtown Wheat
Light to the very dark Muddy Mo
Stout. The food at 75th Street shows
a real artistry, too: Pizzas, sandwiches, and grilled entrées are
served in a *terrazza*-like setting. Live
music on weekends. Lunch and dinner. ঙ (South Kansas City)

BB'S LAWNSIDE BARBECUE
1205 E. 85th St.
Kansas City
816/822-7427
$–$$
Set in a ramshackle roadhouse, BB's
Lawnside combines owner Lindsay
Shannon's dual passions: barbecue
and blues. BB's signature pork ribs
come slathered in a sweet sauce
slightly reminiscent of apples and cinnamon. Side dishes, such as batter
fries and baked beans with green
peppers, fill out the fare. Diners sit
family-style at long tables covered
with checkered tablecloths or in
booths along the walls. Live blues
light up BB's Thu–Sun. No reservations. Lunch and dinner. Closed Mon
and Tue. ঙ (South Kansas City)

EBT RESTAURANT
1310 Carondelet Dr.
Kansas City
816/942-8870
$$$
EBT stands for Emery Bird Thayer,
once an elegant downtown depart-
ment store. Today this restaurant
features some of the store's archi-
tectural treasures, from a gilded el-
evator cage to massive stone pillars.
Diners descend on EBT for special
occasions, from sealing a business
deal to proposing marriage. The
elegant American and French-style
cuisine includes lamb, beef, chicken,
and seafood served in a garden-like
setting. Reservations recommended.
Lunch weekdays; dinner nightly.
Closed Sun. ঙ (South Kansas City)

FIORELLA'S JACK
STACK BARBEQUE
13441 Holmes Rd.
Martin City
816/942-9141
$$
Formerly called Smoke Stack Bar-
B-Q, this Martin City restaurant
changed names when owner Jack
Fiorella opened another restaurant in
Overland Park and decided to set his
places apart from similarly named
eateries. Both restaurants feature
ribs, pork sandwiches, and burnt
ends, all cooked on a hickory wood
grill and guaranteed to satisfy even
the pickiest barbecue aficionado.
Smoked fish is another house specialty. No reservations; expect at
least an hour wait on weekend
nights. Lunch and dinner. Additional
location in Johnson County. ঙ (South
Kansas City)

GUADALAJARA CAFÉ
1144 W. 103rd St.
Kansas City

913/941-4471
$$
This place offers Mexican food in a fine-dining setting. It doesn't get any better than this. Restaurateurs Victor Esqueda and Gilbert Gutierrez base their extensive menu on foods from their native Mexican city. Steak, chicken, and seafood specialties hold center stage, with the standard tacos, enchiladas, and burritos a happy sideline. Dinner reservations recommended. Lunch and dinner. ♿ (South Kansas City)

JESS & JIM'S STEAK HOUSE
517 E. 135th St.
Kansas City
816/941-9499
$$
Since 1938, this south Kansas City restaurant has earned its reputation for great steaks at great prices—and for enormous twice-baked potatoes. Located in Martin City, it continues to attract loyal followers as well as a new crowd looking for the ultimate in grilled beef, pork, and chicken. No reservations. Lunch and dinner. ♿ (South Kansas City)

NEW YORK BAKERY & DELICATESSEN
7016 Troost Ave.
Kansas City
816/523-0432
$
Reminiscent of Manhattan's Lower East Side, the New York Bakery concocts a wonderfully versatile mix of kosher specialties, pastries, and party trays. Sandwiches here come piled high—owner James Holzmark, for example, stacks his rye bread with nearly two pounds of corned beef, as well as sauerkraut, Swiss cheese, and spicy mustard. Lunch and dinner. Closed Sun. ♿ (South Kansas City)

STROUD'S
1015 E. 85th St.
Kansas City
816/333-2132 or 454-9600
$$
Stroud's is one of those Kansas City traditions that soundly deserves its reputation. This humble-looking joint features pan-fried chicken, mashed potatoes, green beans, and cinnamon rolls that attract diners willing to wait as long as two hours for a table. Set in a sprawling wood bungalow, Stroud's epitomizes the days when folks ate real food in real surroundings. No reservations. Lunch and dinner. Additional location Northland. ♿ (South Kansas City)

TASSO'S GREEK RESTAURANT
8411 Wornall Rd.
Kansas City
816/363-4776
$$
Save room for the baklava at this fun-loving spot. At Tasso's, tasty Hellenic meals of moussaka, spring lamb, or gyros come with live Greek music and belly dancing. A small café with its own loyal following, it's the place to go for celebrating like the Athenians. Beware the owner, however, bearing countless glasses of the licorice-like ouzo. Weekend dinner reservations recommended. Lunch and dinner Tue–Sat. ♿ (South Kansas City)

EAST METRO

L.C.'S BAR-B-Q
5800 Blue Pkwy.
Kansas City
816/923-4484
$
This ain't no fancy joint, but L.C.'s smokes up some of the best barbe-

SOUTH KANSAS CITY/EAST METRO

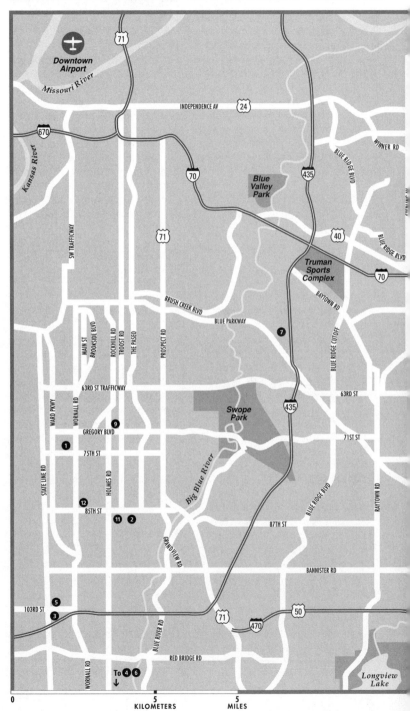

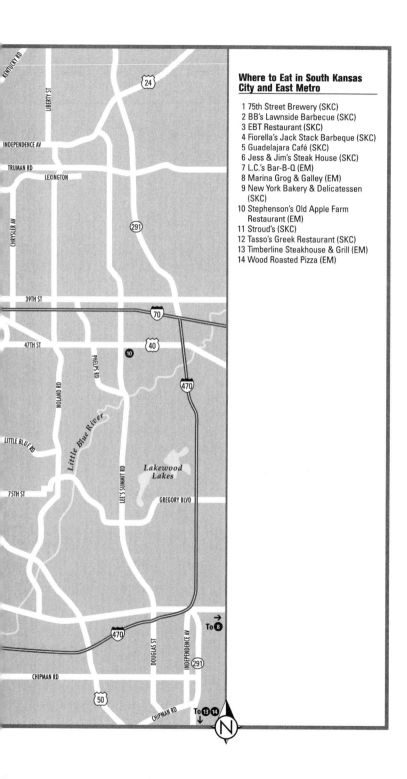

Where to Eat in South Kansas City and East Metro

1 75th Street Brewery (SKC)
2 BB's Lawnside Barbecue (SKC)
3 EBT Restaurant (SKC)
4 Fiorella's Jack Stack Barbeque (SKC)
5 Guadalajara Café (SKC)
6 Jess & Jim's Steak House (SKC)
7 L.C.'s Bar-B-Q (EM)
8 Marina Grog & Galley (EM)
9 New York Bakery & Delicatessen (SKC)
10 Stephenson's Old Apple Farm Restaurant (EM)
11 Stroud's (SKC)
12 Tasso's Greek Restaurant (SKC)
13 Timberline Steakhouse & Grill (EM)
14 Wood Roasted Pizza (EM)

cue in the city. Tucked into a minuscule building with cars speeding by, L.C.'s grabbed attention by smoking its Q outdoors in a homemade steel barrel. The aromatic advertising worked; now those in the know head to this great-smelling smoke hole for huge sandwiches and succulent ribs. Sides such as beans and 'slaw are equally tasty. Lunch and dinner. Closed Sun. & (East Metro)

MARINA GROG & GALLEY
22A North Shore Dr., Gate 1
Lake Lotawana
816/578-5511
$$

About a 30-minute drive east of town—on the shores of residential Lake Lotawana—Marina Grog & Galley provides one of the area's few first-class, waterfront dining opportunities. The shoreline views from this former boat shop are superior, and the cuisine ranges from seafood to steaks. A wall-size saltwater aquarium separates the bar and dining room, enhancing the shoreside theme. Reservations recommended. Dinner Tue–Sun. & (East Metro)

STEPHENSON'S OLD APPLE FARM RESTAURANT
16401 E. 40 Hwy.
Independence
816/373-5400
$$

For more than a half-century, Stephenson's has been the ultimate choice for comfort food. Set in an old roadhouse that's been expanded several times, Stephenson's feels like dining at Grandma's. Entrées include a hickory-smoked half chicken, a smoked beef brisket, and a baked chicken with butter and cream. Stephenson's adds all the fixings, too, from apple fritters and corn relish to

potatoes and green-rice casserole. Desserts here emphasize the restaurant's ties to a family apple orchard. Lunch and dinner daily; Sunday brunch. & (East Metro)

TIMBERLINE STEAKHOUSE & GRILL
920 NE Columbus St.
Lee's Summit
816/554-3323
$$

Like a trip to the slopes of Colorado, this new eatery showcases timbers, from the subtle table design to the tall poles throughout the restaurant. Wooden canoes, skis, and mountain-inspired art round out the decor. The menu at Timberline features hearty portions of delectable grilled food, from steaks to seafood to pork chops. The Loaded Chicken Breast, for example, piles on barbecue sauce, carmelized onions, cheeses, and pepper bacon for a sumptuous taste treat. Lunch Sat–Sun; dinner nightly. & (East Metro)

WOOD ROASTED PIZZA
221 SE Hwy. 291
Lee's Summit
816/246-5611
$

Owner Len Ricci bases his pizza recipes on how the pies were made hundreds of years ago in Naples, Italy. Pizzas are roasted over wood, topped with delicacies such as fresh vegetables and cheese. The method has ensured him success; he's opened another location in Overland Park. Other items include pastas, sandwiches, and salads. Reservations are not accepted. Lunch and dinner. & (East Metro)

5

SIGHTS AND ATTRACTIONS

Every traveler hopes to stumble onto those choice discoveries: a tiny perfect statue tucked beneath a garden's shady foliage, an off-the-beaten-path café where people-watching should be listed on the menu, a golden cathedral spire jutting between glass-and-steel towers. In Kansas City, treasures like these await you at every turn. From north to south, across two rivers and more, bits of history mingle with local scenery and culture, creating a lavish collection of sights and attractions.

The city's complex geography is part of the reason for its wealth of things to see and do. Downtown Kansas City combines its river-town heritage with contemporary castles of commerce. From the waterfront—where shabby storefronts are re-emerging as quaint shops and markets—you can head south into the financial district and government center, which are also rebuilding and reshaping themselves. The hilly canyons between the under-construction civic mall and Bartle Hall yield a trove of sights old and new.

Walking the streets of picturesque Country Club Plaza affords a look into an earlier place and time. An old Spanish mosaic under an eave, a winsome fountain spurting from a side-street wall, a bronze boar with its snout rubbed smooth: The Plaza delivers European style in America's heartland.

Throughout the area, evidence of Kansas City's connection to the past abounds: the place that President Harry Truman called home, in Independence; the Pony Express headquarters on State Line Road; the spread where Jesse James was born, in Kearney. All offer glimpses into a region that remains at the heart of the country.

Whether you're exploring on foot or meandering the streets by car, get ready to make your own River City discoveries.

DOWNTOWN

18TH & VINE DISTRICT
18th and Vine Sts.
Kansas City
816/871-3016
Famous worldwide for its role in the development of jazz, Kansas City's 18th & Vine District recently completed a $22-million redevelopment that enlarged the Negro Leagues Baseball Museum, added a Jazz Museum and 18th & Vine Visitors Center, and incorporated the renovated Gem Theatre into the mix. In this important historic district, sax player Charlie "Yardbird" Parker began his career in the Thirties, Count Basie played with his band, and Joe Turner developed his signature style. ♿ (Downtown)

AMERICAN HEREFORD ASSOCIATION BUILDING
715 Hereford Dr. (a.k.a. W. 11th St.)
Kansas City
Built in 1951, this building is still guarded by the American Hereford Association's massive bovine statue, even though Argus Health Systems now occupies the facility. The building's not open to the public, but in the shadow of the heroic Hereford, a great view overlooks the West Bottoms, the Kansas River valley, and downtown Kansas City, Kansas. (Downtown)

BARTLE HALL
13th St. between Baltimore Ave. and Broadway Blvd.
Kansas City
816/871-3700
When artist R.M. Fischer placed his Sky Stations/Pylon Caps atop the Kansas City Convention Center's expanded H. Roe Bartle Hall, locals ungraciously started referring to them as "hair curlers" and similar descrip-

tive names. Kansas City's most photographed skyline view now includes these space-age creations, however. Bartle (named for a former mayor) offers one of the largest contiguous, column-free exhibit spaces in the country. Lobby open daily. Free. ♿ (Downtown)

BLACK ARCHIVES OF MID-AMERICA
1722 E. 17th Terr.
Kansas City
816/483-1300
Near the historic 18th & Vine District, the Black Archives is home to one of the country's largest collections of African American paintings, sculpture, and research material on famous black leaders of the Midwest. Mon–Fri 10–4. $2 adults, $1 students 12–18, 50 cents children under 12. ♿ (Downtown)

BOULEVARD BREWERY
2501 Southwest Blvd.
Kansas City
816/474-7095
The owners of this small brewery had a tough time finding financing for their venture—especially with beer powerhouse Anheuser-Busch headquartered on the other side of the state. But the entrepreneurs finally prevailed upon family members and opened in 1989, creating fine ales and lagers. Now a local and regional favorite, Boulevard gives free tours at 1:30 every Saturday. Call for reservations. (Downtown)

CATHEDRAL OF THE IMMACULATE CONCEPTION
416 W. 12th St.
Kansas City
816/842-0416
Kansas City's first Catholic church was built in 1856 by Father Bernard

DOWNTOWN KANSAS CITY

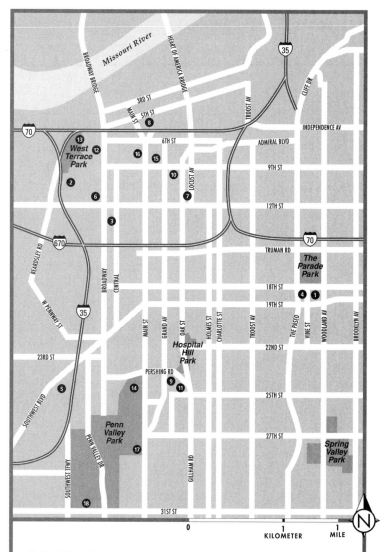

Sights in Downtown Kansas City

1 18th and Vine District
2 American Hereford Association Building
3 Bartle Hall
4 Black Archives of Mid-America
5 Boulevard Brewery
6 Cathedral of the Immaculate Conception
7 City Hall and Observation Deck
8 City Market
9 Crown Center
10 Federal Reserve Bank Visitors Center
11 Hallmark Visitors Center

12 Historic Kansas City Foundation
13 Lewis & Clark Point
14 Liberty Memorial
15 *Muse of the Missouri*
16 New York Life Building
17 *Pioneer Mother*
18 *The Scout*

Donnelly, often called the "builder priest" for his success at luring Irish immigrant laborers and expanding the church's influence. The architecture is commonly labeled neo-Baroque with a Romanesque style. In 1960, 23-karat gold leaf was added to the dome to protect the original copper sheathing. You can enter the building from 11th Street and Broadway. Mass daily. & (Downtown)

CITY HALL AND OBSERVATION DECK
414 E. 12th St.
Kansas City
816/274-2222
Office to Kansas City's mayor and city council, City Hall was built in the depths of the Depression. It remains a renowned example of art deco architecture. Take the elevator to the 28th floor and walk up two flights. From there you can look out in all directions for unmatched views of the Kansas City metro area. The building's open, with the elevator running, Mon–Fri 8:30–4:15. Free. (Downtown)

CITY MARKET
5th St. between
Wyandotte St. and Grand Ave.
Kansas City
816/842-1271
One of Kansas City's original business districts, this area has been revitalized and now plays host to 35 shops,

groceries, and restaurants—and the largest farmer's market in a six-state region. Kansas Citians flock to the Market, primarily on Saturday, to browse through the fresh fruits, veggies, flowers, and crafts. The Arabia Steamboat Museum anchors one side of the square, while Winslow's City Market Smokehouse lures with its barbecue. A great family outing. & (Downtown)

CROWN CENTER
Main St. to Gillham Rd.,
Pershing to 24th Sts.
Kansas City
816/274-8444
Once known as Signboard Hill, this area is now decorated with modern buildings, thanks to Hallmark Cards. The greeting-card giant—privately owned by the philanthropic Hall family—surrounds its world headquarters with retail shops, movie houses, live theaters, restaurants, an outdoor ice skating rink, and two hotels. & (Downtown)

FEDERAL RESERVE BANK VISITORS CENTER
925 Grand Ave.
Kansas City
816/881-2200
Money, money, money. That's the focus at the Federal Reserve Bank Visitors Center. Here, you can see some 30 educational displays that

When You Care Enough . . .

One of Kansas City's most notable companies is the nation's largest greeting-card manufacturer, Hallmark Cards. In fact, Hallmark's $3-billion-plus annual revenues make it the largest player in a $6-billion greeting-card industry.

Founder Joyce C. Hall, a cocky 18-year-old from Nebraska, started the business in 1910 by brazenly delivering postcard packs on spec to Midwestern merchants, while living in a room at the Kansas City YMCA. In the Thirties, Hall decided his company needed more visibility, so he contacted a long list of advertising agencies, all of which laughed at the concept of selling greeting cards under a brand name. Hall prevailed, however, and finally found an agency that linked his company with a radio program, a precursor to the later introduction of television's award-showered Hallmark Hall of Fame.

Under Hall's leadership, Hallmark tapped the talents of artists such as Norman Rockwell, Georgia O'Keeffe, Salvador Dali, and Pablo Picasso. President Dwight Eisenhower commissioned Hallmark to produce the first official White House Christmas card in 1957, and every president until Bill Clinton followed the tradition.

Hallmark has also amassed the world's largest creative team—more than 650 painters, engravers, photographers, stitchery artists, calligraphers, and writers—who pour heart and soul into developing sentiments that speak to the human relationship.

Part of Hall's legacy is on display at the Hallmark Visitors Center in Crown Center.

describe how the Federal Reserve system works, plus view traveling and regional exhibits in the Roger Guffey Gallery. Mon–Fri 8–5. Free. & (Downtown)

HALLMARK VISITORS CENTER
25th St. and Grand Blvd.

Crown Center
Kansas City
816/274-3613
More than just one company's story, the Hallmark Visitors Center touches something in everyone who's ever given or received a greeting card. Exhibits show visitors how Hallmark

Cards has harnessed creativity and craftsmanship to become the largest card company in the world. Videos show clips from award-winning Hallmark Hall of Fame TV productions. Mon–Fri 9–5, Sat 9:30–4:30. Free. &. (Downtown)

HISTORIC KANSAS CITY FOUNDATION
712 Broadway Blvd., Suite 404
Kansas City
816/471-3391
This ardent activist in the preservation of Kansas City's historic buildings and neighborhoods offers extensive knowledge about the area's past. At the foundation's downtown office, you can find brochures and slide programs on historic/preservation areas. The group also gives tours (by reservation only) on topics ranging from art deco architecture to the River Market neighborhood, for a group donation of $25. &. (Downtown)

LEWIS & CLARK POINT
8th and Jefferson Sts.
Kansas City
In 1806, Meriwether Lewis and William Clark camped for three days on this bluff that overlooks the confluence of the Kansas (or Kaw) and Missouri Rivers. It was a well-deserved rest during their return trip from Oregon. From this Quality Hill point, you can read the marker that commemorates their stay and another that notes the importance of French fur traders to the area, while enjoying a view of the rivers, the downtown airport, and Kansas City, Kansas. &. (Downtown)

LIBERTY MEMORIAL
Penn Valley Park
Just south of Pershing Rd.
Kansas City

Liberty Memorial

816/221-1918
President Calvin Coolidge dedicated Liberty Memorial in 1926 to honor those who fought and died in World War I. Over the years, the memorial's museum amassed the only collection specializing in WWI artifacts, including weapons, uniforms, and other memorabilia. Although the 217-foot-high column, walkway, and museum are closed pending renovation, two satellite museums are open: in the Town Pavilion at 12th and Main Streets, and on the lower level of Ward Parkway Shopping Center. You can still stroll the lawn surrounding the Memorial. Town Pavilion museum open Mon–Fri 10–6; Ward Parkway Tue–Sun 10–6. Free. &. (Downtown)

MUSE OF THE MISSOURI
Main St. between 8th and 9th Sts.
Kansas City
She's hard to miss, casting her net from an attractive median on Main

Convention and Visitors Bureau of Greater Kansas City

Neither Sleet nor Snow . . .

In 1860, Alexander Majors, William Waddell, and William Russell, already partners in a successful Santa Fe Trail freight company, launched a new service called the Pony Express. They promised to deliver mail from St. Joseph, Missouri, to Sacramento, California, in only 10 days. To do it, the trio built more than 150 relay stations across nearly 1,900 miles, then hired 80 riders, including Buffalo Bill Cody (then only 15) and young James "Wild Bill" Hickok. After only 18 months, expansion of both the telegraph and railroad systems ended the Pony Express. Today, Majors' home, which once served as headquarters for his freighting operation, is open to the public at 83rd and State Line Road.

Street. Installed in 1961, the 30-foot bronze sculpture pays homage to the Missouri River's importance in the creation and history of Kansas City. Three pools surround the flowing female figure. ♿ (Downtown)

NEW YORK LIFE BUILDING
20 W. 9th St.
Kansas City

When it was completed in 1887, the brick New York Life Building was the city's tallest structure. Its striking bronze eagle was an awesome site along the street, which was the beneficiary of significant corporate investment at the time. Eventually, however, New York Life moved out, and the empty building slowly deteriorated. In 1995, local company Utilicorp United spent more than $30 million transforming the building into its technologically "smart" headquarters. ♿ (Downtown)

PIONEER MOTHER
Penn Valley Park

Southwest of Liberty Memorial
Kansas City
Located southwest of the Liberty Memorial, this sculpture was dedicated in 1927 to honor the spirit of all pioneer women who crossed the Great Plains. The dramatic, multifigured bronze was designed in New York by Alexander Phimister Proctor and cast in Rome. It took four years to complete. ♿ (Downtown)

THE SCOUT
Penn Valley Park
29th and Pennsylvania Sts.
Kansas City

The Scout remains one of Kansas City's most beloved sculptures—in a city filled with sculptures—even though it was originally intended for another location. The memorial to Native Americans was created for San Francisco's 1915 Panama-Pacific Exposition, but during its journey back East, the Sioux brave mounted on horseback appeared temporarily in Penn Valley Park. Locals became so fond of the sculpture that they raised $15,000 to purchase it. ⑤ (Downtown)

PLAZA/WESTPORT

BOARD OF TRADE
4800 Main St.
Kansas City
816/753-7500
Founded before the Civil War, the Board of Trade just south of the Country Club Plaza became a grain exchange in 1869, and now it tracks the region's agribusiness concerns. The world's largest futures market for hard red winter wheat trades here, as do a variety of other commodities. From the third-floor observation deck you can watch as traders deal in Value Line stock index futures. Mon–Fri 8:15–3:30. Free. ⑤ (Plaza/Westport)

CIVIL WAR ROUTE
The Battle of Westport was a bloody conflict that took place October 21–23, 1864. It marked the end of the

Joe Martin/Country Club Plaza Merchants Association

Fountain of Bacchus on the Plaza

Civil War in the West. The major battle occurred in what is now Loose Park, but more than 20 other sites also saw conflict. A self-guided driving tour takes you from Westport to the Big Blue River to the Santa Fe Trail and back, with large markers describing the action at each spot. An explanatory brochure is available in hotel lobby racks or from the Civil War Round Table of Kansas City, 1130 Westport Rd.; 816/931-6620. ⑤ (Plaza/Westport)

COUNTRY CLUB
PLAZA LANDMARKS
46th St. to Ward Pkwy.,
Roanoke Pkwy. to Main St.
Kansas City
Even if you don't shop or eat at any of the Plaza's boutiques or bistros, plan a walking tour through this area. Of special note: The Plaza's tallest tower, at 47th Street and J.C. Nichols Parkway, is a scaled-down replica of the famous Giralda in Seville, Spain. The Fountain of Bacchus in Chandler Court (northwest of the Cheesecake Factory) is a 1911 lead statuary acquired from an estate in Worcestershire, England. The Boy and Frog Fountain, at the corner of Central and Nichols Road, is an original by Raffaello Romanelli of Florence. The Spanish Bullfight Mural, hand-crafted in Seville, is on the east side of Central, between 47th Street and Nichols Road. Free art brochures are available at the Plaza Merchants Association, 450 Ward Pkwy.; 816/753-0100. ⑤ (Plaza/Westport)

EAGLE SCOUT
TRIBUTE FOUNTAIN
39th St. and Gillham Rd.
Kansas City
This fountain to commemorate the

PLAZA/WESTPORT

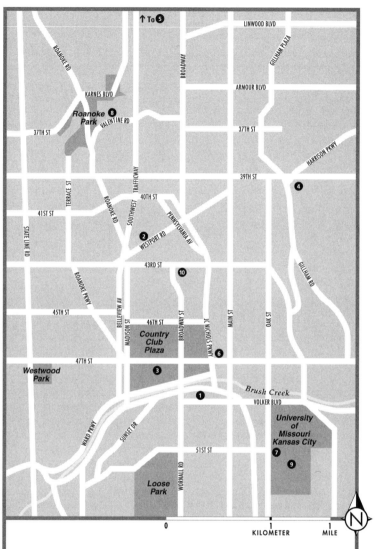

Sights in the Plaza/Westport Area

1 Board of the Trade
2 Civil War Route
3 Country Club Plaza Landmarks
4 Eagle Scout Tribute Foundation
5 Firefighters Fountain
6 J.C. Nichols Memorial Fountain
7 Linda Hall Library
8 Thomas Hart Benton Home
9 University of Missouri–Kansas City
10 Vietnam Veterans Memorial

Steeple of Light

When Frank Lloyd Wright imagined the design for Kansas City's Community Christian Church in the 1930s, he envisioned a shining beacon of light projecting from its rooftop dome. At that time, however, technology wasn't able to produce a sufficiently strong light that would be small enough to fit in the dome. In 1990, church pastor Reverend Bob Hill approached Kansas City artist Dale Eldred regarding the "Steeple of Light." Eldred found a way to install it, but financial restraints kept the project unfinished. Several months after Eldred's death in 1993, Hill approached Eldred's widow and collaborator, Roberta Lord, about the light. As a result, the beam was switched on for the first time in December 1994. The Steeple of Light—which shoots heavenward every weekend and nightly throughout the holiday season—includes four xenon lights, each rated at 300-million candlepower. The church is located at 47th and Main, near the Country Club Plaza.

loftiest of Boy Scouting achievements is appropriate, since more Eagle Scouts are said to reside in Kansas City than anywhere else in the country. Back in 1967, scouting officials procured "Day" and "Night" statues and two bald eagles when New York City dismantled its Pennsylvania Station. The 1900s-era figures were restored and now preside over a fountain in which a book containing the names of 13,943 local Eagle Scouts was embedded. By 1998, the Kansas City area had 35,334 Eagle Scouts. 🚻 (Plaza/Westport)

FIREFIGHTERS FOUNTAIN
31st St. and Broadway Blvd.
Kansas City
Located in Penn Valley Park, the Firefighters Fountain is among the largest fonts in Kansas City. Besides its Tom Corbin sculpture, the fountain fea-

tures plenty of water: Its 80-foot diameter basin holds 76,000 gallons. Dedicated to the city's firefighters in 1991, the tribute also features a memorial terrace area with fallen firefighters' names carved in granite. 🚻 (Plaza/Westport)

J.C. NICHOLS
MEMORIAL FOUNTAIN
47th and Main Sts.
Kansas City
Two years after legendary Plaza developer J.C. Nichols died in 1950, his family purchased a spirited group of heroic figures mounted on rearing horses. Sculpted in 1910 in Paris by Henri Greber, the statuary was designed for a fountain on a Long Island estate. After it came to Kansas City, another eight years passed before the collection was finally functional. Missing parts of the grouping were

created by local sculptor Herman Frederick Simon; architect Edward Tanner designed the fountain itself. One of Kansas City's best-known fonts, the circular pool is a gathering spot from the moment the city turns the water on in the spring until it's doused in early winter. ఈ (Plaza/Westport)

LINDA HALL LIBRARY
5109 Cherry St.
Kansas City
816/363-4600

Though not officially part of the University of Missouri–Kansas City, the Linda Hall Library on its campus is the largest privately funded library of science, engineering, and technology in the United States. The non-lending facility houses more than 1 million volumes, the oldest dating from 1472. Patrons come here to learn about geology, architecture, biology, and much more. Outside, an urban arboretum of more than 450 trees on the library's 14-acre grounds draw visitors, too. At Linda Hall, you can buy a map of the grounds and use it to identify 165 different species of trees—from 30 varieties of oaks to double-flowered horse chestnuts to the Midwest's largest collection of tree peonies. Mon 9–8:30, Tue–Fri 9–5, Sat 10–4. Free; $5 arboretum maps. ఈ (Plaza/Westport)

THOMAS HART BENTON HOME
3616 Belleview Rd.
Kansas City
816/931-5722

Missouri's most famous twentieth-century artist lived in this home from 1939 until he died in 1975, creating many of his colorful depictions of American history and folkways from a carriage-house studio. Benton's late-Victorian-style home was a cen-

One of the many towers on the Plaza, p. 92

ter of creative activity; his studio still holds many of his tools and equipment, as though Benton just walked out yesterday. Guided tours last about an hour. Mon–Sat 10–4, winter Sun 11–4, summer Sun 12–5. $2 ages 13 and over, $1.25 ages 6–12. First floor ఈ (Plaza/Westport)

UNIVERSITY OF MISSOURI–KANSAS CITY
50th to 55th Sts.
between Oak and Troost
Kansas City
816/235-1000

Founded in 1933 as the University of Kansas City, this educational institution joined the University of Missouri system 30 years later. It offers 53 bachelor's, 47 master's, and 28 doctoral degree programs. Specialty areas include nationally recognized programs in health sciences, urban affairs, and performing arts. ఈ (Plaza/Westport)

VIETNAM VETERANS MEMORIAL
43rd St. and Broadway Blvd.
Kansas City

JOHNSON CO./KANSAS CITY, KS

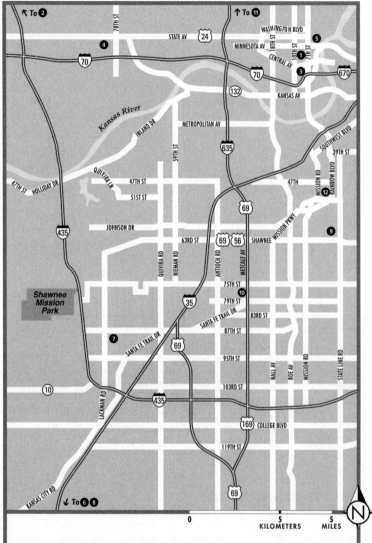

Sights in Johnson County and Kansas City, Kansas

1 Downtown Kansas City, Kansas (KCK)
2 First City of Kansas (KCK)
3 Granada Theatre (KCK)
4 Grinter House (KCK)
5 Huron Indian Cemetery (KCK)
6 Lanesfield School Historic Site (JC)
7 Legler Barn (JC)
8 Mahaffie Farmstead & Stage Coach Stop (JC)
9 Mission Hills, Kansas (JC)
10 Overland Park Farmers Market (JC)
11 Quindaro Ruins/Underground Railroad (KCK)
12 Shawnee Indian Mission State Historic Site (JC)

The Vietnam Veterans Memorial, between the Plaza and Westport, was dedicated in 1986. Resembling the larger memorial in Washington, D.C., the stone wall pays special tribute to the 336 Kansas City–area Vietnam veterans killed or missing in action. The memorial includes restful reflect-ing pools and fountains. & (Plaza/Westport)

JOHNSON COUNTY

LANESFIELD SCHOOL HISTORIC SITE
18745 S. Dillie Rd.
Edgerton
913/893-6645
This one-room school, now on the National Register of Historic Places, dates from 1869, when kids came from miles around to attend the little school on the prairie. Today's visitors can see what it was like back then and even learn from a costumed schoolteacher who gives tours of the restored schoolhouse. Tue–Sun 1–5. Free. & (Johnson County)

LEGLER BARN
14907 W. 87th St.
Lenexa
913/492-0038
Lenexa founding father Adam Legler built it in the 1800s on the Santa Fe Trail. Recent renovations have transformed Legler Barn into an educational and interpretive site. Look for exhibits about Lenexa history, hands-on displays of antique toys, and a train depot next door that also tells a story. Tue–Sat 10–4, Sun 1–5. Free. & (Johnson County)

MAHAFFIE FARMSTEAD & STAGE COACH STOP
1100 Kansas City Rd.

Olathe
913/782-6972
The Santa Fe Trail was one of the highways of its day, and farms became rest stops for stagecoach passengers on their way west. The Mahaffie Farm, established in 1858, was such a spot, serving dinner to travelers between 1863 and 1869. Restoration is ongoing at the limestone home, the last remaining stagecoach stop of its kind. Tours available Mon–Sat 10–4, Sun 12–4 (closed Jan). $3 adults, $1.75 children 3–11. Partially & (Johnson County)

MISSION HILLS, KANSAS
West of State Line Rd., between 55th and 71st Sts.
This neighborhood features rolling hills, winding roads, and multimillion-dollar homes. The Kansas City and Mission Hills Country Clubs provide the area's northern boundary; to the south, you can drive past notable mansions. Candy magnates Russell and Clara Stover, for example, built the enormous hilltop home at Mission Drive and Overhill. The late Ewing Kauffman, former owner of the Kansas City Royals and founder of Marion Merrell Dow, lived on Mission Drive as well. Other current movers and shakers reside here, too. & (Johnson County)

OVERLAND PARK FARMERS MARKET
Between 79th and 80th Sts. and Marty Rd.
Overland Park
Wednesday and Saturday from early May through October, residents crowd Overland Park's quaint downtown area to purchase homegrown fruits and vegetables, flowers, honey, and crafts. It's smaller than the farmers market in the River Market but

Kansas City Skyline

often less crowded. The major action occurs in the covered pavilion, starting about 7 a.m. ⅃ (Johnson County)

SHAWNEE INDIAN MISSION STATE HISTORIC SITE
53rd St. and Mission Rd.
Fairway
913/262-0867

In the 1820s and 1830s, westward expansion forced the Shawnee and other tribes to move from the eastern United States to present-day Kansas. To help the relocated Indian children, the Reverend Thomas Johnson established this mission school in 1839. Later it became a stopping point on the Santa Fe Trail. Guided group tours are given by appointment, and family events are held throughout the year. Tue–Sat 10–5, Sun 1–5. Free. Partially ⅃ (Johnson County)

KANSAS CITY, KANSAS

DOWNTOWN
Around 7th and Ann Sts.
Kansas City, Kansas

913/573-5000 (City Hall)

Kansas City, Kansas, and Wyandotte County have combined many government functions—and when you visit KCK's downtown civic center, it's easy to see why. The two entities live happily side by side, the old Wyandotte County Courthouse across the street from the modern KCK City Hall. The venerable Sailors & Soldiers Memorial Building, "dedicated to the heroes who fought and died for their country," sits next door. Across from Ann Street, Huron Park has a rose garden and offers a quiet place to stop. Partly ⅃ (Kansas City, Kansas)

FIRST CITY OF KANSAS
Towns of Leavenworth–Lansing

Founded in 1854, these neighboring riverfront communities comprised the first incorporated city in the Sunflower State. At Ft. Leavenworth, the oldest fort west of the Mississippi, you can see historic buildings, a museum, and a Buffalo Soldier Monument dedicated to African American soldiers. Partly ⅃ (Kansas City, Kansas)

Ten "Must Do's" in Overland Park

by Mary Birch, president of the Overland Park Chamber of Commerce

1. **Deanna Rose Children's Farmstead** (138th St. and Switzer Rd., 913/897-2360). This popular family experience attracts more than 250,000 visitors a year. The ultimate in interactive fun.

2. **The New Theatre Restaurant** (9229 Foster St., 913/649-7469). Known as one of the best dinner theaters in the country, this 600-seat venue offers food, fun, and excellent entertainment to residents and visitors.

3. **Johnson County Community College Cultural Education Center** (12345 College Blvd., 913/469-4445). A variety of high-quality cultural and community events in 1,400-seat Yardley Hall and a 400-seat theater complement the educational and tourist-related aspects of this facility.

4. **Shopping/dining.** The best in the Midwest, with two regional malls, more than 1,600 retail stores, and 250-plus restaurants to choose from.

5. **Overland Park Arboretum and Botanical Gardens** (17940 Antioch, 913/685-4582). Although only an infant in its development, this 300-acre park is already popular for its trails and water-related areas.

6. **Fall Parade and Craft Show** (Santa Fe Dr. and 80th St., 913/642-2222). For more than 20 years, this event held the last Saturday in September has delighted visitors and residents, showcasing downtown Overland Park to more than 10,000 people.

7. **Corporate Woods Jazz Festival.** For four days in June, this gig brings out the best of Overland Park for more than 30,000 attendees in Corporate Woods Park.

8. **Fourth of July Celebration.** This fireworks display in Corporate Woods remains one of the biggest and best in the region.

9. **Farmers Market.** Located near the clock tower in downtown Overland Park, this Wednesday and Saturday gathering offers the freshest to everyone, with a concert series for atmosphere.

10. **Art in the Woods.** A classy, two-week display of beauty in art in Corporate Woods every May.

GRANADA THEATRE
1019 Minnesota
Kansas City, Kansas
913/281-2087

This grand old movie palace was a 1928 beauty in which films were once accompanied by live organ music. But in 1997, it was destined to be leveled and replaced with a Walgreen's. Instead, Wade Williams and brothers Brian and Ben Mossman—who've developed the Englewood Theater in Independence, the Fine Arts Theatre in Mission, and the Aztec and Rio Theaters in Overland Park—stepped in. The renewed Granada will host films, fine arts concerts, and cultural events when it opens in summer 1999. ⅋ (Kansas City, Kansas)

GRINTER HOUSE
1420 S. 78th St.
Kansas City, Kansas
913/299-0373
The first civilian post office in the Kansas Territory sat on this magnificent bluff overlooking the Kansas River. It was replaced in 1857 by a two-story Southern Colonial home that now provides a small glimpse into pre–Civil War Kansas. Guided tours Wed–Sat 10–5, Sun 1–5. Donation suggested. Partially ⅋ (Kansas City, Kansas)

HURON INDIAN CEMETERY
6th to 7th Sts., Minnesota Ave.
to Ann St.
Kansas City, Kansas
An eerie spot in downtown KCK, the Huron Indian Cemetery is the final resting place for at least 400 members of the Huron tribe. Forced from Canada to Ohio to Kansas, the Hurons (who became known as the Wyandotte Indian Nation) were instrumental in establishing the first free school in Kansas and the first territorial government in their adopted homeland. The cemetery was created in 1843 and is now maintained as a city park. Eleven explanatory markers provide a fascinating look into the lives of these early residents. (Kansas City, Kansas)

QUINDARO RUINS/
UNDERGROUND RAILROAD
27th St. and Sewell Ave.
Kansas City, Kansas
913/342-8683 for tour appointment
A life-sized statue dedicated to John Brown overlooks what's left of the old town of Quindaro, a refuge established in the five years preceding the Civil War. This was where runaway slaves disembarked from their journeys to hide in a labyrinth of limestone tunnels and caves in the abolitionist state of Kansas. The largest known underground railroad archeological site in the country, the Quindaro Ruins/Underground Railroad recently was designated a National Historic Site. Set in a bend of the Missouri River, it affords a moving account of the essence of freedom. (Kansas City, Kansas)

NORTHLAND

CLAYBROOK HOUSE
HISTORIC SITE
Opposite the Jesse James Farm
Kearney
816/628-6065
This restored pre–Civil War mansion is best known as the home of Jesse James' daughter, Mary James Barr. Virginian George Claybrook originally developed it as a Southern-style plantation in 1858, although the architecture is more indicative of mid-1800s rural Missouri. Spring and Christmas events are held each year. June–Aug Sat–Sun 10–4. Free. Partially ⅋ (Northland)

GLADSTONE TEACHERS
MEMORIAL
70th St. and N. Holmes Rd.
Gladstone
816/436-2200

NORTHLAND

Christa McAuliffe, the teacher-crew member who died in the 1986 space shuttle *Challenger* disaster, is honored in this special memorial. Located near Gladstone's City Hall and Central Park, the monument is dedicated to the heroic efforts of all teachers. ♿ (Northland)

JESSE JAMES FARM AND VISITORS CENTER
21216 James Farm Rd.
Kearney
816/628-6065

In 1847, Jesse James was born at this Kearney, Missouri, farm. At age 16, he followed his older brother Frank into the Civil War, fighting under the notorious William Quantrill—but the James boys would become even more legendary themselves: When they returned home, they joined other former Confederates to rob banks. James' restored birthplace features the home's original furnishings, an audiovisual presentation recapping his life, and the world's largest display of James family artifacts. I-35 north to Exit 26 (Kearney), two miles east on Hwy. 92, then two miles north. May–Sept daily 9–4; Oct–Apr Mon–Sat 9–4, Sun 12–4. $4.50 adults, $3.75 seniors, $2 ages 8–15. Partially ♿ (Northland)

SHOAL CREEK, MISSOURI
7000 NE Barry Rd. in Hodge Park
Kansas City
816/792-2655

This fascinating nineteenth-century living-history museum comprises 17 period structures, each furnished with books, clothing, and special items that people made or took with them on their journey west. Some buildings were original and have been restored; others are replicas. Shoal Creek provides a way to step

back in time through tours, special events, and the native animals on site. Tue–Sat 9–3, Sun 12–4. $2 guided tours and special events, free children under 6; free all other times. Partially ♿ (Northland)

WILLIAM JEWELL COLLEGE
500 College Hill
Liberty
816/781-3806

Three decades after Liberty was settled, town fathers founded William Jewell College in 1849. It is now one of the oldest private colleges in Missouri. The fully accredited liberal arts school sits proudly on a hill overlooking Liberty, its 2,000 students within walking distance of the town square. The college is known throughout the metro area for its outstanding music and dramatic performance series. ♿ (Northland)

SOUTH KANSAS CITY

ALEXANDER MAJORS HOUSE
8201 State Line Rd.
Kansas City
816/333-5556

It's hard to imagine now, but Pony Express co-founder Alexander Majors once lived out in the middle of nowhere. His home, just north of today's Ward Parkway Shopping Center, served as the headquarters for the Pony Express (during the 18 months it was in operation) and two early freight operations. Preservationists restored the 1856 farmhouse and now offer tours and special events. Mar–Dec Sat–Sun 1–4. $3 adults, $1 children under 12. First floor ♿ (South Kansas City)

JOHN WORNALL HOUSE MUSEUM

Top Ten African American Sights in Kansas City

by Frances Hill, president of CWT/Accent Travel, one of the area's largest minority-owned businesses

1. **Negro Leagues Baseball Museum** (1601 E. 18th St., Kansas City; 816/221-1920)
2. **The Black Archives of Mid-America** (2033 Vine, Kansas City; 816/483-1300)
3. **Bruce R. Watkins Cultural Heritage Center** (3700 Blue Pkwy., Kansas City; 816/923-6226)
4. **18th & Vine Historic District**
5. **Metropolitan Baptist Church** (2310 E. Linwood Blvd., Kansas City; 816/923-3689)
6. **St. Stephen Baptist Church** (1414 E. Truman Rd., Kansas City; 816/842-6311)
7. **Epicurean Lounge** (7502 Troost, Kansas City; 816/333-8383)
8. **Bodyworks Unlimited** (8625 Troost, Kansas City; 816/363-6910)
9. **Gates Bar-B-Q** (several locations)
10. **The Hitching Post Restaurant** (3448 Prospect, Kansas City; 816/924-9579)

61st Terr. and Wornall Rd.
Kansas City
816/444-1858
Although the Wornall House is now surrounded by residential neighborhoods, it sat on 500 acres of farmland when built in 1858. The Greek Revival house was originally owned by John Bristow Wornall and his wife, Eliza, and was considered the most prestigious house in the region. During the 1864 Battle of Westport, the house was commandeered as a field hospital by the Confederate and Union armies. Special event weekends are held throughout the year. Open for tours Tue–Sat 10–4, Sun 1–4 (closed in Jan, shortened hours in Feb). $3 adults, $2.50 seniors, $2 children 5–12. First floor &. (South Kansas City)

SEA HORSE FOUNTAIN
Meyer Circle on Ward Pkwy.
Kansas City
For the past decade or so, officials have tried various methods to straighten the curves that circle Ward Parkway's Sea Horse Fountain. But frankly, the residents don't mind the obstruction. One of the best examples of developer J.C. Nichols' blend of water and statuary, the fountain was fashioned from a seventeenth-century Venetian cherubim

Favorite Historic Buildings

by Jane Fifield Flynn, past president of the Jackson County Historical Society and author of several history books on the region

1. **Kansas City Power and Light Company Building** (1330 Baltimore Ave.). For more than 30 years, this building dominated Kansas City's skyline as the tallest building in the state. A series of set-backs and stylized geometric architectural detailing characterize its art deco style. The building is most resplendent after dark, when floodlights, concealed at each recessed step, are directed up toward the six-story crowning shaft with its multicolored light display.

2. **Pierce Street Houses** (48th St., Locust St. to Rockhill Rd.). The adage of "power in numbers" is exemplified by this block of identical houses located in the historic Rockhill neighborhood. The design, using shingle siding and native limestone, is but one of several architectural styles within the neighborhood. All buildings came from William Rockhill Nelson, who published the *Kansas City Star*.

3. **Apartments** (E. 43rd, Oak, and McGee Sts.). Dignified, symmetrical, and massive describe these three-story apartments with their handsome columns and front porches. Once a part of many streetscapes, the apartments are a dying type among the city's residential structures. A stone wall defines the site on which a 20-room mansion once stood before it was razed for the apartments' construction.

4. **Walter E. Bixby Residence** (6505 State Line Rd.). When this residence was completed in 1937, the local citizenry enjoyed a wonderful example of the international style of architecture. Horizontal lines and geometric forms complement the white stucco exterior. The original landscape, designed by Hare & Hare, greatly enhanced the appearance of this less-than-traditional home.

5. **Boley Clothing Company Building** (1124 Walnut St.). When architect Louis Singleton Curtiss first announced his intention to "wrap" a building in a glass skin, skeptics and traditionalists must have had a field day. But in 1908, Curtiss did indeed wrap this building. Cited for his unique design and pioneering construction materials, Curtiss recessed the building's supporting columns several feet from the facades, which allowed the glass wrap. The columns were made of steel, the first ever rolled in the United States.

6. **Mutual Musicians Foundation** (1823 Highland Ave.). A duplex when it was built in 1906, this building at first glance reveals little of its

importance. Located in the 18th and Vine Historic District, it has been the home of the Black Musicians Union Local 627 since 1928. Jazz greats including Charlie "Yardbird" Parker, Count Basie, Bennie Moten, and Mary Lou Williams came here for jam sessions. The building was designated a National Historic Landmark— Kansas City's only one—in 1982.

7. **Pendergast Headquarters** (1908 Main St.). This unassuming building is unchallenged in its contribution to Kansas City history. For almost 30 years, this was the base of Thomas J. Pendergast, the city's all-time most influential political figure. For decades, Pendergast's Democratic machine controlled the activities of the city, dispensing favors for patronage. Ironically, income-tax evasion caused his downfall.

8. **New York Life Building** (20 W. 9th St.). It was the 1880s, the decade of one of Kansas City's greatest building booms. Eastern money poured into the city, creating confidence and stylish architecture. Most obvious was the construction of the New York Life Building. Adorned with a magnificent bronze eagle cast in the studio of Augustus Saint-Gaudens, the building remained the city's tallest structure for many years.

9. **John B. Wornall House** (146 W. 61st Terr.). Originally surrounded by 500 acres of farmland, this antebellum Greek revival–style house has become a rarity in Kansas City. John Bristow Wornall, who built the house in 1858 for his bride, Eliza, made a comfortable living selling agricultural products to the fortune-seekers heading west. During the Civil War Battle of Westport (in 1864), the brick mansion served as a hospital for Union and Confederate wounded. The house has been cited for its architectural and historical significance. Open to the public, it is owned by the Jackson County Historical Society.

10. **Union Station** (Pershing Rd. and Main St.). When the building opened to the public on October 30, 1914, crowds pushed their way into the massive 400-foot-by-800-foot Grand Hall and then into the North Waiting Room, which exceeds the length of a football field. Once the third-largest passenger station in the country (it has risen to second-largest), Union Station served for more than 30 years as the city's public square. On June 17, 1933, local newspaper headlines read, "Union Station Massacre!" That day, during an attempt to free a notorious federal prisoner, four people were killed in the crossfire. A stray machine-gun bullet is still lodged in a wall to the west of the east entrance.

On the Right Track

When it opened in 1914, Union Station was one of the most modern railway terminals in the country. Already Kansas City was making impressive strides toward becoming a U.S. transportation hub, and the $5.8-million station ranked as the third-largest railroad facility in the world, second only to New York's Grand Central and Pennsylvania Stations.

By the end of the 1950s, however, airline and automobile travel had supplanted the rails, and fewer than two dozen trains passed through the station each day. Soon, Kansas City's enormous terminal was abandoned in favor of a tiny depot attached to one side.

In 1974, the city agreed to grant tax incentives to a developer who wanted to construct two new buildings on land east of the station in return for restoring the grande dame. Unfortunately the company reneged on the deal, and the city spent two more decades filing and settling expensive lawsuits. Finally an independent civic group bought Union Station and started raising funds to renovate the building and create a science museum inside. In a historic union of Missouri and Kansas taxes, voters on both sides of the state line overwhelmingly approved a sales tax to renovate the vacant facility. Although other metropolitan areas had passed multicounty taxes, this was the first time a tax had crossed a state line.

When Science City opens in November 1999, visitors will be able to experience everything from space stations to medical labs to a prehistoric environment—in addition to marveling at a monumental structure that was once given up for dead.

---

and sea horse figures he had purchased in Italy. & (South Kansas City)

EAST METRO

1827 LOG COURTHOUSE
117 W. Kansas Ave.

Independence
816/325-7111
It's only a two-room log cabin, but this humble building on Kansas Avenue was the first courthouse in Jackson County. In the 1930s, Judge Harry S. Truman held court here while the main courthouse was being reno-

vated. Apr–Oct Mon–Sat 10–4, Sun 1–4. Free. &. (East Metro)

BINGHAM-WAGGONER ESTATE
313 W. Pacific Ave.
Independence
816/461-3491
The stately Bingham-Waggoner Estate was built in 1855 by John Lewis, an Independence pioneer. But artist George Caleb Bingham made it famous. Also a community activist, Bingham painted his popular *Martial Law* in his studio on the estate's 19 acres. In 1879, Peter Waggoner purchased the home, then remodeled it extensively. When the last Waggoner died in the 1970s, the nonprofit Bingham-Waggoner Historical Society was formed to acquire and operate the home. Much of the mansion's interior remained as it had been during Peter's residence. Tours Apr–Oct Mon–Sat 10–4, Sun 1–4. $3 adults, $2.50 seniors, $1 ages 6–16; $6 combination ticket includes the Vaile Mansion and the 1859 Jail, Mar-

shal's Home & Museum. Partially &. (East Metro)

CAVE SPRING INTERPRETIVE CENTER
8701 E. Gregory Blvd.
at Blue Ridge Blvd.
Kansas City
816/358-2283
At the Cave Spring Interpretive Center, you've landed at one of the Santa Fe Trail's early stops. Rotating exhibits describe the nature and cultural history of Kansas City, while nature trails feature a cave, spring, and wildlife habitats. The Interpretive Center offers special programs and field trips. Tue–Sat 10–5. Free. &. (East Metro)

CHARLIE PARKER GRAVE SITE
8604 E. Truman Rd.
Kansas City
Charlie "Yardbird" Parker was only 34 years old when he died in New York. He'd expressly stated that he didn't want to return to Kansas City, but his family brought him back anyway and buried him in Lincoln Cemetery. A

Bingham-Waggoner Estate

Independence Department of Tourism

SOUTH KANSAS CITY/EAST METRO

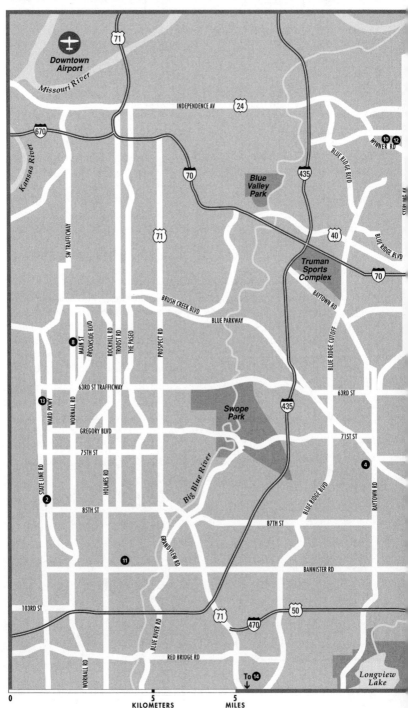

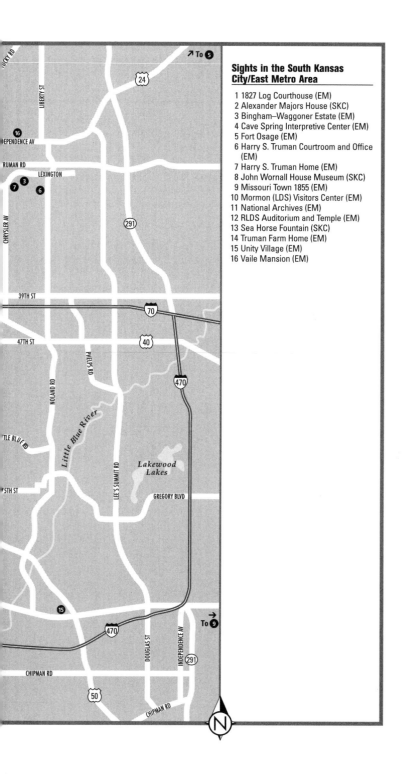

Sights in the South Kansas City/East Metro Area

1 1827 Log Courthouse (EM)
2 Alexander Majors House (SKC)
3 Bingham–Waggoner Estate (EM)
4 Cave Spring Interpretive Center (EM)
5 Fort Osage (EM)
6 Harry S. Truman Courtroom and Office (EM)
7 Harry S. Truman Home (EM)
8 John Wornall House Museum (SKC)
9 Missouri Town 1855 (EM)
10 Mormon (LDS) Visitors Center (EM)
11 National Archives (EM)
12 RLDS Auditorium and Temple (EM)
13 Sea Horse Fountain (SKC)
14 Truman Farm Home (EM)
15 Unity Village (EM)
16 Vaile Mansion (EM)

statue of the legendary jazzman is slatted to be installed in the 18th & Vine Historic District, where it is hoped even more Bird devotees will visit their hero. (East Metro)

FORT OSAGE
BB Hwy.
Sibley
816/795-8200
Operating from 1808 to 1827, Fort Osage was the first U.S. outpost in the Louisiana Purchase. Overlooking the Missouri River, the site was chosen by Lewis and Clark and built under William Clark's personal direction. A full-scale replica of the fortification showcases a variety of artifacts in the blockhouse, trading house, officers' quarters, and soldiers' barracks. Fort Osage hosts special events year-round. Take Highway 24 east to Buckner, Missouri; turn north at BB Highway (a.k.a. Sibley Street), travel two to three miles and watch for signs. Apr–Nov Wed–Sun 9–4:30, Nov–Apr Sat and Sun only. $3 adults, $2 seniors and children 5–13. Partially ♿ (East Metro)

HARRY S. TRUMAN COURTROOM AND OFFICE
Old Courthouse at
Main St. and Lexington Ave.
Independence
816/795-8200, ext. 1260
President Truman began his political career as a judge in this spot, overseeing a $10-million road program during the Depression and initiating the Jackson County park system. At his restored courtroom and office, visitors can view a multimedia presentation, *The Man from Independence*, and see a pictorial history of Truman's early years. Mar–Nov Fri–Sat 9–4:30 (closed Dec–Feb). $2

adults, $1 seniors and children 5–13. ♿ (East Metro)

HARRY S. TRUMAN HOME
219 N. Delaware St.
Independence
816/254-9929
Bess Wallace lived here with her mother and grandparents. When she married her childhood sweetheart, Harry Truman, in 1919, he moved in, too. During President Truman's administration the residence was familiarly known as the "Summer White House," and after Truman left office in 1953, he and Bess returned to this Victorian mansion. The 33rd president died in 1972, but his First Lady kept the house as it had been during his lifetime. Bess died a decade later, bequeathing the home to the country. Guided tours daily 9–5 (closed Mon Labor Day–Memorial Day). $2 at the Truman Home ticket center, at Main Street and Truman Road. All visitors must go to the ticket office first. Partially ♿ (East Metro)

MISSOURI TOWN 1855
Lake Jacomo/Fleming Park
Blue Springs
816/795-8200, ext. 1260
Ever wonder about life in the 1850s? At Missouri Town 1855, more than 35 period buildings cover about 30 acres, giving you the opportunity to visit old houses, an antique church, a blacksmith shop, and reconstructed barns. Living-history interpreters show how people lived back then, as they quilt, garden, or work at the general store. Look for reenactments and other special events throughout the year. Take Highway 70 to the Blue Springs exit, on the east side of Lake Jacomo. Wed–Sun 9–4:30 (Nov–Apr weekends only). $3 adults, $2 seniors and ages 5–13. ♿ (East Metro)

Reorganized Church of Jesus Christ of Latter-Day Saints Temple in Independence

MORMON (LDS) VISITORS CENTER
937 Walnut St.
Independence
816/836-3466

Independence was an important destination for Mormons after founder Joseph Smith indicated that this was where Jesus Christ would return to earth. Countless members of his faithful flocked to the area. At the Mormon Visitors Center, you can view an historic display of Mormon life in Missouri between 1831 and 1839. The center houses plenty of artifacts; a slide show and laser disc presentation describing church beliefs are also available. Daily 9–9. Free. & (East Metro)

NATIONAL ARCHIVES
2312 E. Bannister Rd.
Kansas City
816/926-6272

One of 12 field branches of the U.S. National Archives and Records Ad-ministration, this branch is noted for its genealogy information, diplomatic dispatches, and war documents. It's a favorite place for people research-ing their family trees. Mon–Fri 8–4, every third Sat 9–4. Free. & (East Metro)

RLDS AUDITORIUM AND TEMPLE
1001 W. Walnut St.
Independence
816/833-1000, ext. 1318

The Reorganized Church of Jesus Christ of Latter-Day Saints was offi-cially launched in 1852, when Joseph Smith III took the helm of the largest Mormon splinter group. In Inde-pendence, the massive Auditorium and the newly built Temple—with its 300-foot spiral roof that resembles a seashell—house the RLDS world headquarters. In addition to being a place of worship, the buildings fea-ture museum displays and guided tours. Organ recitals daily June–Sept at 3 p.m. on the 110-rank, 6,000-pipe, Aeolian-Skinner organ, one of the

Why is the RLDS in Independence?

As founder of the Mormon church, Joseph Smith believed that Independence was his "City of Zion," the place where Jesus would first appear at his second coming. The leader was so convincing that converts hastened to establish a settlement in the Missouri town.

Smith, however, was killed in 1844, which sent the faithful into a tailspin. His eldest son was only 11 when Smith died; other leaders arose but couldn't attract a sufficient following. As many as 20 splinter groups formed in the eight years following this leader's death.

By 1852, Joseph Smith III heard the call. Now 19, the prophet's son led a dissident group that refused to follow newly emerging leader Brigham Young and his doctrines, one of which was polygamy. Calling themselves the Reorganized Church of Jesus Christ of Latter-Day Saints, the group claimed theirs to be the original church organized by Joseph Smith in 1830.

Now numbering some 200,000 members in more than 1,000 churches across the United States, the RLDS still believes that Independence is its spiritual home.

largest in the United States. Daily 9–5. Free. ♿ (East Metro)

TRUMAN FARM HOME
12301 Blue Ridge Blvd.
Grandview
816/881-4431

When he was a boy, Harry Truman often stayed here on his grandparents' farm. He returned as a young adult during his budding political career. The family farm has been restored and is now run by the National Park Service. Free tours of the house. June–Aug Sat–Sun 9–4. Partially ♿ (East Metro)

UNITY VILLAGE
Hwy. 350 and Colbern Rd.
816/524-3550

Another religious world headquarters in the area, Unity Village is the 1,400-acre home of the Unity School of Christianity. Founded in 1889 by American clergyman and educator Charles Fillmore and his wife, Myrtle, the nondenominational religion combines teachings from Christian Science, New Thought, Hinduism, Theosophy, and others. Visitors can roam Unity's well-kept grounds, which include fountains, lakes, formal gardens, a bell tower, and a cafeteria that's open to public. Tours and 20-minute slide presentation. Hours vary by season; roughly Mon–Fri 8–5, Sat–Sun 10–5. Free, but goodwill offerings are accepted. ♿ (East Metro)

VAILE MANSION
1500 N. Liberty St.
Independence
816/325-7111
Built in 1881 by entrepreneur Harvey Vaile, this 31-room mansion is one of the finest and most well-preserved examples of Victorian architecture's Second Empire style in the United States. Ceiling murals and opulent furnishings adorn the building's interior; its exterior makes for dramatic photos. Apr–Oct Mon–Sat 10–4, Sun 1–4 (closed Nov–Mar). $3 adults, $1 ages 6–16; $6 combination ticket with the Bingham-Waggoner Estate and the 1859 Jail, Marshal's Home & Museum. Partially ఉ (East Metro)

Convention and Visitors Bureau of Greater Kansas City

6

MUSEUMS AND GALLERIES

Kansas City boasts a surprising number of fascinating museums exploring everything from history and art to tiny toys. You can view some of the finest Asian art in the country, the entire cargo of a pre–Civil War paddlewheeler, and even Victorian jewelry made from human hair. Kansas City's art galleries also show an array of talented regional, national, and international artists, whose work—from traditional to cutting edge—adds to the area's creative ambiance.

ART MUSEUMS AND PUBLIC GALLERIES

JOHNSON COUNTY COMMUNITY COLLEGE GALLERY OF ART
12345 College Blvd.
Overland Park
913/469-8500, ext. 3972
The Gallery of Art at Johnson County Community College concentrates its exhibitions and educational programming on contemporary art and periodically exhibits historic work and American Indian art. Under director Bruce Hartman, the gallery has started an acquisition program for contemporary outdoor sculpture, including the dramatic *Running Man* atop the school's Commons Building.

Mon–Fri 10–5, Sat–Sun 1–5. よ (Johnson County)

KEMPER MUSEUM OF CONTEMPORARY ART
4420 Warwick Blvd.
Kansas City
816/561-3737
The Kemper Museum, opened in 1994 through the efforts of its civically active namesake family, contains permanent and rotating exhibits by international contemporary artists. The modern glass, granite, and stainless steel building provides a harmonious setting for works by Jasper Johns, Frank Stella, and David Hockney, among others. A sculpture courtyard and the colorfully delightful Café

Art and Soul

William Rockhill Nelson was a zealous patron of the arts. Founder of the Kansas City Star *and financial proponent of the parks-and-boulevard system, Nelson bequeathed $11 million to the city specifically for art acquisitions when he died in 1915. His gift, combined with another $1 million from reclusive art patron Mary Atkins for land and a building, eventually launched the now-famous Nelson-Atkins Museum of Art.*

Unlike most great museums, the Nelson-Atkins was not created from existing art collections. The trustees began buying in earnest in the early Thirties, under the direction of art historians such as Laurence Sickman, who amassed one of the most important collections of Asian art in the United States. Because they started the museum during the Depression, the trustees were able to acquire excellent pieces at relatively low prices. The Nelson, as it's known locally, opened its doors in 1933.

Sebastienne make the Kemper a rewarding place to visit. Tue–Thu 10–4, Fri 10–9, Sat 10–5, Sun 11–5. Free. Café Sebastienne open Tue–Sun 11–2:30, Fri 6–9; call 816/561-7740 for reservations. ᭥ (Plaza/Westport)

**NELSON-ATKINS
MUSEUM OF ART
4525 Oak St.
Kansas City
816/561-4000**
Considered one of the finest art museums in the country, the Nelson contains prestigious collections of European and American art, from Caravaggio, Monet, and Rembrandt to Homer, Sargent, and Bingham. Its renowned Oriental Collection includes the Chinese Temple Room, galleries displaying furniture and porcelain, and an array of glazed T'ang Dynasty tomb figures. Outside, the Henry Moore Sculpture Garden comprises 13 larger-than-life works in a landscaped setting, while four giant shuttlecocks by Claes Oldenburg and Coosje van Bruggen decorate the lawns. The Rozelle Court Restaurant serves lunch in a romantic setting straight from Tuscany. Tue–Thu 10–4, Fri 10–9, Sat 10–5, Sun 1–5. $5 adults, $2 adult students, $1 ages 6–18, free to all on Sat. ᭥ (Plaza/Westport)

**UNIVERSITY OF
MISSOURI–KANSAS CITY
GALLERY OF ART
51st St. and Holmes Rd.
Kansas City
816/235-1502**
This gallery at the University of Missouri–Kansas City is a forum for contemporary art and issues. Gallery

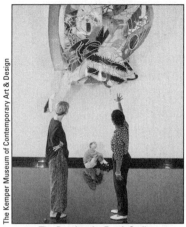

The Prophet *by Frank Stella*
at the KM, p. 114

director Craig Subler assembles six exhibitions a year that are geared toward exploring topics of our time. The gallery also sponsors regular lectures, visiting artists, and art historians. During the school year, Tue–Fri 12–5, Sat–Sun 1–5. Call for summer hours. & (Plaza/Westport)

SCIENCE AND HISTORY MUSEUMS

1859 JAIL, MARSHAL'S HOME & MUSEUM
217 N. Main St.
Independence
816/252-1892
Built before the Civil War, this historic jail once held outlaws Frank James and William Quantrill. Within the jail, with its barred windows and double iron doors, it's possible to step into a cell and experience the sinking feeling of early frontier justice. Apr–Oct Mon–Sat 10–5, Sun 1–4; Mar, Nov, Dec Tue–Sat 10–4, Sun 1–4; closed Jan and Feb. $3 adults, $2.50 seniors, $1 ages 6–16. & (East Metro)

AGRICULTURAL HALL OF FAME & FARMING MUSEUM
630 N. 126th St.
Bonner Springs
913/721-1075
As the nation's largest exhibit of artifacts relating to American farm life, the 270-acre Agricultural Hall of Fame & Farming Museum was chartered by Congress in 1960. It's now the only such institution honoring farmers. Built entirely with private funds, the museum's three major buildings chronicle the evolution of American agriculture, from the first farm truck to the steam threshing engine to ice harvesting tools. It's a rural extravaganza. Mid-Mar–Dec 1 Mon–Sat 9–5, Sun 1–5. $5 adults, $4 seniors, $2.50 ages 5–12. & (Kansas City, Kansas)

AMERICAN JAZZ MUSEUM
1616 E. 18th St.
Kansas City
816/474-8463
The new American Jazz Museum celebrates the African American community that thrived at 18th and Vine for more than four decades. Set in the heart of the place where Kansas City jazz was born, the Jazz Museum is one of the most interactive museums in the country. Here you can listen to rare tunes from the Thirties, watch a video featuring early jazz greats, or create your own music. In the same building is the Negro Leagues Baseball Museum (see listing below). Tue–Thu 9–6, Fri–Sat 9–9, Sun 12–6. $6 adults, $2.50 under 12; combination tickets with the Negro Leagues museum $8 adults, $4 under 12. & (Downtown)

ARABIA STEAMBOAT MUSEUM
400 Grand Ave.
Kansas City

Treasure Hunters of the Midwest

It started as a dream. It became an obsession.

Back in 1988, three families decided they would try to salvage the 180-foot sidewheeler Arabia, *which sank in 1856, after hitting a Missouri River snag. The river channel had shifted, leaving the boat beneath a farm field. Earlier recovery efforts—in 1877, 1897, and 1974—had failed, but the Hawleys, Mackeys, and Luttrells believed they could succeed. Skeptics claimed the boat was empty; nevertheless, these Independence natives remained committed.*

First, Bob Hawley designed a system to lower the water table at the riverfront field. Then the team started digging, spending four months excavating a 40-foot deep pit. Finally they hit pay dirt: perfectly preserved—albeit wet and mud-caked—top hats, eyeglasses, tobacco, glass beads, canned pickles, and much, much more. After cleaning and preserving the 200 tons of booty with water and polyethylene, the families opened the Arabia *Steamboat Museum in 1991. It's one of Kansas City's unique and most popular attractions.*

816/471-4030
The mighty Missouri River swallowed hundreds of steamboats during the vessels' heyday, catching many on snags lurking just beneath the murky surface. The *Arabia* was among them, but the boat was recovered—more than a century after its sinking by a group of determined treasure-seekers. This museum highlights more than 200 tons of recovered goods salvaged from the 1850s steamboat, including china, jewelry, hardware, cookware, and food. A full-scale reproduction of the 171-foot boat deck features a 28-foot working paddle wheel. Located on the east side of the City Market complex. Mon–Sat 10–6, Sun 12–5. $7.50 adults, $7 seniors, $3.75 ages 4–12. &
(Downtown)

HARRY S. TRUMAN LIBRARY AND MUSEUM
U.S. 24 and Delaware Ave.
Independence
816/833-1225
Harry S. Truman's presidential library provides a fascinating look at the leader considered by many to be one of the finest U.S. presidents of the twentieth century. This site contains approximately 30,000 Truman-related objects, from gifts to personal possessions to memorabilia. Visitors can see Truman's Oval Office and witness his legacy of leadership, from his stints as a captain in World War I to

judge to president. Rotating exhibits and programs illustrate the Truman presidency and the world that the Missouri native helped build and shape. Mon–Sat 9–5, Thu to 9, Sun 12–5; closed Thanksgiving, Christmas, New Year's Day. $5 adults, $4.50 seniors, $3 ages 6–18. ⅙ (East Metro)

HISTORIC LIBERTY JAIL AND VISITOR CENTER
216 N. Main St.
Liberty
816/781-3188
In this small building, Joseph Smith— the first prophet and president of the Church of Jesus Christ of Latter-Day Saints (Mormons)—was incarcerated from 1838 to 1839. The museum is operated by the Mormons, who also offer exhibits, an audiovisual presentation, and information about church history at the site. Guided tours daily 9–9. Free. ⅙ (Northland)

JESSE JAMES BANK MUSEUM AND HISTORIC SITE
Historic Square
Liberty

816/781-4458
Step back in time and imagine conducting your bank business in this tiny brick building. Then imagine outlaw Jesse James barreling in, ready to relieve you of your cash. This is the site of the first successful daylight bank robbery during peacetime in the United States. The original 1858 vault and hand-scribed ledger books are on display. Mon–Sat 9–4. $3 adults, $2.50 seniors, $1.50 ages 8–15. ⅙ with advance notice. (Northland)

JOHNSON COUNTY HISTORICAL MUSEUM
6305 Lackman Rd.
Shawnee
913/631-6709
Life was hard back in the pioneer days, and this museum shows just how difficult it truly was. Exhibits and hands-on activities depict life on the plains; one display is dedicated to the pioneer trails experience in what is now Johnson County. On a quite different note, you can also tour a 1950s house—a donated model home rebuilt by Kansas City Power & Light to

The Jesse James Bank Museum

From Lumber to Science

The Kansas City Museum opened its doors in 1940, in a mansion once called Corinthian Hall. Built in 1910 as the home of Robert Alexander Long, founder of the Long-Bell Lumber Company, the home was named for the six Corinthian columns that support the front portico.

Over the years, the museum increased its emphasis on exhibits that highlight science, technology, and history. Today the facility's planetarium remains the only public planetarium in the area; its Challenger Learning Center offers simulated, hands-on space flights to stimulate interest in math, science, and technology.

The museum has also launched plans to rocket into the future. Scheduled to open in late 1999, the Kansas City Museum's Science City will occupy a portion of the renovated Union Station. Other exhibits will still be on view at Robert Long's gracious three-story home in northeast Kansas City.

demonstrate all the modern electrical conveniences of the time. Tours are given by 1950s-clad guides. Museum open Tue–Sat 10–4:30, Sun 1–4:30. Free. 1950s house open Tue–Sun 1–4:30. $2 adults, $1 kids. ⅋ (Johnson County)

KANSAS CITY MUSEUM
3218 Gladstone Blvd.
Kansas City
816/483-8300
This museum features high-touch science and history exhibits that appeal to kids of all ages. The National History Hall, a working soda fountain, the planetarium, and the Challenger Learning Center are only four of the major attractions. Chief exhibits in 1999 include *Dear Mr. Ripley: Treasures from the Believe It or Not Archives* (June 5–Sept 5) and

Inside Out: The Visible Human (Oct 2–Jan 2, 2000). Tue–Sat 9:30–4:30, Sun 12–4:30. Suggested donations: $2.50 adults, $2 seniors and students, $1.50 children. Planetarium tickets $3.50. ⅋ (Downtown)

NATIONAL FRONTIER TRAILS CENTER
318 W. Pacific Ave.
Independence
816/325-7575
The National Frontier Trails Center has become the nation's foremost museum and research facility on the West's exploration and settlement. It's a natural, since Independence was the principal jumping-off point for the Santa Fe, California, and Oregon Trails. Rotating and permanent exhibits—including two nineteenth-century wagons—as well as an interpretive center, films, and archives

explain the "Go West" call popular in the mid-1800s. Mon–Sat 9–4:30, Sun 12:30–4:30. $2.50 adults, $1 students 6–17. ♿ (East Metro)

NEGRO LEAGUES BASEBALL MUSEUM
1616 E. 18th St.
Kansas City
816/474-8463
When it opened in 1994, the Negro Leagues Baseball Museum was dedicated to preserving and illuminating the history of African American baseball in America, a mission it fulfills admirably. Through interactive computer stations, uniform displays, and a photo gallery, visitors can learn about the contributions made by these gifted players. Tue–Sat 9–6; Sun 12–6. $6 adults, $2.50 under 12; combination tickets with the jazz museum $8 adults, $4 under 12. ♿ (Downtown)

OLD SHAWNEE TOWN
57th St. and Cody Rd.
Shawnee
913/268-8772
In this re-creation of an early Kansas pioneer community, visitors can wander through a variety of original and reconstructed buildings, including Kansas' first jail (built in 1843), a chapel, a farmhouse, and a one-room school, among others. An adjacent park reassembles the town in miniature. Tue–Sat 12–5. $1 adults, 50 cents children. ♿ (Johnson County)

STRAWBERRY HILL MUSEUM
720 N. 4th St.
Kansas City, Kansas
913/371-3264
Built for a prosperous family in 1887, this three-story, red brick home later became St. John's Orphanage. Now it houses exhibits that detail the lives

The Nelson-Atkins Museum of Art, p. 115

and history of the Slavic people who immigrated to this area. The museum (named for its Strawberry Hill neighborhood) provides an intimate look at an often-overlooked ethnic group in America. Sat–Sun 12–5. $3 adults, $2 ages 6–12. (Kansas City, Kansas)

WYANDOTTE COUNTY HISTORICAL MUSEUM
631 N. 126th St.
Bonner Springs
913/721-1078
Located near the Agricultural Hall of Fame in Bonner Springs, the museum presents local and regional history. Exhibits include a 1903 horse-drawn fire engine and a variety of other turn-of-the-century artifacts. Tue–Sat 10–5, Sun 1–5. Free. ♿ (Kansas City, Kansas)

SPECIALTY MUSEUMS

AMERICAN ROYAL MUSEUM & VISITORS CENTER
1701 American Royal Ct.
Kansas City

Ten Favorite Displays to See at the Toy & Miniature Museum

by William R. Robertson, renowned miniaturist and Kansas City resident

There are tens of thousands of things to see at this museum but here goes, starting with the smallest . . .

1. An American Indian bowl with a pair of ⅛-inch-long frogs for handles, made by Theresa Wildflower.

2. A carved and gold-gilded picture frame with a 60-mesh needlepoint painting by Jim Mormon.

3. Carved boxwood skeletons: a 2.5-inch-high human and a seven-inch-long velociraptor, with separate teeth and claws carved from holly. Made by Lloyd McCaffery.

4. An eight-inch-high English Georgian secretary desk with working locks and 19 secret compartments.

5. A sidesaddle, three-wheeled velocipede, circa 1870s.

6. An American Gothic–style fretwork cabinet doll house with mid-nineteenth-century painted metal furniture. Don't miss the felt "penwipes" shaped like a bulldog with pups.

7. Twin Manors, a Georgian-style miniature house made from 75,000 pieces. Be sure to see its exploded-view front door.

8. A nine-foot-tall, nineteenth-century French music box in the shape of a château, with stained glass windows and floor, working gutters and downspouts, and gold gilt details.

9. GeeGee's room, a full-scale Victorian nursery filled with toys and dolls. Don't miss the Noter-Growlers, toy dogs you could rent to walk on the boardwalk in the 1890s.

10. The maze, a winding hallway lined with miniature room settings ranging from a turn-of-the-century architects' classroom to the Palace of Versailles' study.

816/221-9800
The American Royal spent $34 million for an expansion that included a visitors center. Through interactive displays and a 20-minute film, visitors learn about the American Royal Livestock, Horse Show, and Rodeo, an annual fall event commemorating Kansas City's historic role as a crossroads of the cattle industry. Tue–Sat 10–4, Sun by appointment. $3 adults, $2.50 seniors, $2 ages 2–12. ⚹ (Downtown)

**BRUCE R. WATKINS
CULTURAL HERITAGE CENTER
3700 Blue Pkwy.
Kansas City**

816/923-6226

Named for a much-beloved city councilman, this center was erected to honor the contributions of Kansas City's African American residents. In addition to seasonal exhibits and a research library, the center hosts cultural events. Tue–Sat 10–6. Free. ♿ (East Metro)

KANSAS CITY FIRE MUSEUM
1019 Cherry St.
Kansas City
816/474-0200

Set in a retired fire station, the Kansas City Fire Museum houses 10 hand-drawn chemical and hose carts that date from 1855. In addition, visitors can see antique hooks and ladders, buckets, ropes, poles, vintage posters, sirens, and various motorized apparatus. Kids will enjoy ringing the firebell and learning about fire safety. Mar–Oct Sat 9–1. $2.50 adults, $1 ages 6–12. ♿ (Downtown)

LEILA'S HAIR MUSEUM
815 W. 23rd St.
Independence
816/252-4247

Leila Cohoon, owner of the Independence College of Cosmetology, opened this museum in 1989 to feature a collection she'd begun in the Fifties. About 500 displays chronicle decorative uses for hair, most predating 1900. Among Cohoon's most-prized pieces are a scrapbook dating from 1725 to 1900, with calling cards and locks of hair; a delicately woven hair brooch; and a Victorian-era hair wreath valued at $10,000. Tue–Sat 8:30–4:30. $3 adults, $1.50 seniors. ♿ (East Metro)

TOY & MINIATURE MUSEUM
5235 Oak St.

Kansas City
816/333-2055

On the University of Missouri–Kansas City campus, this restored 1911 mansion contains an eye-popping 24-room collection of fine miniatures, antique doll houses, Victorian playthings, and much, much more. Far from just a children's attraction, the museum takes you through winding vistas of objects that amaze with their detail and artistry. Be sure to check out the selections from Hallmark's Jerry Smith Toy Collection, a series primarily for boys. Wed–Sat 10–4, Sun 1–4. $4 adults, $3.50 seniors and students over 12, $2 ages 3–12. ♿(Plaza/Westport)

GALLERIES

Home to the annual Plaza Art Fair, the Kansas City Art Institute, and Hallmark Cards, Kansas City has become a hotbed for artistic endeavors. Galleries exist throughout the area, most holding frequent Friday-night openings. What follows is only a small sampling.

BYRON COHEN GALLERY
2020 Baltimore Ave.
Kansas City
816/421-5665

This contemporary gallery features rotating shows highlighting newly created paintings, sculpture, drawings, ceramics, photography, and video. Thu–Sat 11–5 and by appointment. (Downtown)

CENTRAL PARK GALLERY
1644 Wyandotte St.
Kansas City
816/471-7711

Run by husband and wife Jim and

Ten Great Public Sculptures in the Kansas City Area

by Heidi Bilardo, art consultant and former public art administrator for the Municipal Art Commission

1. *Shuttlecocks*, by Claes Oldenburg and Coosje van Bruggen, at the Nelson-Atkins Museum of Art. Envision the museum's building and grounds as a badminton court for giants.

2. *Sky Stations*, by R.M. Fischer. Huge aluminum sculptures placed atop the Bartle Hall Convention Center's pylons, and interior sculptures installed throughout this building.

3. *J.C. Nichols Memorial Fountain*, by French sculptor Henri L. Greber, located at 47th and Main Streets. The four equestrian figures are battling a variety of elements: an alligator, a bear, and two fish-tailed human figures. The grouping is thought to represent an allegory of rivers.

4. *Always*, by Clement Meadmore. Large, bold sculpture located in front of the Cultural Education Center at Johnson County Community College, Quivira and College Boulevard.

5. *Muse of the Missouri* sculpture and fountain, by Wheeler Williams, 9th and Main Streets. Bronze Greek goddess evokes the mythology and history of the Missouri River.

6. *The Scout*, by Cyrus Dallin, in Penn Valley Park, 29th and Pennsylvania. Expressive historic bronze sculpture dedicated as a memorial to the local Native Americans tribe in the Kansas City area.

7. *Bull Wall*, by Robert Morris, at the American Royal Center, 1800 Genessee St. Unique sculpture combining references to Kansas City's stockyard era as well as to neolithic cave paintings in France and Goya's *Flying Bulls*. This work is at its full glory when the steam element is turned on, primarily during November's American Royal events.

8. *Meridian and Bonfire*, by Deborah Butterfield, at the Kansas City Zoo. First formed from tree vines and driftwood, these cast-bronze horses represent the animal that humans worldwide have relied upon most heavily throughout history.

9. *Three Figures/15 Elements*, by Joel Shapiro, at KCI Airport, along the median strip on Cookingham Drive. Three-part geometric sculptures represent the human form.

10. *Triple Crown*, by Kenneth Snelson, at Main and 27th Streets. Stainless steel, cabled tension sculpture captures an intensity of light and reflects it back onto the confluence of many roadways.

Brenda Miles, this nine-year-old gallery features original works and prints in nearly all media. Local, regional, national, and international artists are represented. Tue–Fri 9–5, Sat 10–4. ♿ (Downtown)

DIRT GALLERY
1323 Union Ave.
Kansas City
816/471-3278
The West Bottoms was once the heart of Kansas City's economy and identity. But now a real artists' community has started taking root in old factories and warehouse space. Dirt Gallery is only one of a half-dozen up-and-comers. None have regular hours, so call ahead. (Downtown)

DOLPHIN GALLERY
1901 Baltimore Ave.
Kansas City
816/842-4415
Look for budding art talent at this gallery owned by John O'Brien, including a significant representation from the Kansas City Art Institute. Artists here have created everything from modern sculpture to traditional landscapes. Tue–Fri 9–5, Sat 12–5, and by appointment. (Downtown)

ETHNICART
1601 E. 18th St.
Kansas City
816/472-8463
This gallery features art from around the world but specifically taps the ethnic traditions and cultural creativity of resident artists in its new location in the 18th & Vine Historic District. Tue–Sat 10–6. ♿ (Downtown)

GRAND ARTS
1819 Grand Blvd.
Kansas City

816/421-6887
A nonprofit gallery, Grand Arts shows numerous works by developing artists and renowned contemporary professionals. The facility includes a working sculpture studio. Thu–Sat 10–5 and by appointment. (Downtown)

KANSAS CITY ARTISTS COALITION
201 Wyandotte St.
Kansas City
816/421-5222
This group was formed in 1972 as an artist-run organization. It presents exhibitions, performances, lectures, and readings in its professional gallery space. It also publishes *Forum*, a journal of art news and reviews. ♿ (Downtown)

SHERRY LEEDY CONTEMPORARY ART
2004 Baltimore Ave.
Kansas City
816/474-1919
Sherry Leedy anchors an area that's exploding with distinctive galleries. Glass, ceramics, paintings—this modern gallery has it all. Artists from the area, as well as national and international creators, show in this downtown space. Thu–Sat 11–5 and by appointment. (Downtown)

SOCIETY FOR CONTEMPORARY PHOTOGRAPHY GALLERY
2012 Baltimore Ave.
Kansas City
816/471-2115
This gallery has earned its reputation for bringing in the photographic works of a variety of artists, from Seydou Keita's photographs of Mali to Bill Gaskins studies on good hair and bad hair. Thu–Sat 11–5 and by appointment. (Downtown)

© Hallmark Cards, Inc.

7

KIDS' STUFF

Kansas City is a kids' kind of town, from the area's many parks and play-grounds to the countless sights to learn from. Do they want to see a sea lion? Head for the Kansas City Zoo. Take a turn in the wave pool? Try Kansas City's Oceans of Fun. The region offers amusement rides to try, exotic animals to touch, and educational exhibits to explore. Whether they like science, art, or tree-climbing, kids can find it all—and have a ball—in Kansas City.

ANIMALS AND THE GREAT OUTDOORS

DEANNA ROSE CHILDREN'S FARMSTEAD
138th St. and Switzer Rd.
Overland Park
913/897-2360
This five-acre farm contains an amply stocked barnyard where kids can get close to buffalo, chickens, rabbits, pigs, and other animals. Many farm residents are friendly enough to pet. The farmstead also includes picnic shelters and a na-ture trail. Apr–Sept daily 9–8; Oct daily 9–5 (closed Nov–Mar). Free; hayrides $2 per person. & (Johnson County)

ERNIE MILLER PARK AND NATURE CENTER
909 N. Kansas
Olathe
913/764-7759
Preserved in its natural state, this 113-acre park showcases ecologi-cal habitats such as grassland, upland meadow, and bottomland forest. Three short trails wind through and between the areas, giv-ing kids an opportunity to see the wildlife living there. Pocket-sized reference guides make the experi-ence even more educational. At the Nature Center, exhibits include a wildlife diorama and ecology dis-plays. Tue–Sat 9–5; Sun 1–5. Free. & (Johnson County)

KANSAS CITY ZOO
I-435 and 63rd St.
Kansas City
816/871-5700

With its $71-million expansion, the Kansas City Zoo offers a fascinating range of natural settings for all kinds of animals, from rhinos to gorillas to meerkats. Among the zoo's newest additions are the African Safari and Australian exhibits. The zoo's IMAX Theatre, one of the few in a zoo setting, shows films such as *Everest* and *Alaska: Spirit of the Wild*. Other fun stuff includes train, camel, and pony rides; year-round sea lion presentations; and several restaurants. Early Apr–mid-Oct daily 9–5; mid-Oct–early Apr 9–4. $5 ages 12 and over, $2.50 ages 3–11, $1 everyone all day Tue. Parking $2. ⅍ (South Kansas City)

LAKESIDE NATURE CENTER
Elmwood St. and Gregory Blvd.
Kansas City
816/444-4656

Like the zoo, the Lakeside Nature Center is located in Swope Park.

This educational center features native Missouri animals, including birds of prey, mammals, and reptiles. Kids can learn from the center's hands-on exhibits and enlightening Saturday classes, or by hiking one of the two trails nearby. Tue–Sat 9–5; also Apr–Oct Sun noon–4. Free; nominal fee for Saturday courses. ⅍ (South Kansas City)

RIVERVIEW GARDEN CENTER
7851 Riverview Ave.
Kansas City, Kansas
913/299-6184

Kids from grade school to junior high will find this commercial growing emporium a fascinating way to learn. The center cultivates annuals and perennials, from chrysanthemums to poinsettias, and keeps water ponds, too. An affable host, owner Mike Murray will show kids around the 10-acre garden and the 45,000-square-foot greenhouse, either by reservation or whenever families drop in. Mon–Sat 9–5. Free. ⅍ (Kansas City, Kansas)

A cheetah at the Kansas City Zoo

Ollie MacMillen/Kansas City Zoological Gardens

FUN AND EDUCATIONAL

FARMLAND INDUSTRIES RESEARCH FARM
3705 N. 139th St.
Bonner Springs
913/721-2600

The area's largest agribusiness company, Farmland Industries operates a 360-acre farm that gives a fascinating in-depth look at how the enterprise develops feed for cows, calves, pigs, and pets. This is a research facility, so tours are given only on Tuesday and Thursday during the third week of each spring and summer month. By reservation only. Free. ⅍ (Kansas City, Kansas)

Top Ten Favorite Animals at the Kansas City Zoo
by Dr. Mark Wourms, Zoo Director

1. **Chimpanzees.** All kinds of social interactions can be viewed through a 40-foot wall of glass.

2. **Meerkats.** These animals form curious colonies with guards, babysitters, and foragers. Always a great photo.

3. **African Elephants.** The majesty and power of the largest terrestrial animal is quite amazing.

4. **Red Kangaroo.** The mob can be on the path with our visitors. Joeys sticking out of pouches are wonderful discoveries.

5. **Cheetah.** Visitors eating lunch can enjoy watching the graceful cheetah in Nanyuki Market.

6. **Giant Hornbill.** These amazing, colorful, and rare birds live in the Tropical Asia section.

7. **African Lions.** The "King of Beasts" can be viewed outdoors or through glass.

8. **River Otters.** These native North American "clowns" are known for their playful interactions.

9. **Scottish Highland Cow.** Our cow, Warf, is worth seeing because he is just so cute.

10. **Warthogs.** Look in the mud. These *Lion King* stars are so ugly, they're beautiful.

KALEIDOSCOPE
25th St. and Grand Blvd.
Crown Center
Kansas City
816/274-8300
Run by Hallmark next door to its Visitors Center, the Kaleidoscope program exists to encourage creativity in kids 5 to 12. Through various senuous and imaginative hands-on activities, Kaleidoscope helps children develop their creativity. Reservations required Mon–Fri during the school year (816/274-8301); open sessions Sat at noon, 1:15, and 2:30. Free. 𝅉 (Downtown)

RIDE THE AMTRAK
2200 Main St.
Kansas City
816/421-3622
During the holidays, parents often take their kids to Lee's Summit, Independence, or Warrensburg to board the Amtrak train for a ride to Kansas City. From there, it's a short walk to Crown Center to see Santa before the return train trip. It's possible to give the kids a real train-riding experience any time of year by making these short journeys. A round-trip ticket between Independence and Kansas City: $8–$10 adults, $7–$8.50 seniors,

half price ages 2–15 when accompanied by an adult. Limit two children
per adult. Call for train schedule. &
(Downtown)

PUPPETS AND THEATER

THE COTERIE THEATRE
25th St. and Grand Ave.
Crown Center
Kansas City
816/474-6552
Located on Crown Center's Level 1,
the Coterie is a professional theater
presenting dramatic works for the
entire family. Kids particularly enjoy
the stage company's mission: to
present inspiring plays that challenge stereotypes and get the audience talking. Plays set for 1999
include *Free to Be. . . You and Me*,
Of Mice and Men, *The Seven
Dwarfs*, *Lord of the Flies*, along with
the Young Playwrights' Showcase.
Call for dates and times. Tickets are
$6. & (Downtown)

PAUL MESNER PUPPETS
Unity Temple on the Plaza
707 W. 47th St.
Kansas City
816/235-2700 or 816/756-3500
Started in 1982, Paul Mesner's puppet
shows run the gamut from classic
stories to learning experiences. Off-
beat characters energize the shows,
making them enjoyable for adults,
too. Morning and early afternoon performances during the season range
from the *Heartland Puppetry Festival*
to *The Dinosaur Show*. Tickets are $6.
& (Plaza/Westport)

THEATRE FOR YOUNG AMERICA
4881 Johnson Dr.
Mission
913/831-1400

TRIVIA

What to do with teens? Try an
underground game of paint-
ball (Chapter 10), a concert at
Sandstone (Chapter 11), or a
watery day at Oceans of Fun
(this chapter). Teens in Kansas
City also head to the Country
Club Plaza (Chapter 9) and to
Crown Center's ice rink
(Chapter 10).

In addition to its regular lineup of
first-rate plays for children, TYA offers
classes for aspiring actors ages 3½
and up throughout the year. In summer, special workshops teach dramatic skills such as storytelling and
improvisation. Plays in 1999 range
from *Mother Hicks* to *Little Red*. Located on Mission Mall's second level.
$6 all ages; group rates available. &
(Johnson County)

MUSEUMS AND LIBRARIES

CHILDREN'S MUSEUM OF
KANSAS CITY
4601 State Ave.
Kansas City, Kansas
913/287-8888
Located on the lower level of the
Indian Springs Shopping Center, the
Children's Museum emphasizes art,
history, and science with engaging
exhibits such as the Magic School
Bus, a mock radio station, and a
model grocery. Kids learn from and
enjoy this storehouse of knowledge. Tue–Sat 9:30–5, Sun 1–5. $3
ages 2 and up. & (Kansas City,
Kansas)

Convention and Visitors Bureau of Greater Kansas City

Toy and Miniature Museum

KANSAS CITY MUSEUM
3218 Gladstone Blvd.
Kansas City
816/483-8300
For a description, see Chapter 6, Museums and Galleries. ♿ (Downtown)

TOY AND MINIATURE MUSEUM
5235 Oak St.
Kansas City
816/333-2055
For a description, see Chapter 6, Museums and Galleries. ♿ (Plaza/Westport)

WONDERSCOPE CHILDREN'S MUSEUM
5705 Flint St.
Shawnee
913/268-4176
913/268-8130 (recording)
Here kids will find interactive exhibits that feature everything from a television studio to a weather station to a "What if You Couldn't" display. Set in the former Flint Elementary School, Wonderscope is a colorful facility that encourages parents and kids to explore together. Mon–Sat 10–5, Sun 12–5. $4 ages 3 and up, $2 ages 1–2. ♿ (Johnson County)

STORES KIDS LOVE

BITTERMAN FAMILY CONFECTIONS
1625 Oak St.
Kansas City
816/221-2922
With its wood floors and old-fashioned shelves stacked to the ceiling, Bitterman looks like a kids' paradise. The store—owned by the Bitterman family since 1936—features hard candies, chocolates, and novelty sweets. A newly installed candy museum showcases the family's collection of jars, tins, gum boxes, and other candy memorabilia. Mon–Fri 10–4. ♿ (Downtown)

FAO SCHWARZ
235 W. 47th St.

Ten Best Things to Do with Kids in the Kansas City Area

by Pam Elliott, owner of Pam's Day Care and a 1998 Child Care Professional Gold Medal Award–Winner

1. Visit the **Deanna Rose Children's Farmstead.** Kids can pet and feed farm animals and go on hayrides in a horse-drawn wagon. Good for kids ages 1 to 10.

2. See a play at **Theatre for Young America**. For 25 years, TYA has been producing professional theater for young audiences in the Kansas City area. Good for ages preschool to grade 8, depending on the play. Group rates available.

3. Tour the ***Arabia* Steamboat Museum**. Children can touch some exhibits and view artifacts taken from a Civil War–era paddle-wheeler. Ages 8 and up.

4. Take a hike at the **Ernie Miller Park and Nature Center**. Offers hiking trails for all ages, with varying degrees of difficulty. The center has hands-on activities and animals on display. Kids ages 3 to 12 will enjoy these trails.

5. Visit the **Kansas City Zoo**, one of the Midwest's best. Visit the newer sites: Africa and Australia. Also, take a break at the IMAX Theatre. Good for kids ages 3 and up.

6. Ride the **Smoky Hill Railway** (502 S. Walnut, Belton). Kids can experience lifelike history as they ride a real train down a former Frisco Railroad line, past a hobo village. The conductor will give a history lesson, and a 30-minute train movie is shown prior to the ride. Good for kids ages 4 and up.

7. Enjoy **Carrousel Park**. When the weather's bad, try this indoor amusement park, with rides, shows, ice cream, pizza, and other snacks. Good for kids ages 3 and up.

8. Visit **Wonderscope Museum**. Hands-on activities focus on arts, sciences, and technology. Features include a TV studio, space station, and hospital exhibit. The Small Wonders room is great for younger kids.

9. Eat at **Fritz's Union Station Restaurant**. Kids can order meals by table telephone and watch as food is delivered via a model train that runs above the tables. All ages.

10. Check out **Kauffman Stadium**. Visit the locker rooms, sit in the dugout and press box, see the Hall of Fame. Call for tour schedule (816/921-2200). Good for ages 4 through teens.

Kansas City
816/931-9090

Kids will love the giant bear that stands sentinel at the FAO Schwarz door. Inside, they can roam the huge store and play with the electronic floor keyboard, the interactive rain forest, and the animated candy store, FAO Schweetz. Mon–Sat 10–8, Thu to 9, Sun 12–6. ♿ (Plaza/Westport)

KCPT STORE OF KNOWLEDGE
4705 Broadway Blvd.
Kansas City
816/960-0480

Sure it's for kids, but grown-ups also find plenty to play with here. The public TV–affiliated shop stocks more than 5,000 toys, games, puzzles, videos, software selections, hobby kits, and other merchandise. More than 60 subjects include the arts, science, history, and foreign languages. Naturally a special section is dedicated to PBS programs. Mon–Sat 10–9, Sun 11–5. (Plaza/ Westport)

PRIMARY COLORS
5344 W. 95th St.
Overland Park
913/341-6789

When kids want to get creative, they head to Primary Colors, where art reigns supreme. Launched by twenty-something Scott Novorr in 1997, this store carries kids' art supplies and projects, offers walk-in art workshops, and encourages budding Botticellis to paint, draw, and color at several hands-on displays. Mon–Fri 10–5:30, Sat 10–5. ♿ (Johnson County)

READING REPTILE
4120 Pennsylvania St.
Kansas City
816/753-0441

The ultimate kids' bookstore, Reading Reptile carries fun and educational titles, and provides places for children to look over the inventory. This charming Westport store also hosts storytimes and activity hours that attract kids from throughout the metro area. Children who enjoy reading will want to spend ample time in this book haven. The Reptile sponsors a weekly movie on Friday at 7. Mon–Thu 10–6, Fri–Sat 10–8, Sun 12–5. ♿ (Plaza/ Westport)

U.S. TOY COMPANY/
CONSTRUCTIVE PLAYTHINGS
2008 W. 103rd Terr.
Leawood
913/642-8247

Get ready to spend an enjoyable afternoon for all ages at this educational toy emporium. Within its two enormous warehouses set behind Gates Bar-B-Q on State Line Road, U.S. Toy stocks games and toys for learning, plus a carnival section, one of the largest magic shops in the world, and a host of costumes. Hours

The Detonator at Worlds of Fun, p. 132

Dan Feicht/Worlds of Fun

Kids Just Wanna Have Fun

Not all men with money like to have so much fun. But Lamar Hunt, owner of the NFL's Kansas City Chiefs and founder of the American Football League, also developed the dual theme parks Worlds of Fun and Oceans of Fun.

Worlds of Fun opened in 1973 with 60 rides, shows, and attractions. Based on Jules Verne's Around the World in Eighty Days, *the park covers five continents, including Europe, Africa, Asia, and the Americas. Rides within the 170 acres number more than 140; the most popular these days include the Orient Express, the Zambezi Zinger, and the Mamba. The Stax of Wax Rock & Roll Revue is one of the favorite shows, while the Vittle Griddle is the most popular eatery.*

Oceans of Fun opened in 1982 and remains the Midwest's largest tropically themed water park. Within its 60 acres, Oceans of Fun features the million-gallon Surf City Wave Pool. A long list of water-related rides keeps the kids coming back all summer.

Although Hunt has sold the two parks, his legacy remains at Worlds and Oceans of Fun. Unconfirmed reports have it that the Dallas-based entrepreneur has even been spotted whooshing down the Aruba Tuba!

vary seasonally, so call ahead. ♿ (Johnson County)

THEME PARKS

OCEANS OF FUN
I-435 Exit 54
Kansas City
816/454-4545
Water, water everywhere: Oceans of Fun features watery attractions on more than 60 acres, including a million-gallon wave pool, children's water playgrounds, giant water slides, and an adults-only pool with swim-up refreshments. Generally open late May–early Sept daily at 10 a.m.; closing times vary. $18.95 adults and children at least 48 inches tall, $13.50 seniors, $5.95 children under 48 inches tall and over age 3; after 4 p.m., all ages $13.50. Prices rise slightly each year and don't include tax. ♿ (Northland)

WORLDS OF FUN
I-435 Exit 54
Kansas City
816/454-4545

This internationally themed park features more than 140 rides, shows, and attractions, including the Sea Dragon, the Wacky Worm kiddie coaster, and the Detonator. Among the newest rides, the Mamba is one of the tallest, longest, and fastest roller coasters in the world. Generally open mid-Apr–mid-May and early Sept–early Oct weekends from 10 a.m.; late May–early Sept daily at 10 a.m. Closing hours vary. $26.95 adults and children at least 48 inches tall, $13.50 seniors, $5.95 children under 48 inches tall and over age 3; after 4 p.m., $13.50 all ages. Prices rise slightly each year and don't include tax. ♿ (Northland)

PLACES TO PLAY

CARROUSEL PARK
95th St. and Metcalf Ave.
Overland Park
913/385-7275
Set inside the Metcalf South Shopping Center, Carrousel Park draws families with its rides, games, prizes, food, and entertainment. The indoor amusement park is available for parties during the week and open to the public Wed–Sun 10–9. $9 children for a multiple-ride pass or $1 for single rides; adults free. (Johnson County)

COOL CREST FAMILY FUN CENTER
10735 E. Hwy. 40
Independence
816/358-0088
Within Cool Crest's 4.5 acres, families can enjoy four 18-hole miniature golf courses, an exotic bird display, a game room with video machines and pinball, and several party and patio areas. The Patterson family has operated this Independence gathering spot since 1950. Summer: 10–11 daily. Winter: Mon–Thu noon–9:30, Fri–Sat noon–11, Sun noon–9:30. Prices vary depending on games played. ♿ (East Metro)

DISCOVERY ZONE
7594 W. 119th St.
Overland Park
913/469-1838
An enormous room filled with elevated tunnels and slides, Discovery Zone encourages kids to expend some energy and enhance their coordination skills. Parents can join the romp through the 4,000-square-foot play center. Another Discovery Zone is at 4420 S. Noland Rd. in Independence (816/373-4445). Mon–Thu 10–8, Fri–Sat 10–9, Sun 11–7. $5.99 children ages 3 and up, $3.99 under age 3; adults free. (Johnson County)

FAMILY GOLF PARK
1501 NE Hwy. 40
Blue Springs
816/228-1550

This family fun center boasts 36 holes of miniature golf, bumper boats, a game room, a par-3 golf course, a putting green, and golf lessons from professionals. The boats aren't the only water-related activity; the miniature golf course winds through a landscaped lake setting, and the par-3 course hugs the water. The park also provides a lighted golfing practice facility that's open year-round. Mon–Thu 8:30 a.m.–10:30 p.m., Fri–Sat 8:30 a.m.–11:30 p.m., Sun 9 a.m.–10:30 p.m. Rates vary depending on activities. & (East Metro)

JEEPERS!
20070 W. 151st St.
Olathe
913/393-1346
Located in the Great Mall of the Great Plains, Kansas City's discount center, this indoor family amusement park could stand alone. Part of a national chain, Jeepers! includes rides; a soft playground with tunnels, tubes, and chutes; as well as giant slides and skill games. Smaller children enjoy the creative play area, where they can cavort in the dinosaur dig sandbox. Mon–Thu 10–9, Fri–Sat 10–10, Sun 11–8. An all-day, unlimited pass is $6.99 weekdays, $10.99 weekends and holidays, $3.99 kids under 40 inches; single ride tickets also available. & (Johnson County)

8

PARKS, GARDENS, AND RECREATION AREAS

From one of the largest city parks in the country to a swath of tiny pocket pre-serves, Kansas City lays claim to a remarkable variety of outdoor spaces. Some contain lakes within their rolling acreage, while others offer gardens filled with towering trees and blooming perennials. Whatever the season, the metropolitan area presents plenty of places to play and revel in nature.

ANTIOCH PARK
6501 Antioch Rd.
Merriam
913/831-3355

This 44-acre preserve is one of the most beautiful and popular commu-nity parks in the area. Its Old Dodge Town play area appeals to kids, while parents especially enjoy the Helen S. Cuddy Rose Garden and Memorial Arboretum. Walking paths lead visi-tors through a nature area and near two ponds. A basketball court, tennis courts, and picnic shelters add to the park's amenities. Apr–Oct daily 5 a.m.–11 p.m., Nov–Mar daily 7:30 a.m.–8 p.m. ♿ (Johnson County)

BRUSH CREEK PARK
Roanoke and Ward Pkwys.

Kansas City
816/871-5600

Once a concrete-lined embarrass-ment, Brush Creek Park now encom-passes 286 revitalized acres. Along pathways, visitors can walk, run, or skate past numerous statues and fountains, or stop off at the Bruce R. Watkins Cultural Heritage Center, the Plaza Tennis Center, the Wheeler Amphitheater in Theis Park, or the Martin Luther King Jr. Square at Swope Parkway and Woodland. Fi-esta Cruises' 48-passenger boats began cruising Brush Creek in 1998, offering 40-minute tours for $6.50. ♿ (Plaza/Westport and East Metro)

FLEMING PARK
South of Hwy. 40 on Woods

Chapel Rd.
Blue Springs
816/795-8200 (general information)
816/795-1112 (Blue Springs Lake)
816/795-8888 (Lake Jacomo)
Fifteen minutes east of Kansas City proper, Fleming Park's 7,809 acres contain three lakes with swimming beaches, marinas, and picnic shelters, as well as Missouri Town 1855, a native hoofed-animal enclosure, an archery range, camp sites, and hiking trails. On summer weekends, the two largest bodies of water—Lake Jacomo and Blue Springs Lake—are magnets for boaters, anglers, and sailors. Seven trails wind through the area, offering blufftop and lakefront vistas. Stop at park headquarters for maps and information. ♿ (East Metro)

HERITAGE PARK
16050 Pflumm Rd.
Olathe
913/831-3355
Heritage Park's 1,160 acres used to be a reservation for the Black Bob Indians, a small band of Shawnee led by Chief Black Bob. Today this park features a 45-acre lake with a marina and places to fish, sailboard, and canoe. Three children's play areas, an equestrian center, softball and soccer parks, and an 18-hole golf course also provide ample outdoor activities. Picnic areas dot the landscape. Apr–Oct daily 5 a.m.–11 p.m., Nov–Mar daily 7:30 a.m.–8 p.m. ♿ (Johnson County)

HIDDEN VALLEY PARK
N. Russell Rd. and
N. Bennington Ave.
Kansas City
816/871-5600
Covering 174 acres, Hidden Valley Park straddles NE Parvin Road just north of the Missouri River. An observation deck, playground, and hiking trails give outdoorsy types a way to escape without going far from downtown. (Northland)

HODGE PARK
7000 NE Barry Rd.

Rollin' on the River

One of Kansas City's newest green spaces is the Richard L. Berkley Riverfront Park, which officially opened in late 1998. Set along the Missouri River between the Heart of America and Paseo Bridges, the 17-acre greenspace includes a paved walkway and thousands of trees planted to beautify the area. The park was immediately popular with bicyclists and walkers, who have long wanted a way to enjoy the riverfront.

Named for a beloved former mayor, the park eventually will include a walkway linking the River Market to Riverfront Park. City officials hope to build a waterfront restaurant and aquarium as anchors for a $30-million riverfront development.

Kansas City
816/871-5600
Within Robert H. Hodge Park's 801 acres, you can see a realistic reconstruction of an 1850s Missouri village, as well as view a native-animal enclosure. The park also features an 18-hole golf course, sliced by the east fork of Shoal Creek. Hodge's picnic areas are particularly scenic. &. (Northland)

LINE CREEK PARK ARCHEOLOGICAL RESERVE
NW 56th St. and
NW Waukomis Dr.
Kansas City
816/587-8822
This 137-acre park encompasses the Line Creek Archeological Museum, which features a slide presentation and a replica of the prehistoric Hopewell Indian village. The museum also offers classes and occasional archeological digs for kids. In addition, the park has nature and hiking areas, playgrounds, picnic areas, and ball fields. Keep your eyes open for buffalo and wildlife at the park.

Sat–Sun 11–4; group reservations only on weekdays. &. (Northland)

LONGVIEW LAKE PARK
South of I-470 on Raytown Rd.
Kansas City
816/795-8200 (general information)
816/966-8976 (marina)
The U.S. Army Corps of Engineers created Longview Lake for flood control and recreational purposes. Open since 1986, the 4,852-acre park features a four-mile nature trail, a six-mile paved bicycle trail, camping, boat rentals, a marina, softball, and a golf course. Like Fleming Park, Longview also offers a fishing dock for handicapped anglers. &. (East Metro)

LOOSE MEMORIAL PARK
51st St. and Wornall Rd.
Kansas City
816/871-5600
Now an urban park, the Jacob Loose Memorial Park was once a country club for the suburban elite. Today its 74 acres attract nearby residents, Plaza employees, and

Powell Gardens, p. 140

Powell Gardens

TOP TEN

Ten Favorite Roses to Grow and View in Kansas City

by Judy Penner, rosarian at the Laura
Conyers Smith Municipal Rose Garden, Loose Park

1. **Chrysler Imperial.** A red hybrid tea rose with a strong scent, nice form, and long-lasting bloom.

2. **Gold Medal.** With its spicy aroma, this yellow grandiflora is great for its fragrance alone.

3. **Mr. Lincoln.** This red hybrid tea reaches heights of five to six feet and has a nice scent.

4. **Double Delight.** A red and white rose; each bloom on the bush has some color variation.

5. **Sunsprite.** Growing about three feet tall, this bright yellow floribunda produces lots of blooms on a single stem and maintains its color.

6. **Care Free Wonder.** I like this pink shrub rose for its hardiness.

7. **Rio Samba.** A yellow blend with pink and orange, this hybrid tea bears blooms with interesting color variations and patterns.

8. **Peace.** Its healthy strong foliage and large blooms make this yellow-blend hybrid tea a popular plant.

9. **White Lightnin'.** This rose stays very white and has a sweet fragrance.

10. **Sweet Surrender.** With pretty pink blooms, this hybrid tea dries well for potpourri.

metro-area folks who want to bask in its rose garden, walk the path that circles the park, dip into the wading pool, swing a tennis racquet, enjoy the playground, or have a picnic. Set in the park's northwest corner, the Laura Conyers Smith Municipal Rose Garden overflows with gorgeous, fragrant blooms from spring through fall. A full-time rosarian keeps the circular plot healthy and vivacious. ♿ (Plaza/Westport)

**MAPLE WOODS
NATURE PRESERVE
N. Prospect Rd. and 76th St.
Gladstone
816/436-2200**
Kansas City sports plenty of nature preserves in and around its boundaries, but this one contains nearly 40 acres of virgin maple forest. In addition, a wildlife habitat and six miles of nature trails within walking distance of a residential area make Maple Woods a special place to get

Pocket Parks

Kansas City's pocket parks are small respites of less than an acre. Here are a few examples:

1. **Murray Davis Park** *(40th and Main Sts.), .09 acre*
2. **Andrew Drips Park** *(16th St. and Belleview Ave.), .16 acre*
3. **Santa Fe National Historic Trail** *(6201 E. 93rd St.), .24 acre*
4. **Ewing Park** *(107th St. and Ewing Ave.), .28 acre*
5. **Douglas Park** *(2632 Jarboe St.), .5 acre*
6. **Garment District Place** *(8th St. between Washington and Broadway), .76 acre*
7. **Lafayette Traber Garden** *(Woodland Ave. and Pendleton St.), .78 acre*
8. **Manheim Green** *(Manheim Rd. and 40th St.), .99 acre*

away without going too far. &. (Northland)

MARTHA LAFITE THOMPSON NATURE SANCTUARY
407 N. Lafrenz Rd.
Liberty
816/781-8598
The word *sanctuary* aptly describes this 100-acre preserve that's located east of Liberty. A privately owned nonprofit facility, the park was founded by Martha Lafite Thompson, who wanted to protect wildlife and provide a place for people to appreciate nature. Three easy hiking trails wind through a restored tall-grass prairie, mature hardwood timber, and a meadow. Take Mill Street past William Jewell College and veer right onto Richfield Road. Make a left on Lafrenz. Nature Center Tue–Sat 9–5, Sun 1–5 (closed Mon). Sanctuary daily 8 a.m.–sunset. Free. &. (Northland)

MILL CREEK STREAMWAY PARK
Along Mill Creek
Shawnee, Lenexa, and Olathe
913/831-3355
Mill Creek Streamway Park has been in development for more than a decade. It's an ambitious project linking eight of the county's major streamways. Currently the peaceful 400-acre park provides a total of 15 miles of noncontiguous hiking and biking trails. Seven access points: Lenexa (Shawnee Mission Park near shelter 8; 95th Street, approximately one mile west of I-35; and 87th Lane, just east of the intersection with Woodland); Shawnee (west of I-435 at Shawnee Mission Parkway and Midland Drive, and north of Shawnee Mission Parkway at 5946 Barker Rd.); Olathe (a half-mile west of Ridgeview Road on 114th Street, and east of Woodland Avenue on Northgate Road). (Johnson County)

MINOR PARK
Holmes and Red Bridge Rds.
Kansas City
816/871-5600
Local families come to this park for
baseball games and picnics—and
for the get-away-from-it-all atmosphere close to town. Set on 235
acres just off the Big Blue River's
western bank, Minor Park also includes a golf course, a Santa Fe Trail
historic site, and a playground. &
(South Kansas City)

OVERLAND PARK ARBORETUM &
BOTANICAL GARDENS
17940 Antioch Rd.
Overland Park
913/685-3604
In the early phases of a 20-year development plan, Overland Park Arboretum & Botanical Gardens is a
300-acre preserve at 179th and Antioch. Visitors can walk through several ecological environments on trails
that wind among gardens and along
the bank of Wolf Creek. In the Erick-
son Water Garden, stop to enjoy the
four waterfalls as well as plant life

Penn Valley Park

that includes ornamental grasses,
wildflowers, ground covers, and decorative trees and shrubs. The pre-
ferred-species demonstration area
gives homeowners, landscapers, and
arborists an opportunity to view and
evaluate a range of plants appropriate to the area. & (Johnson County)

PENN VALLEY PARK
Pershing Rd. and Main St.
Kansas City
816/871-5600
Penn Valley Park was created at
the turn of the century, as part of
the comprehensive parks-and-
boulevard system. Visionary architect George Kessler proposed
replacing the shanties that dotted
the bluffs and ravine at Penn Valley,
and the public agreed with his plan.
Today the 176-acre park contains
Liberty Memorial and its World War
I museum (closed pending renovation), a jogging path, tennis courts
and a ball field, and the statues *The
Scout* and *Pioneer Mother*. Penn
Valley Park and Memorial Hill Park,
on the slope at Pershing Road and
Main Street, are the popular locations for the Kansas City Symphony's Radio Days Concert on
Labor Day, the Blues and Jazz Festival in July, and the Spirit Fest in
August. & (Downtown Area)

POWELL GARDENS
1609 NW Hwy. 50
Kingsville
816/697-2600
Founded and funded chiefly by
Kansas City's Powell Family Foundation, Powell Gardens occupies more
than 800 acres. It offers visitors the
chance to wander through one of
the largest perennial gardens in the
Midwest. A Rock and Waterfall Garden intermingles ornamental trees,

Ten Favorite Birding Spots in Kansas City
by Kevin Sink, president emeritus of the Burrough's Audubon Society

1. **Lake Jacomo and Fleming Park.** Visit the Audubon nature center and library to see a native prairie and the incredible bird-feeding station. Tour the lake roads to see waterfowl and woodland species.

2. **Lakeside Nature Center and Swope Park.** This is a bird and wildlife rehabilitation center with surrounding woodlands. Call the nature center (816/444-4656) for more information on specific birding sites.

3. **Ernie Miller Nature Park.** Along a wooded creek, these 113 acres are a great spot for woodpeckers, sparrows, and woodland songbirds. Impressive nature center with interpretive displays.

4. **Burr Oak Woods.** With more than 1,000 acres of oak forest and prairies, this diverse habitat provides homes for a broad spectrum of birds. One of the best nature centers in the state, it's a great place to take the whole family.

5. **Wyandotte County Lake.** At this particularly nice fall and winter birding site, visitors can view gulls, waterfowl, sparrows, eagles, and other raptors.

6. **Shawnee Mission Park.** A very accessible park with woodlands, fields, and a large body of water for waterfowl. Bluebirds, hawks, Canada geese, sparrows, and other woodland species can be seen along the trails.

7. **Martha Lafite Thompson Nature Sanctuary.** This outstanding nature center has a good feeding station, interpretive displays, helpful staff, and a network of trails. It's an entertaining place to take the family to see woodland species or to go on "owl prowls" with the staff.

8. **Smithville Lake.** Mid- to late November this very large lake is a stopover for thousands of snow geese and other waterfowl. If your timing is right, you may see eagles. A variety of habitats near the lake support woodland and grassland species.

9. **The Prairie Center.** A good example of native prairie near the metro area, these 300 acres of grasslands are home to sparrows, meadowlarks, bluebirds, and more. Of particular interest are the many species of prairie wildflowers. From spring to fall, something is almost always in bloom on this prairie.

10. **Weston Bend State Park.** About 15 minutes north of the KCI Airport, this is a great place to bird. Lots of heavily timbered hills and an extensive trail system make this one of the best places to see warblers in the spring and fall.

shrubs, perennials, and native woods with winding streams and gentle cascades as accents. Powell Gardens also hosts summer music and dance performances. The Visitor Education Center serves as an orientation and education area; its Café Thyme is a favorite lunch spot (11–2). Daily 9 a.m.–sunset. $5 adults, $4 seniors, $2 children under age 13. & (East Metro)

SAR-KO-PAR TRAILS PARK
87th St. and Lackman Rd.
Lenexa
913/541-8592
Anchored by the historic Legler Barn Museum, this 53-acre park also features jogging trails, a lake, the Indian Trails Family Aquatic Center, a sand volleyball court, and a restored railroad depot and caboose. The park—whose name comes from a Creek Indian warrior who died in 1849—has become a gathering place in this southwest Johnson County community. At Sar-Ko-Par Trails Park, thousands converge for annual events such as the Lenexa Great Barbecue Battle, the Lenexa Spinach Festival, and the Heartland Trails Festival. (Johnson County)

SHAWNEE MISSION PARK
7900 Renner Rd.

Lenexa–Shawnee
913/831-3355
Johnson County's largest park spans 1,250 acres, with a lake that attracts people who want to canoe, sail, and fish. In addition, the park, dedicated in 1964, includes horseback and nature trails, an archery range, a swimming beach, a visitor center, marina, and an outdoor theater in which lively summer productions are held. Shawnee Mission Park is a popular family picnic spot. & (Johnson County)

SMITHVILLE LAKE
Northeast of Smithville on
U.S. 169 and Hwy. 92
Smithville
816/532-0803
Smithville Lake covers more than 7,200 acres. Its shoreline offers two full-service marinas that provide boat rentals, equipment sales, and dining facilities. In addition, the lake has two swimming beaches and two campgrounds, encompassing more than 750 campsites (including electrical hookups, shower, laundry, and other facilities). For a day trip, choose from a waterfowl refuge, sailboat facilities, golfing, 200 picnic sites with 11 shelter houses, horseback riding, hiking trails, a visitors center, and a hand-

---

A Brief Park Comparison

	Swope Park, KC, MO	*Central Park, NYC*
Size	*1,769 acres*	*843 acres*
Animals	*Zoo with IMAX theater*	*Two zoos*
Drama	*Broadway-style shows*	*Shakespeare, puppets*
Chip shots	*Two 18-hole golf courses*	*Lawn bowling*

A Garden of Bronze

Henry Moore was a renowned British sculptor whose enormous bronze pieces ranged from reclining figures to mother-and-child scenes to animal forms. Born in 1898, Moore intended for his large sculptures to be viewed in nature, set against rocks, trees, and sky.

Kansas City's Henry Moore Sculpture Garden achieves that goal. Located on the south grounds of the Nelson-Atkins Museum of Art, the sculpture sanctuary comprises the largest collection of monumental bronze pieces by Moore outside of his native country. Works include Reclining Figure, Hand, Seated Woman, *and* Three Part Object. *Another sizable group of Moore's maquettes and working models are installed in the Rozelle Court Gallery.*

In addition to the 13 outdoor sculptures, the 22-acre Nelson-Atkins Sculpture Garden contains an array of natural sights. More than 100 American linden, ginkgo, crab apple, Norway spruce, and river birch trees, as well as 50,000 daffodils and 10,000 Japanese yew, decorate the area.

icapped-accessible fishing dock. ❧ (Northland)

SWOPE PARK
Swope Pkwy. and Meyer Blvd.
Kansas City
816/871-5600
Among the country's largest city parks, Swope Park includes 1,769 acres. Within its undulating landscape are the Kansas City Zoo and its IMAX Theatre; the 7,795-seat Starlight Theatre, home to summer plays and concerts; two golf courses; the Lakeside Nature Center; athletic fields for softball, soccer, rugby, Frisbee, and more; hiking and horseback-riding trails; picnic and fishing areas; and a daycamp for kids. ❧ (South Kansas City)

WATERWORKS PARK
NE 32nd St. and N. Oak Tfwy.
Kansas City
816/871-5600
A relatively small 57 acres, Waterworks Park is most popular for its skyline views of downtown Kansas City. In addition, its close-to-town location and steep hills make it a favorite spot for wintertime inner-tubing and sledding. In the summer, kids gather to play ball at the park's baseball diamonds. ❧ (Northland)

WYANDOTTE COUNTY LAKE PARK
91st St. and Leavenworth Rd.
Kansas City, Kansas
913/299-0550

Wyandotte County Lake Park isn't far from town, but it certainly seems remote once you get there. The park's 1,500 acres include a 330-acre lake with marina, boat rentals, picnic shelters, tennis courts, horseback trails, and the Pierson Community Center. Kids can ride a model train on the second Saturday of each month. The National Park Service designed the lakeside boathouse. Construction began in 1935, which explains its old-time feel. From the East Lookout shelter, you can see Lansing and Leavenworth, Kansas. ⅍ (Kansas City, Kansas)

Henry Moore Sculpture Garden, p. 143

9

SHOPPING

Although Kansas City was born near the Missouri River, commerce has spread like floodwaters to encompass districts throughout the metropolis. From the Country Club Plaza's stylish boutiques to Johnson County's booming retail regions, the area now provides residents and visitors with places to buy everything from designer apparel to fishing supplies, from souvenirs to home-improvement gadgets.

SHOPPING AREAS

Downtown

Many people think downtown Kansas City lacks shopping opportunities. Actually, the numerous stores in the area count downtown workers among their most loyal customers. Within the central business district, both City Center Square and the Town Pavilion offer boutiques and restaurants and serve as convenient places for light shopping. The River Market, several blocks closer to the Missouri River, includes antiques malls, housewares boutiques, specialty shops, and the City Market.

ABDIANA
2001 Grand Blvd.
Kansas City
816/421-5577

Nicholas Abnos was doing quite well as the proprietor of a popular futon business. But when Midtown's famed Firestone building faced demolition, the entrepreneur decided he would renovate it for office space. One thing led to another, and Abnos found himself launching a new home-furnishings store on seven floors of the refurbished edifice. Everything about this store is high class, from the unique furniture, accessories, and fabrics to the care Abnos took in restoring his new space to the professional designers

City Market

Whether you want a lime or a live chicken, you can find it at the City Market in the River Market. Every Saturday and Wednesday, numerous farmers head to the historic district near downtown to peddle their produce and stock. Choices abound in the warmer months; between April and October you can work your way through a cornucopia of seasonal produce. Also, during the summer, look for the Sunday Art Market, where painters, sculptors, and craftspeople set up their wares.

on hand to help. The most delightful feature: The inventory is actually affordable. (Downtown)

ALL NATIONS FLAG COMPANY
114 W. 5th St.
Kansas City
816/842-8798
Founded in 1924, this locally owned flag company stocks an enormous inventory within its turn-of-the-century brick building in the River Market. All Nations carries flags from around the world as well as holiday and special-occasion banners. You can even buy the flagpole to hoist your new purchase. Prices at All Nations are reasonable, and quality is high. (Downtown)

ANTIQUITIES AND ODDITIES
2045 Broadway Blvd.
Kansas City
816/283-3740
Corinthian columns, brass doorplates, gargoyles from demolished buildings: Antiquities and Oddities' two locations are jam-packed with treasures that make for a delightful browsing experience—especially for anyone renovating an old house. The Broadway location (formerly Old Theatre

Architectural Salvage) offers three floors of treasure hunting. The other store, at 1732 Cherry St., 816/842-4606, is similarly expansive. Broadway location open Thu–Sat 10–4, Cherry St. location open Sat 9–2, and both open by appointment. (Downtown)

CHEEP ANTIQUES
500 W. 5th St.
Kansas City
816/471-0092
The folks at Cheep Antiques are experts at refinishing the furniture they buy, so don't expect to cull through stacks of junk. Cheep Antiques specializes in good-quality American antique furniture, from armoires to rockers to pie safes. There's nothing stuffy about this three-story, 30,000-square-foot emporium. (Downtown)

CY RUDNIK'S
CROWN CENTER FABRICS
2450 Grand Ave.
Kansas City
816/842-7808
Whether you want glittery taffeta for a stunning ball gown or tough-but-colorful corduroy for kidswear, Cy Rudnik's Crown Center Fabrics probably carries it. Although this store is

small in square footage, its range of fabrics is impressive. And the best part? You can actually imagine yourself wearing these textiles in a host of situations, from formal to casual. (Downtown)

MEIERHOFF'S ANTIQUE STAINED GLASS
210 Wyandotte St.
Kansas City
816/421-4912
Step back in time, to a place where the ambiance is almost holy. In her pre–Civil War building in the River Market area, former restaurateur Jan Meierhoff has amassed a jaw-dropping collection of stunning stained glass from old churches, mansions, and other buildings. From doors, windows, lamps, mantles, and transoms, Meierhoff's specializes in restoring antique glass and creating custom art pieces. A sign in the proprietor's office says it all: Queen of Stained Glass. (Downtown)

OGGI
600 Central St.
Kansas City
816/421-1010
Contemporary furnishings, lighting, and decor fill the four floors of Oggi's restored brick building. It's fun to wander from setting to setting, admiring the lava lamps, resting in the overstuffed faux-leather chairs, browsing the mirrors adorned with sea glass. Oggi (say "OH-gee")

charges a pretty penny for its wares but does hold regular sales. (Downtown)

PLANTERS SEED & SPICE CO.
513 Walnut St.
Kansas City
816/842-3651
Set in an antique brick building at the entrance to the City Market, Planters Seed & Spice has served customers since 1924. With an old-time country-store atmosphere, this retailer stocks bulk seeds and spices, plus such gardening highlights as brass plaques, redwood planters, and small statuary. You can also buy hand tools to use outdoors and live herbs to plant in the yard in springtime. Planters also carries farm supplies, including livestock feed. (Downtown)

Westport

Although you wouldn't know it now, the area along Westport Road between Main Street and Southwest Trafficway was once the place where wagon trains loaded up before heading west. Kelly's Westport Inn and the adjacent Stanford & Sons restaurant are original buildings, owned at one time by Daniel Boone's nephew, who operated them as supply stores. Now Westport is home to unusual shopping opportunities as well as a string of restaurants and night clubs. The neighborhood hops on Friday and Saturday nights.

While shopping in Westport, stop at Murray's, purveyor of some of the region's best-tasting—and most cleverly named—ice cream.

Historic Westport District, p. 147

ACCENTS
4135 Pennsylvania St.
Kansas City
816/753-2320
Women who love earrings visit Accents regularly just to see what's new. Within the store's intimate space they find one of the Midwest's largest selections of affordable handcrafted jewelry. Many of the pieces—necklaces and bracelets, too—are made by regional artists. (Plaza/Westport)

BACKWOODS
3936 Broadway Blvd.
Kansas City
816/531-0200
This cozy store stocks all sorts of outdoor gear, from tents to hiking shoes to day packs, even though high-end rugged duds overrun much of the floor space. Look for regional outdoor books here, too. Located just north of Westport Road, Backwoods is staffed by a knowledgeable group who can help you find the appropriate accoutrements for any excursion. (Plaza/Westport)

LOMA VISTA HARDWARE
311 Westport Rd.
Kansas City
816/931-5846
Todd Dean wanted to run his own business, but he wasn't sure it was the hardware store owned by his dad, Chuck. Instead, the artistic young man set up a clothing shop in the hardware store's empty second floor. Now Todd's reputation as a high-style couturier has exploded nationwide. Young models, celebrities, and other hipsters come to Loma Vista for its natural fabrics, clean lines, and trendy men's and women's wear— not to mention the hardware. (Plaza/Westport)

MIDTOWN HATTERS
4120 Pennsylvania St.
Kansas City
816/753-7274
Once upon a time, no one would have dared to venture outside without a hat on his or her head. If Doug West has his way, those days will come again. In 1996, the successful salesman chucked it all to open a hat

store, and now he stocks fedoras, homburgs, berets, derbies, top hats, borsalinos, and unique women's hats, among others. A friendly man who's following his dream, West enjoys helping his customers find the right look. (Plaza/Westport)

NATURAL WEAR
435 Westport Rd.
Kansas City
816/531-9082
Mother Earth gone stylish: That's the best description of Natural Wear. Earthy colors such as beige, olive, and cayenne predominate in Natural Wear's loose and chic inventory. Accessories from earrings to handbags complete the fashion picture. (Plaza/Westport)

PERFECT SCENTS
4116 Pennsylvania St.
Kansas City
816/753-8117
At this little shop you can mix and match your own shampoos, perfumes, and hand lotions from a variety of interesting scents such as rain, patchouli, and "Chinese nights." Another store in Johnson County's Hawthorne Plaza brings the far-out to the 'burbs. (Plaza/Westport)

PRYDE'S OLD WESTPORT
115 Westport Rd.
Kansas City
816/531-5588 or 800/531-5588
The ultimate kitchen store, Pryde's anchors the east end of Westport Road in a funky old building. Inside, you'll find the latest in cookware, dishes, linens, and must-have kitchen gadgets. Pryde's will gift-wrap for free and ship to anywhere in the United States. Its toll-free number lets you order more goodies no matter where you live. (Plaza/Westport)

Country Club Plaza

Kansas City's shopping mecca also provides an enjoyable place just to hang around. Clothing boutiques such as Armani and Ann Taylor, department stores like Mark Shale and Halls Plaza, housewares boutiques from Williams–Sonoma to Pottery Barn—the list of places where you'll gladly spend your money is seemingly endless. In addition, the Plaza lures folks who want to wine and dine at its many bistros. In the summer, sidewalk cafés do a booming business.

ACT II
1507 W. 47th St.
Kansas City
816/531-7572
Perhaps the finest women's apparel consignment shop in town, Act II also runs a store for men on 45th Street. The Store has strict standards, which means its clothes are almost like new. (Plaza/Westport)

THE BETTER CHEDDAR
604 W. 48th St.
Kansas City
816/561-8204
Look for something other than Velveeta at this Plaza gourmet grocery store, including cheeses galore, wines from famous regions, myriad brands of extra-virgin olive oil, and pasta in countless shapes and sizes. If it's food-related, Better Cheddar probably has it. Walking through the store will make you hungry, but there's plenty here to satisfy that urge. (Plaza/Westport)

EDDIE BAUER PREMIER STORE
325 Nichols Rd.
Kansas City
816/756-5390

Annual Art Fair on the Plaza

It's not Seattle, but this enormous Plaza department store stocks everything from rugged boots to dressier evening wear. You'll find all the great stuff from Eddie Bauer's catalog, as well as items that were chosen just for the company's retail operations. An Eddie Bauer Home Collection, AKA Eddie Bauer, and an outdoor gear selection complete the picture. (Plaza/Westport)

GRANDEUR GARDENS
223 W. 47th St.
Kansas City
816/561-2212
Kansas Citians love their gardens. Even in winter, they're either planning for spring or decorating their homes in garden styles. This shop targets all outdoor addicts with elegant pottery, distinctive paving stones, and items gardeners can hide in their gardens—from gargoyles to the Green Man. Just stepping inside Grandeur Gardens elicits

that old springtime rush. (Plaza/Westport)

LUYBEN MUSIC
4318 Main St.
Kansas City
816/753-7111
Kansas City's sheet-music central. In this store near the Plaza, you'll find a complete inventory of music from classical masters to contemporary composers, from vocal to piano to orchestral. If Luyben doesn't have it, they can order it. (Plaza/Westport)

POTTERY BARN
400 W. 47th St.
Kansas City
816/753-3252
An elegant store that makes the Pottery Barn catalog come alive. This Plaza retailer stocks trendy furniture, dishes, glassware, and lighting in a setting that's become a favorite for shoppers throughout the area. What's more, a professional, on-site design studio can help customers decide from among the many styles and colors available and can assist them in creating a chic Pottery Barn atmosphere in their own home. (Plaza/Westport)

THREE DOG BAKERY
612 W. 48th St.
Kansas City
816/753-3647
Three Dog Bakery has made its hometown owners rich and famous because the concept is so . . . bow-wow bizarre! At this first-of-its-kind store, you can find the perfect gift for every woofie, from fresh-baked birthday biscuits to all-natural doggie chews. The store is so elegant, some first-timers think it's a haven for humans in search of pastry. Check it

out—even if you're a confirmed cat person. (Plaza/Westport)

TOSCANO LTD.
610 W. 48th St.
Kansas City
816/756-0222
Step through the doors of this Plaza establishment, and it's as though you've entered the light-drenched hills of Tuscany. At Toscano, owners Tony Grimaldi and Daniela Short have collected a colorful array of Majolica dishware made by ceramicists in the Tuscany and Umbria districts of Italy. Handmade and hand-painted, these pieces—such as small boxes, lidded jars, and large bowls—are truly collectors' items. (Plaza/ Westport)

Brookside

Throughout older Kansas City neighborhoods, you'll come upon rows of shops built in the Twenties, Thirties, and Forties. One of the most magnetic areas sits at the crossroads of 63rd Street and Brookside Boulevard, where residents can find everything from fabrics to Halloween costumes to lawn sprinklers. Two grocery stores, a drugstore, and several lively neighborhood pubs round out the scene. Those not on diets regularly patronize Foo's Fabulous Frozen Custard for its wickedly rich desserts.

THE BEST OF KANSAS CITY
6233 Brookside Plaza
Kansas City
816/333-7900
Set in a space the size of a walk-in closet, the Best of Kansas City combines locally made products into stunning gift baskets. Topsy's popcorn, Stephenson's jellies, and barbecue sauce from nearly everyone in town are only a few of the staples at this specialty shop. You can buy items individually as well. (South Kansas City)

THE DIME STORE
314 W. 63rd St.
Kansas City
816/444-7207
Time seems to have stopped at about 1950 here. Undulating wooden floors hold ceiling-high shelves stocked with everything from old-fashioned toys to cookware to scrapbooks. Chances are excellent that you'll find stuff at the Dime Store that you thought had long disappeared. (South Kansas City)

THE FIDDLY FIG
22 W. 63rd St.
Kansas City
816/363-4313
Originally a florist shop, the Fiddly Fig has expanded into a larger space with a growing inventory to match.

Three Dog Bakery

The Original Shopping Master

Back in the early part of this century, real estate developer Jesse Clyde (J.C.) Nichols built stylish homes that captivated the upwardly mobile. His plans included neighborhood amenities such as sidewalks, nearby shops, and expansive landscaping. People flocked to his then-suburban communities for the chance to purchase a Nichols home.

By 1922, however, Nichols announced a scheme that was outright revolutionary. He had purchased acreage on either side of Brush Creek, just north of his carefully manicured neighborhoods. On this property, Nichols believed he could create a retail district that would appeal to his residents and bring in the big bucks for him.

Nichols decided to limit the buildings in his retail district to three stories, except for the Spanish-style towers he would build as decoration. In fact, the entire Country Club Plaza would be created with a Spanish Renaissance and Baroque theme, using adornments such as artwork, ironwork, and fountains. The Plaza would be accessible by car but would dovetail with the nearby neighborhoods, too.

When it opened in March 1923, the Country Club Plaza became the first master-planned shopping district in the country. And, needless to say, J.C. Nichols did become an even wealthier businessman.

Unique gifts, such as candles, frames, and dried arrangements, decorate the place in a stylish yet casual fashion. This is also the best place in the neighborhood for fresh flowers, jungle plants, and arrangements for any occasion. (South Kansas City)

¡Ay, caramba! This colorful shop simply gushes with goodies from our neighbors to the south. Piñatas, candelabra, chairs, tables—Latin American Imports pulls together an impressive selection of decorative details. (South Kansas City)

LATIN AMERICAN IMPORTS
324 W. 63rd St.
Kansas City
816/361-5115

THE WORLD'S WINDOW
332 W. 63rd St.
Kansas City
816/361-2500

Take an around-the-world trip without ever leaving Kansas City. This interesting shop mixes ethnic art, apparel, jewelry, and furnishings from places as diverse as Indonesia and South America. A special children's section gets kids into the global perspective, too. (South Kansas City)

Johnson County

A current building boom in the Kansas City area focuses on the area around Johnson County's College Boulevard and 119th Street. Town Center Plaza, for example, opened in mid-1996, with stores such as Pottery Barn, Williams-Sonoma, and Abercrombie & Fitch. The mall sits on 119th Street between Roe and Nall, surrounded by other malls featuring everything from sporting goods to maternity wear to toys. The Metcalf Avenue area, although older, is similarly lined with shopping opportunities. Out in Olathe, the Great Mall of the Great Plains, with its eight anchor stores and 175 outlet stores, has become the largest entrant in another retail explosion farther south.

BEARDEN'S STAINED GLASS & DOOR
7600 Metcalf Ave.
Overland Park
913/381-4527
Bearden's is a great spot to buy a stained glass lamp, window, or door—but it's also the premier place to learn how to make them yourself. Classes run regularly throughout the year, teaching students the secrets of copper foiling, leaded glass, and even mosaic stepping stones. Run by the affable Bearden brothers, this Johnson County shop turns many Kansas Citians into stained glass aficionados every year. (Johnson County)

D&D STATUARY
3415 Merriam Dr.
Merriam
913/262-2279
The plethora of cast concrete objects at D&D Statuary is simply mind-boggling. The company's owners have filled their huge yard with shelves and rows of birdbaths, pots, and all manner of yard art. Choose from everything from roosters to religious figures. Objects come naturally gray or stained with a green or black patina. (Johnson County)

DEAN & DELUCA
4700 W. 119th St.
Leawood
913/498-3131
For more than two decades, Dean & DeLuca has remained a New York City institution. When it opened at the Town Center Plaza in 1997, the purveyor of gourmet specialties— from caviar to coffee, chutney to chocolates—was soundly welcomed by everyone in the metro area. Here, patrons can find that unusual kitchen implement, enjoy a cup of fresh-brewed espresso, and shop for those special items to make tonight's party special. (Johnson County)

FOB KANSAS CITY
9024 Metcalf Ave.
Overland Park
913/381-8910
Tables that resemble long-legged cranes, chairs that look like monkeys, vases from China and Indonesia: FOB Kansas City imports unusual furnishings from Pacific Rim countries. At FOB (which stands for "fresh off the boat"), you're as likely to find a carved teak gazebo as a set of teak salad spoons. (Johnson County)

Ten Great Places to Shop

by Tammy Edwards, a professional shopper and owner of Signature Image Inc., a wardrobe consulting firm

1. **Act II** (1507 W. 47th St., Kansas City). Designer consignment fashions for women at bargain prices.

2. **Button Boutique** (8971-B Metcalf Ave., Overland Park). The widest selection of exquisite clothing buttons in the area.

3. **Country Club Plaza.** One of the finest upscale outdoor shopping experiences in the world.

4. **Crown Center** (2450 Grand Ave). A good mix of shops set in a casual environment.

5. **Designer Shoe Warehouse** (7345 Quivira, Overland Park). Extensive selection of men's and women's shoes at discount prices.

6. **Dillard's Clearance Center** (Great Mall of the Great Plains, Olathe). Department-store finds at a fraction of the original prices.

7. **Genny's Women's Apparel** (College Blvd. and Antioch, Overland Park). Unique clothes and accessories for all occasions.

8. **Hawthorne Plaza** (119th and Roe, Leawood). Find everything from special scents to unique fashions for the entire family.

9. **Town Center Plaza** (Between Nall and Roe on 119th St., Leawood). A distinctive array of upscale shops in a contemporary outdoor setting.

10. **Westport** (Westport Rd. and Broadway, Kansas City). An eclectic mixture of specialty clothing and jewelry shops.

GALYAN'S
119th St. and Nall Ave.
Leawood
913/661-0200
Mouths drop open when people first enter this sporting goods store. That's because Galyan's resembles a giant tree house, its soaring entrance flanked by tree trunks reaching toward a second-story shopping balcony. At the back of the sports emporium, a climbing wall gives intrepid souls a place to practice their sport, much to the delight of other less-courageous patrons. They've got clothing, shoes, boats, backpacks, and tons of other gear for sale, too. (Johnson County)

JACOBSON'S
Town Center Plaza
Leawood
913/696-1500
One of the most deluxe department stores in town, Jacobson's features a full line of designer wear for men,

Tom's Exotic Aquatics

This store, at 10215 E. Hwy. 350, 816/353-3279, in the center of Raytown, is not for the faint-hearted. Here, Tom and Bonnie Searcy have created an establishment that lures reptile fanatics or, as they call themselves, "herp people." At Tom's Exotic Aquatics, you'll find boa constrictors, iguanas, chameleons, corn snakes, bearded dragons, and other bizarre animals. The Searcys also sell a wide variety of fish, as well as food for their unusual inventory.

women, and children. In addition, this relatively new retailer in town provides special services to its clientele, including personal shoppers, complimentary gift wrap, baby and bridal gift registries, free in-store alterations, and an espresso bar. (Johnson County)

K&K FLYFISHER'S SUPPLY
8643 Grant St.
Overland Park
913/341-8118
This former convenience store now houses one of the Midwest's largest selections of fly-fishing equipment and angling paraphernalia. Expert advice on casting and fly-tying; courses available, too. (Johnson County)

MUNDY AND YAZDI
5905 Slater St.
Merriam St.
913/362-2006
Forget that trip to Turkey. Mundy and Yazdi carries an amazing selection of antique handwoven rugs from Turkey, Persia, Afghanistan—just name your rug-making region. Proprietor Carol Mundy also teaches courses, complete with slides from her buying trips abroad. (Johnson County)

NOMADIC NOTIONS
9264 Metcalf Ave.
Overland Park
913/642-3131
Beads, beads, everywhere. Nomadic Notions sells thousands of multicolored beads, with all the supplies you need to create necklaces, earrings, and other jewelry. The shop also offers classes and restringing, and the staff will custom design jewelry, too. (Johnson County)

ORGANIZED LIVING
11940 Metcalf Ave.
Overland Park
913/498-2600
Anyone trying to organize a closet, an office, a kitchen—or any other room they inhabit—will want to visit Organized Living. The store stocks furniture as well as handy gadgets such as stacking baskets, lift-top garbage pails, and sealable canisters. (Johnson County)

THE PERUVIAN CONNECTION
9256 Metcalf Ave.
Overland Park
913/648-1981
Owned by a friendly mother-daughter

team, the Peruvian Connection features unusually stylish clothing made in South America from soft alpaca or silky pima cotton. At this catalog and outlet store, you'll find scrumptious vests, sweaters, coats, and handcrafted jewelry. (Johnson County)

RESTORATION HARDWARE
Town Center Plaza
Leawood
913/327-7121
Steven Gordon launched Restoration Hardware in Eureka, California, when he couldn't find parts to restore an old home. He opened his Kansas City store in late 1996—smack dab in new-home territory. Oh well, Kansas Citians with old houses flock there anyway, looking for the perfect light fixture, doorknob, and paint hue. Restoration also carries soft goods such as linens. (Johnson County)

ANTIQUES DISTRICTS AND MALLS

45TH & STATE LINE ANTIQUES DISTRICT & DESIGN CENTER
Around 45th St. and State Line Rd.
Kansas City
913/362-2002
Within the little bungalows that hug State Line Road west of Westport, you'll find some 20 antiques

shops and galleries. Anderson's Antiques specializes in the eighteenth and nineteenth centuries; Barkwell Antiques covers American, European, and Asian furnishings; and Cumming's Corner concentrates on turn-of-the-century lighting. (Plaza/ Westport)

BRASS ARMADILLO ANTIQUES MALL
1450 Golfview Dr.
Grain Valley
816/847-5260
Located east of Kansas City between Grain Valley and Blue Springs, the Brass Armadillo ranks among the metro area's largest antiques malls. This newly built fourth mall in a Des Moines-based chain rents space to some 600 vendors in a 42,000-square-foot facility. You can find everything from armoires to Zippo lighters. Locked cases carry some of the smaller offerings, but the bulk is available for up-close inspection. (East Metro)

COUNTRY MEADOWS ANTIQUES MALL
4621 S. Shrank Dr.
Independence
816/373-0410
Situated near Old Stephenson's Apple Farm, this rambling, two-story space carries a plethora of antiques in a general-store atmosphere. Fre-

T I P

Think it's just a rumor that antiques are cheap in the Midwest? In fact, you can find plenty of bargains at area antiques malls. However, the best deals usually come from the many auctions held throughout the region. The *Kansas City Star* runs columns of auction notices on Sunday, generally for the following week.

quent sales are a hallmark of the Country Meadows mall, and regulars know to check back often. (East Metro)

MISSION ROAD ANTIQUES MALL
4101 W. 83rd St.
Prairie Village
913/341-7577
The Mission Road Mall presents the collections of 250 dealers in a 50,000-square-foot area. The mall winds through two floors of adjoining buildings, giving antiques aficionados plenty to look at. A small café nestles in one corner. (Johnson County)

RIVER MARKET ANTIQUE MALL
115 W. 5th St.
Kansas City
816/221-0220
Like many antiques malls, this one runs the gamut in goods. One dealer likes treasures from the Fifties, another collects handwoven rugs from Iran. The 25,000-square-foot mall rises several floors in a slowly renovated building near the City Market, and it's a fascinating place to browse and search out hidden treasures. (Downtown)

WALDO ANTIQUES DISTRICT
Around 75th St. and Wornall Rd.
Kansas City
816/523-9314
A smaller district than the one at 45th Street and State Line Road, the Waldo area also features less expensive goods. Still, there are several small antiques malls and individual shops whose shelves contain some mighty unusual finds. (South Kansas City)

BOOKSTORES

BARNES & NOBLE
400 W. 47th St.
Kansas City
816/753-1313
This bookseller has opened stores all over the country, but Kansas City's first Barnes & Noble occupies a special four-story renovated building in the heart of the Country Club Plaza. Cushy chairs and Starbucks coffee make for a great book-buying getaway. Other locations in in Johnson County, Northland, and East Metro zones. (Plaza/Westport)

BLOOMSDAY BOOKS
6227 Brookside Blvd.
Kansas City
816/523-6712
One of the city's best used book stores, Bloomsday is run by novelist and former lawyer Tom Shawver, who likes to know his customers and what they read. Books here are gently used, prices are reasonable, and the coffee cart serves up delicious lattes. (South Kansas City)

THE COMPLETE TRAVELER
7321 W. 80th St.
Overland Park
913/648-1560
In Kansas City, savvy travelers head

to the Complete Traveler whenever they're planning their next trip. Bill Abram stocks a wide range of travel guides and maps, as well as a choice selection of luggage and travel gear. In addition, the Complete Traveler sells rail passes for a variety of European destinations. (Johnson County)

RAINY DAY BOOKS
2706 W. 53rd St.
Fairway
913/384-3126
Kansas City's grande dame of independent bookstores, Rainy Day Books attracts a loyal following in part because of its commitment to hosting big-name writers. Well-known authors such as Ray Bradbury, Jane Smiley, Newt Gingrich, and Anne Rice are only a few of the folks Rainy Day owner/founder Vivian Jennings has brought to town. The Fairway store also carries an impressive selection of varied books. (Johnson County)

SPIVEY'S BOOKS
825 Westport Rd.
Kansas City
816/753-0520
When it comes to antiquarian tomes, David Spivey is the master of his domain. On three floors in Westport, Spivey has laid out a fascinating selection of used and rare books, old maps, collectible autographs, and fine prints. The scholarly proprietor also offers appraisals, rebinding, and paper conservation services. (Plaza/Westport)

MAJOR DEPARTMENT STORES

DILLARD'S
This ubiquitous Kansas City depart-

ment store features a range of men's and women's apparel, as well as kids' clothing, housewares, and furniture. Famous brands range from Liz Claiborne to Ralph Lauren, but Dillard's offers less-expensive house brands as well. Dillard's can be pricier and a more luxurious shopping experience than Jones (see below), but the store marks down frequently, so it pays to head straight for the sale racks. (South Kansas City, Johnson County, Northland, East Metro)

HALLS
The locally owned Halls department stores provide fine shopping opportunities at two locations, Crown Center and the Country Club Plaza. Designers such as Armani, Buccelatti, and Lagerfeld reign in the clothing departments, while housewares are filled with the likes of Wedgwood and Waterford. Expect excellent quality and high prices. (Downtown, Plaza/Westport)

JONES STORE
Recently acquired by May Co., Jones also rules the Kansas City area; you'll notice that nearly every mall has either a Jones or Dillard's as an anchor. In general, Jones displays the same kind of inventory as its competitor and also holds frequent metrowide sales. Jones can provide at least a half-day experience for the truly dedicated. (Johnson County, Northland, East Metro)

SHOPPING MALLS

Kansas City's malls span the area geographically, but they're not always obviously located. Prairie Village Shopping Center, for example,

sits in the middle of a tree-lined residential district but features a re-
spectably sized Jones Store as its
anchor. Antioch Shopping Center
provides 700,000 square feet of
shopping to residents north of the
Missouri River, with stores such as
Sears and Burlington Coat Factory.
Some of the largest and most centrally located are listed below.

INDEPENDENCE CENTER
I-70 and Hwy. 291
Independence
816/252-0608
A fairly new mall in the growing area
east of town, Independence Center
boasts anchors such as Jones Store,
Dillard's, and Sears within its 1.1 million square feet. (East Metro)

METCALF SOUTH
SHOPPING CENTER
95th St. and Metcalf Ave.
Overland Park
913/649-2277
Although malls to the south have
grown in size, Metcalf remains a stalwart presence in Johnson County.
Stores at this 950,000-square-foot
mall include Gap, Jones Store, and
Kids at Heart. (Johnson County)

METRO NORTH
SHOPPING CENTER
Hwy. 169 and Barry Rd.
Kansas City
816/436-7800
Metro North is the prime mall north of
the river, serving a growing popula-
tion that's headed toward the airport.
Within its 1.2 million square feet,
Metro North shops include Music-
land, Brandsmart, and Dillard's.
(Northland)

OAK PARK MALL
95th St. and Quivira

Overland Park
913/888-4400
Oak Park Mall was enormous before
it attracted the area's first Nordstrom;
now it's the largest in the region. In
addition to the upscale Seattle-based
retailer, stores at the 1.4-million-
square-foot mall include Bailey
Banks & Biddle, Aveda Lifestyle
Store, and Dillard's. (Johnson County)

TOWN CENTER PLAZA
119th St. between Roe
and Nall Aves.
Leawood
913/498-1111
The place to see and be seen, Town
Center Plaza probably houses the
largest collection of yuppie-oriented
stores in the metro area, including
Abercrombie & Fitch, Restoration
Hardware, and Jacobson's (750,000
square feet so far). (Johnson County)

WARD PARKWAY CENTER
86th St. and Ward Pkwy.
Kansas City
816/363-3545
One of the original enclosed malls in
the region, Ward Parkway was also
home to the very first multiscreen
movie theater in the country. These

days, anchors include Montgomery Ward, Dillard's, and Stein Mart—in addition to a 22-screen AMC movie theater within its 860,000 square feet. (South Kansas City)

DISCOUNTERS/ FACTORY OUTLETS

BOB JONES SHOES
1914 Grand Blvd.
Kansas City
816/474-4212
Nothing but shoes and more shoes greets you as you enter this gigantic store near downtown. Bob Jones stocks everything from designer labels to off-brand shoes for men and women. The back racks are where you'll find the biggest bargains. Look for the wooden Indian standing outside. (Downtown)

GREAT MALL OF THE GREAT PLAINS
20700 W. 151st St.
Olathe
913/829-6277
When this mall opened in 1997, it immediately became a shopping destination for folks throughout the region. The mall winds through several specialty areas, from fashion to sports to home and hobby. Stores include

everything from the Burlington Coat Factory to Linens 'n' Things to Dillard's Clearance Outlet. Restaurants run the gamut from Applebee's to Red Lobster, and a 16-screen movie theater entertains those who'd rather skip the sales. (Johnson County)

PRIME OUTLETS AT ODESSA
1306 W. Old Hwy. 40
Odessa
816/230-5662
You've got to drive 20 miles east to reach this factory outlet mall, but plenty of folks do it regularly. Once there, you'll find 45 stores, including Spiegel, Mikasa, and Nine West shoes. There's a food court midway in the mall, so you can rest before tackling the second half. (outside East Metro)

RECOVERY SALES OUTLET
13900 E. 35th St.
Independence
816/252-9212
The inventory at RSO changes daily, depending on the salvaged goods that come through its doors. At this freight reclaimer, you'll find everything from designer wedding gowns at half price to $2 compact discs. Regulars come often, just so they don't miss anything. (East Metro)

Convention and Visitors Bureau of Greater Kansas City

10

SPORTS AND RECREATION

Kansas Citians love the outdoors. Besides the natural greenways that course through the city's heart, the area boasts lakes perfect for fishing, links ideal for golfing, and trails tailor-made for hiking. Even in winter, Kansas City's natural side beckons locals and visitors to stretch their legs, breathe some fresh air, and play.

Professional sports are also a popular diversion here. In this Midwestern metropolis, you can attend an NFL Kansas City Chiefs game, watch Major League Baseball's Kansas City Royals, or opt for tennis, soccer, or hockey.

PROFESSIONAL SPORTS

Auto Racing

KANSAS CITY INTERNATIONAL RACEWAY
8201 Noland Rd.
Kansas City
816/358-6700
This is the Kansas City area's drag-racing capital. Fans, including many of the drivers' and crews' families, meet at the raceway from the end of May through October for bracket drag racing. Gates open Saturday at 2:30 p.m., and races generally run until 10 p.m. Grudge, or practice, rac-

ing takes place each Wednesday and Friday beginning at 6 p.m. Sat $10, Wed $9; children under 12 free. &. (East Metro)

LAKESIDE SPEEDWAY
5615 Wolcott Dr.
Kansas City, Kansas
913/299-2040
Lakeside features a half-mile, semi-banked asphalt track with stand seating for 5,000. Racing fans come at 8 on Friday nights between April and September to watch four car classes: NASCAR/Winston Racing series modifieds, 4-cylinder pony stocks, street stocks, and charger

stocks. $10 adults; children under 6 free. ॐ (Kansas City, Kansas)

Baseball

KANSAS CITY ROYALS
1 Royal Way
Kansas City
816/921-8000
The Kansas City Royals have undergone a youthful resurgence of late, releasing veteran stars in favor of up-and-comers. The team continues to work at rebuilding, always reaching for a repeat of that glorious 1985 season, when the Royals won the World Series. $6–$15. ॐ (East Metro)

Football

KANSAS CITY CHIEFS
1 Arrowhead Dr.
Kansas City
816/924-9400
Members of the National Football League, the Kansas City Chiefs play their home games at Arrowhead Stadium in the Harry S. Truman Sports Complex. A majority of the stadium's 79,451 seats are occupied by season-ticket holders, but true gridiron fans will want to try landing a seat anyway. Ticket prices average about $40; parking's extra. For pregame festivities, Arrowhead is the site of one of the world's largest tailgate parties, as countless fans arrive early to picnic before the contest begins. ॐ (East Metro)

Hockey

KANSAS CITY BLADES
1800 Genessee St.
Kansas City
816/842-1063
The Kansas City Blades, members of the International Hockey League, have made Kemper Arena their home since 1990. Fans can watch the IHL's 1992 Turner Cup Champions as they demonstrate their incredible skating and puck-handling skills, backed by a truly competitive spirit. The Blades' season runs Oct–Apr. $10–$18. ॐ (Downtown)

Truman Sports Complex

Convention and Visitors Bureau of Greater Kansas City

TRIVIA

Kansas City football fans are rabid; tens of thousands show up for games clad in red-and-gold Chiefs gear to passionately cheer on their team . . . despite the fact that the Chiefs—even with revered quarterback Joe Montana in the 1993–94 seasons—haven't made it to the Super Bowl since 1970. Still, fans haven't given up hope. Arrowhead Stadium remains sold out for years to come, and the search for another Len Dawson–like quarterback continues.

Horse and Greyhound Racing

THE WOODLANDS
9700 Leavenworth Rd.
Kansas City, Kansas
913/299-9797
This dual-track racing complex features horses and dogs. Two modern buildings are fully enclosed, making the grandstands and clubhouses all-season facilities. The Woodlands stages greyhound racing year-round, while thoroughbred and quarter horses race in the fall. Wed and Sat 1 and 7 p.m., Thu–Fri 7 p.m., Sun 1 p.m. $1.50 general admission, $3.50 clubhouse. ♿ (Kansas City, Kansas)

Soccer

KANSAS CITY ATTACK
1800 Genessee St.
Kansas City
816/474-2255
You know about outdoor soccer; how about indoor soccer? The Kansas City Attack belongs to the National Professional Soccer League, which combines the high-scoring shootouts of basketball and the fast-paced, hard-hitting action of hockey in an Americanized version of soccer. Oct–Mar at Kemper Arena. $11, $13, $15. ♿ (Downtown)

KANSAS CITY WIZARDS
706 Broadway Blvd.
Kansas City
816/472-4625
This major league soccer team, launched by Kansas City Chiefs' owner, Lamar Hunt, and his family, provides nonstop action on the field. The Wizards play at Arrowhead Stadium in a season that runs Mar–Sept. $10–$15 adults, $6–$9 children. ♿ (East Metro)

Tennis

KANSAS CITY EXPLORERS
1800 Genessee St.
Kansas City
913/362-9944
This World Team Tennis group has played in Kansas City since 1993 at Hale Arena, next to Kemper. The Explorers' guest-player roster includes the likes of Jimmy Connors, John McEnroe, and Martina Navratilova. $9–$50. ♿ (Downtown)

RECREATIONAL ACTIVITIES

Biking

Kansas City is packed with two-wheel enthusiasts. For more infor-

America's Stadium Capital

Today's sports fans file into multilevel arenas filled with super suites, concierge service, gourmet dining, and high-tech sound and video systems. They have three Kansas City sports architecture companies to thank for the experience.

In the late Sixties, the Kansas City Chiefs Football Club ordered the first-ever U.S. stadium dedicated solely to a professional football team. For design, the owners tapped Kivett & Myers of Kansas City, Missouri. After local officials asked, "What about baseball?" the architects suggested two separate stadiums, one for each sport, which would operate as a single entity.

Despite running $20 million over budget, the projects were deemed a success. Arrowhead Stadium debuted in the fall of 1972; Royals Stadium (later renamed Kauffman Stadium) opened the next spring and was the last baseball-dedicated facility built until Chicago's Comiskey Park opened in 1991. The dual facilities were dubbed the Harry S. Truman Sports Complex.

Since then, Kivett & Myers' protégés have created the nation's big three sports architecture firms, all still based in Kansas City: HOK Sports, Ellerbe Becket, and HNTB Corp. All compete for commissions from major- and minor-league teams, colleges, and Olympic committees around the world. From England to Malaysia, Manitoba to Hong Kong, these firms set the cutting edge.

HOK has created, among others, Chicago's New Comiskey Park, Miami's Joe Robbie Stadium, and the New Hong Kong Stadium. HNTB has designed Vancouver's Place Stadium and Indianapolis' Hoosier Dome, and Ellerbe Becket was responsible for Jack Kent Cooke Stadium for the Washington Redskins and the 1996 Olympic Stadium/Atlanta Braves Ballpark.

---

mation, see the "Biking in Kansas City" section in Chapter 2.

INDIAN CREEK AND TOMAHAWK GREENWAY BIKING & HIKING TRAILS

I-435 and Lee Blvd.
Leawood
913/451-9165
These urban-suburban paths run about 10 miles along the northern edge of I-435 and the surrounding

area. But once you're riding, it seems like the world is far away. Get on the trail at Leawood Park or at many points including Corporate Woods and Indian Creek Recreation Center. The Tomahawk Trail ends at College Boulevard and Highway 69. Riders and hikers will find nature information and exercise stations along the path. & (Johnson County)

LITTLE BLUE TRACE
Hwy. 78
Independence
816/795-8200
Among the many areas for trail bicycling, the Little Blue Trace provides a relatively easy opportunity to get out into the wilds. An eight-mile round trip, the trail starts at the Blue Mills Road shelter off Highway 78. The crushed-rock surface takes some of the hazard out of the off-road trip. (East Metro)

LONGVIEW LAKE
South of I-470 on Raytown Rd.
Kansas City
816/795-8200
Longview Lake is a popular destination for all kinds of outdoor enthusiasts, including those who want to experience nature on a street bike. A paved, 6.5-mile bicycle trail traverses much of the western side of the lake, between O'Donnell Park and picnic shelter 14 near the marina. Cyclists pass through wooded areas and across a wooden bridge. & (East Metro)

Boating

BLUE SPRINGS LAKE
South of Hwy. 40 on Woods
Chapel Rd.
Blue Springs
816/795-1112 (marina)
Blue Springs Lake is one of three lakes within Fleming Park, and the only one available for unlimited powerboating. People flock to the lake's 725 liquid acres for powerboating, water-skiing, tubing, and Jet-skiing. The lake features a full-service marina with rental boats and slips, concessions, tackle and bait. Rental prices for fishing and pontoon boats range from $10–$25/hour to $45–$150/day. & (East Metro)

LAKE JACOMO
East of I-435 on Woods Chapel Rd.
Lee's Summit
816/795-8888
At 970 acres, Fleming Park's Lake Jacomo is one of Jackson County's prime boating lakes. Jacomo includes a full-service marina, concessions, lakeside gasoline pumps, and fishing bait and tackle. Those eager to navigate the waters can rent crappie boats, bass boats, canoes, and two- and four-seat pedal boats. Rental prices range from $6–$25/hour to $20–$150/day. & (East Metro)

LONGVIEW LAKE
South of I-470 on Raytown Rd.
Kansas City
816/966-8976
Set between Kansas City and Grandview, Longview Lake covers 930 acres, with ample opportunities for powerboaters, water-skiers, Jet-skiers, and pontoon boaters. At the lake's marina, you can rent a variety of vessels, and stock up on marine supplies. The carp that school around the marina love to be fed. Rental prices for fishing and pontoon boats range from $10–$25/hour to $45–$150/day. & (East Metro)

SHAWNEE MISSION PARK LAKE
7900 Renner Rd.

Sailboats at Lake Jacomo, p. 165

Lenexa–Shawnee
913/888-4713
Shawnee Mission is Johnson County's largest park and includes a 150-acre stocked fishing lake. It's a serene setting in which wooded slopes come down to the shoreline. A boathouse on the north shore rents canoes, fishing boats with trolling motors only, and pedal boats. Canoes rent for $4/half-hour, fishing boats $10/hour, pedal boats $4/half-hour, and Sunfish sailboats $12/hour. ♿ (Johnson County)

SMITHVILLE LAKE
Northeast of Smithville on U.S. 169 and Hwy. 92
Smithville
816/532-0803
Compared to other lakes in the area, Smithville is gigantic, covering 7,200 acres. Families come here to enjoy the relatively uncrowded lake and the easy access (five multilane boat-launch ramps). Its southern half is available for water-skiing and inner-tubing throughout the year. Two full-service marinas offer boat rentals, equipment sales, and dining facili-

ties. Rentals range from $30– $65/ two-hour minimum to $75– $210/day. ♿ (Northland)

WYANDOTTE COUNTY LAKE
91st St. and Leavenworth Rd.
Kansas City, Kansas
913/299-8488
A 60-plus-year-old boathouse sits along Wyandotte County Lake's shore, offering concessions and boat rentals (canoes, paddleboats, and fishing boats). The 330-acre lake is small but provides a relaxing way to spend time on the water. Boats rent for $7–$14 per hour. Boathouse open 8 a.m.–8 p.m. Closed Tue. ♿ (Kansas City, Kansas)

Bowling

Thousands of Kansas City area residents love to bowl, joining leagues or taking their kids to the lanes on Saturday afternoons. For more information about leagues or the 23 bowling centers represented on the Missouri side, call the Greater Kansas City Bowling Association, 816/358-5470. A similar group, the Wy-Jon Bowling Association, 913/ 262-7574, oversees 12 additional facilities in Wyandotte and Johnson Counties in Kansas.

AMF COLLEGE LANES
10201 College Blvd.
Overland Park
913/451-6400
Bowling buffs will find 32 lanes, seven billiards tables, and a lounge among the many amenities of this popular Johnson County center across the street from the Double-tree Hotel. League play is popular, but open lanes are usually available. Sun–Thu 9 a.m.–midnight, Fri–Sat 9 a.m.–3 a.m. $3.15 per game; shoe

rental $2.50 adults, $2 children. &
(Johnson County)

AMF PRO BOWL
505 E. 18th Ave.
North Kansas City
816/221-8844
With 48 lanes, this is by far the largest
bowling facility in the Kansas City
area, a fact that's made it popular for
more than four decades. AMF also offers nine pool tables, go-carts, miniature golf, and four batting cages.
Mon–Thu 9 a.m.–midnight, Fri–Sat 9
a.m.–3 a.m., Sun 9 a.m.–11 p.m. Lane
prices average $3; shoe rental $2.25.
& (Northland)

PREMIER BOWLING &
RECREATION
11400 E. Hwy. 350
Raytown
816/356-5955
This ranks as one of the area's
newest bowling centers. Besides 32
lanes, you'll find pool tables, a large
dart area, and a 75-game arcade
room. When the games become too

Arrowhead Stadium, home of the Chiefs

much, you can relax in Premier's
150-seat sports bar and watch the
big-screen TV. Note: League play
occupies all lanes nearly every night
from 6–8:30. Sun–Thu 10 a.m.–midnight, Fri–Sat 10 a.m.–2 a.m. $2.35
per game during day hours, $2.60 at
night; shoe rental $1.50. & (East
Metro)

Camping/Backpacking

*In addition to campgrounds listed in
Chapter 3, the Kansas City area offers
several wilderness reserves with hiking and primitive camping.*

LANDAHL PARK RESERVE
E. Truman Rd.
Independence
816/795-8200
The scenic Landahl Park Reserve includes trails that range from .6 to 3.6
miles, traversing wooded hills and
hidden vales. In warm weather,
the Conservation Department holds
target-shooting and outdoor education courses in several open areas.
But campers can easily avoid the
groups on this 1,330-acre reserve.
The park also includes playing fields,
picnic shelters, and restrooms. Landahl is two miles west of Highway 7
on Truman Road. (East Metro)

MONKEY MOUNTAIN RESERVE
South of I-70
Grain Valley
816/795-8200
On this 855-acre reserve you'll find
hiking trails, fishing ponds, and
places to picnic, cross-country ski,
and ride horses. Even the most dedicated primitive campers will be glad
for the reserve's restrooms. Head
east from I-70 until you're just past
Grain Valley; take old U.S. 40 south to
Monkey Mountain. (East Metro)

Canoeing and Kayaking

Avid canoeists and kayakers abound throughout the Kansas City area, which offers plenty of paddling opportunities. The Missouri River is best left to experienced paddlers who know the local waters, but residents often head to one of the many central or southern Missouri rivers for scenic trips down spring-fed waters. Numerous companies rent canoes along waterways such as the Gasconade, Buffalo, and Niangua Rivers. Conditions range from white water to mirror smooth, depending on the river and the time of year.

For a list of canoe-rental companies, call the Missouri Division of Tourism at 800/877-1234 and request its Missouri Get-Away Travel Guide. *For more information on paddling and clubs, contact the Kansas Canoe Association (Mike Caldwell), 913/383-9490; the Kansas City Whitewater Club, 816/478-8524; the Ozark Wilderness Waterways Club, 816/861-7737; and the Kansas City Paddler, a boat and gear store at 412 Delaware, 816/283-0800.*

BLUE RIVER PARKWAY
Blue River
Kansas City
816/795-8200

A greenbelt lines the Big Blue River, beginning at Swope Park and winding southward approximately 12 miles to the Kansas–Missouri state line. The parkway is a special spot for hikers, and local canoeists treasure the waters of the Blue, too. A put-in ramp is located near 131st Street and Holmes Road. Beware: The normally quiet waters can rise quickly and become treacherous during sudden rainstorms. (South Kansas City)

KANSAS RIVER
Johnson County Parks & Recreation District
DeSoto
913/438-7275

At normal flow levels, the Kansas— or Kaw—River provides one of the area's premier canoeing opportunities. Put in at the Cedar Creek Kaw River Access boat ramp (just east of DeSoto), make the four- to five-hour lazy float downstream, and pull out 11 miles later at Mill Creek's Wilder Road Access ramp. River birds, fish, and picnic-perfect sandbars can be found along the way. (Johnson County)

Fishing

Kansas City is riddled with lakes, streams, and rivers—which makes fishing a popular pastime. In these parts, fisherfolk reel in largemouth bass, walleye, crappie, and channel cat, among others.

Since the region covers two states and 11 counties, fishing permits vary.

In general, however, Missouri requires a $3 daily nonresident fishing permit, and Kansas sells a $3.50 daily nonresident fishing license. Aside from major waters such as Smithville, Jacomo, Blue Springs, Longview, and Wyandotte County Lakes (see Boating section), fervent fishers may try the following spots.

JAMES A. REED MEMORIAL CONSERVATION AREA
13101 Ranson Rd.
Kansas City
816/524-1656
This wildlife refuge contains 11 lakes connected by easily accessible roads. Regular catches here include crappie, bluegill, and catfish; a catch-and-release trout season occurs in the fall. Take Hwy. 50 east to Ranson Road, then head south. Just east of Lee's Summit. ق (East Metro)

LAKE OLATHE
625 Lakeshore Dr.
Olathe
913/764-6163
Fish stalkers have 170 watery acres at this south Kansas City lake. With any luck they'll find catfish, crappie, bass, and even trout. The area near the fishing pier is sown annually with Christmas trees, providing new cover and nesting areas for the fish. ق (Johnson County)

SHAWNEE MISSION PARK
7900 Renner Rd.
Lenexa–Shawnee
913/831-3355
This 150-acre Johnson County lake regularly attracts anglers seeking everything from bluegill to bass to carp. Rainbow trout, however, draw the biggest crowd, soon after the fish are stocked each spring and fall.

Boat rental is available. ق (Johnson County)

Fitness Clubs

GOLD'S GYM FAMILY FITNESS CENTERS
816/931-9888
Gold's sports five locations in the Kansas City metro area, offering workout equipment such as stationary bicycles, stair-steppers, Nautilus machines, and free weights. Some also have swimming pools. $10 per day or $25 for seven days. Mon–Fri 6 a.m.–11 p.m., Sat 8–8, Sun 9–7. ق (all zones except South Kansas City and Kansas City, Kansas)

MOFFETT'S GYM
12244 W. 63rd St.
Shawnee
913/268-6808
This local gymnasium features circuit training, aerobics classes, free weights, and massage. In addition, the fitness club provides childcare. No towels or locks. $5/day or $20/week. Mon–Fri 5 a.m.–10 p.m., Sat 6 a.m.–7 p.m., Sun 10–5. ق (Johnson County)

YMCAS
816/561-9622 or 913/371-4400
The YMCA of Greater Kansas City includes 10 branches, some with pools. You'll also find weight rooms, indoor and/or outdoor tracks, and locker-room facilities at many of the clubs. The YMCA of Kansas City, Kansas, has two facilities, similarly equipped. Hours and fees vary. ق (all zones)

Gambling

ARGOSY'S RIVERSIDE CASINO
I-635 and Hwy. 9
Riverside

816/746-7711

Argosy launched Kansas City's first riverboat casino, brought to the area from Illinois in late 1993. This was one of the only vessels that actually cruised the river with gambling underway, in the days before moored boats were allowed. Now set in Riverside, five minutes from downtown Kansas City, Missouri, the boat offers aisles of gaming tables, along with several restaurants. Daily 8 a.m.–2 a.m. & (Northland)

FLAMINGO HILTON CASINO KANSAS CITY
1800 E. Front St.
Kansas City
816/855-7777

The first Kansas City casino on the south bank of the Missouri River, the colorful Flamingo Hilton puts all its gambling on one floor. The facility offers two restaurants and a lounge, as well as live entertainment. In early 1999, Donald Trump announced his plans to purchase the Flamingo, which could mean that changes lie ahead. Sun–Thu 7 a.m.–5 a.m., Fri–Sat 24 hours. & (Downtown)

HARRAH'S CASINO NORTH KANSAS CITY
Hwy. 210 and Chouteau Tfwy.
North Kansas City
816/472-7777

Harrah's opened its North Kansas City facility in late 1994 and now offers gaming aboard the *North Star* and the *Mardi Gras*. With four on-site restaurants, the 200-room Harrah's hotel allows visitors to stay close to the action. Sun–Thu 8 a.m.–2 a.m., Fri–Sat until 3 a.m. & (Northland)

STATION CASINO
I-435 and Birmingham Rd.
Kansas City

816/414-7000

When it opened in early 1997, Station Casino became Kansas City's largest riverboat-gambling operation. The twin-boat complex features 13 restaurants, a hotel, movie theaters, a children's play zone, a 1,350-seat arena, and a microbrewery—in addition to a substantial gaming area. Sun–Thu 8 a.m.–2 a.m.; Fri–Sat 24 hours. & (Northland)

Golf

CRACKERNECK GOLF COURSE
18800 E. Hwy. 40
Independence
816/795-7771

Whether you believe this course's distinctive name derives from a "hanging tree" once used by Jesse James or from the Southern "crackers" who moved into the area in the late 1800s, this 18-hole course offers both challenges and easy access. It's found where Hwys. 291 and 40 intersect, just south of I-70. & (East Metro)

DEER CREEK GOLF CLUB
7000 W. 133rd St.
Overland Park
913/681-3100

Deer Creek has a noble heritage: The 18-hole course was designed by Robert Trent Jones Jr. In addition, it's received several *Golf Digest* rankings, including "Top 3 Best New Public Courses in 1989" and 3½ stars for Places to Play in 1993. & (Johnson County)

HERITAGE PARK GOLF COURSE
16445 Lackman Rd.
Olathe
913/829-4653

One of the newer public golf courses in the metro area, Heritage Park includes a variety of water features among its 18 holes. Indeed, the course crosses and parallels three lakes and Coffee Creek. ♿ (Johnson County)

HODGE PARK GOLF CENTER
7000 NE Barry Rd.
Kansas City
816/781-4152
This 18-hole, Kansas City–run course is especially scenic, winding through wooded, rolling hills. The east fork of Shoal Creek also cuts a small swath, lending a natural air to the game. ♿ (Northland)

LONGVIEW LAKE GOLF COURSE
South of I-470 on Raytown Rd.
Kansas City
816/761-9445
Jackson County's first golf facility sits on the east side of Longview Lake, providing vistas of the water. The complex includes a total of 27 holes—an 18-hole championship course and a 9-hole executive course—plus a driving range and clubhouse. ♿ (East Metro)

PARADISE POINTE CHAMPIONSHIP GOLF COURSE
18212 Golf Course Rd.
Smithville
816/532-4100
Sculpted out of the hilly land that surrounds Smithville Lake, Paradise Pointe combines relaxing play with geologic challenges. This is the only public golf complex in the Kansas City area with two 18-hole championship courses, a driving range, and a 4-hole golf academy. ♿ (Northland)

TOMAHAWK HILLS PUBLIC GOLF COURSE
17501 Midland Dr.
Shawnee
913/631-8000
Built in 1910, Tomahawk Hills is the oldest golf course still played in the metro area. Set among rolling hills adjacent to Shawnee Mission Park, Tomahawk Hills ranks as one of Kansas City's most challenging public courses. Its 18-hole championship layout runs 6,000 yards. ♿ (Johnson County)

Hiking

BLUE AND GRAY PARK RESERVE
Hwy. 50, near Lone Jack
816/795-8200
This Jackson County park offers two wooded trails, but the most interesting is the Lone Jack Civil War Trail. Approximately 15 miles long, the trail follows county roads from the Blue and Gray Park Reserve to Missouri Town 1855. Hikers pass through oak and hickory hardwood forests and encounter a variety of wildlife. (East Metro)

BLUE RIVER PARKWAY
Blue River
Kansas City
816/795-8200
Among the parkway's trails is the very scenic and moderately easy 4.5-mile (one way) Blue River Parkway Nature Trail between Kenneth Rd. and Red Bridge. Much of the trail follows the river, allowing hikers to see wildlife that includes birds, rabbits, squirrels, and the occasional deer and beaver. (South Kansas City)

FLEMING PARK
South of Hwy. 40 on Woods Chapel Rd.
Blue Springs
816/795-8200
Fleming Park features seven trails,

Ten Favorite Hikes in the Kansas City Area

by William B. Eddy and Richard O. Ballentine, coauthors of *Hiking Kansas City*

1. **Watkins Mill State Park Trail**. A paved circuit through varied terrain around Williams Creek Lake north of Kansas City. The quiet walker stands an excellent chance of seeing deer (six miles east of Kearney off Hwy. 92).

2. **The Landahl Nature Preserve**. Northeast of Blue Springs, the area contains several trails through woods and uplands, including the nature trail with the Indian name Washingsabba.

3. **The Bethany Falls Trail at Burr Oak Woods**. Walk past the remains of settlers' cabins and below limestone bluffs, where you may find spring-blooming columbine.

4. **Larry Mattonen Memorial Trail**. One of Fleming Park's seven trails, this one travels through deep woods and along the lake shore.

5. **Blue River Parkways Trail**. The north segment of the trail, in the Red Bridge area, follows an abandoned railroad right-of-way along bluffs with views of the Blue River.

6. **The Mill Creek Streamway Trail**. This Johnson County system is a paved route that extends from Olathe to the Kansas ("Kaw") River. The north segment, from Shawnee Mission Park to and around Nelson Island in the river, is a favorite.

7. **West Ridge and Harpst Valley Trails**. These connecting trails at Weston Bend State Park pass up, down, and through wooded hills and along high bluffs that offer spectacular views of the Missouri River.

8. **Wallace State Park**. The well-developed loop trail system, just south of Cameron, Missouri, provides a deep-woods experience close to that found in national forests, with valleys, thick forests, and open hilltops.

9. **Clinton Lake**. This 12,000-acre preserve near Lawrence has nearly 100 miles of trails. The George Latham Trail, in the Woodbridge Primitive Area, provides an excellent hike around a peninsula, with woods, meadows, rock outcroppings, and birds and other wildlife.

10. **Prairie Center**. West of Olathe, this native prairie grasslands preserve has a trail through the prairie and adjacent forest. The trip includes streams, lakes, old stone fences, and a buffalo wallow.

from the .75-mile Missouri Town–Clermont Nature Trail to the 1.5-mile Rock Ledges Nature Trail, a loop that begins at shelter 14. Look for directions to these paths at park headquarters on Woods Chapel Road. (East Metro)

PRAIRIE CENTER
26325 W. 135th St.
Olathe
913/856-7669
Much of this preserve's 300 acres is open prairie with nature trails through wildflowers such as larkspur, sunflowers, and goldenrod. Animals also frequent this verdant prairie; you might see owls, deer, or coyote. The buffalo wallow dates back an estimated 150 years. ⅃ (Johnson County)

RIVER BLUFF TRAIL
Hwy. 291
Kansas City
816/795-8200
The River Bluff Trail, in River Bluff Park near Courtney, is a twisting, hilly, 2.4-mile trek. You'll encounter a 100-foot dropoff at one point. A walkable, historic 13.5-mile section of the Lewis & Clark Trail starts at River Bluff Park as well. The trail heads east, often following county roads, to the mouth of the Little Blue River, then follows the levee to Fort Osage. (East Metro)

Horseback Riding

BENJAMIN RANCH WEST
6401 E. 87th St.
Kansas City
816/765-1100
Russian immigrant Hyman Benjamin started with 40 acres in 1885. Today the 250-acre Benjamin Ranch maintains about 200 acres of its property as a preserved natural wilderness, with riding trails winding through the rugged terrain. Reservations requested. Daily 9–7. $15.99 for a 45-minute guided trail ride. (East Metro)

Hot-Air Ballooning

AERONAUTICAL ADVENTURES
103rd St. and Metcalf Ave.
Overland Park
913/649-0004
The St. Louis–based Petrehn family has flown balloons since 1972, and several members hold world flying records. In Kansas City, between six and ten passengers can fly together in one of the company's 15 balloons. One-hour flights include refreshments, followed by a champagne reception on the ground. Year-round flights, subject to weather conditions. $155/person; packages available. (Johnson County)

Hunting

Hunters relish the opportunities available in Kansas and Missouri. Both states offer a variety of game seasons, including deer, turkey, pheasant, quail, dove, rabbit, squirrel, duck, and goose. Additionally, many areas offer firearm, muzzleloader, and archery seasons. Hunting licenses are required for all but those who hunt on land they own.

A Missouri resident license costs $9 small-game, $15 combined small-game and fishing, $11 deer or turkey, and $15 archery deer and turkey. Nonresidents pay $5 daily small-game, $60 annual small-game, $75 turkey, $75 archery deer, and $110 firearm deer. For more information, contact the Missouri Department of Conservation, Kansas City Metro Office, 8616 E. 63rd St., Kansas City; 816/356-2280.

An annual Kansas general hunting

Top Ten Kansas City Running Routes

by Garry Gribble, owner of Garry Gribble's Running
Sports and a marathon finisher in all 50 states

1. **Indian Creek Trail** in Overland Park, is on the east side
   between Switzer and Mission Road.

2. **Shawnee Mission Park Trails** offer a variety of scenery.

3. **Martha Lafite Thompson Nature Trail**. This Liberty trail is
   beautiful.

4. **Loose Park**. This run features a view of the Plaza; go through
   scenic neighborhoods by heading south on Summit to Valley
   Road.

5. **Mill Creek Park** is a circular trail at J.C. Nichols Parkway.

6. **Overland Park Arboretum**. This one offers much in southern
   Johnson County, near 179th Street and Antioch.

7. **Longview Lake**. The trails here provide a scenic view of eastern Jackson County.

8. **Burr Oak Trails**. In Blue Springs off Highway 7, these are a
   must-run.

9. **The Levee Run**. This Lawrence route is rural but provides
   good running.

10. **Parkville River Trail**. This Parkville, Missouri, route hugs the
    Missouri River.

---

license costs $15.50 for residents and
$65.50 for nonresidents; a 48-hour
nonresident waterfowl license is
available for $20.50. Additional deer
tag and state and federal waterfowl
stamp fees may apply. Kansas Department of Wildlife and Parks,
Kansas City District Office, 14639 W.
95th St., Lenexa: 913/894-9113.

Hunting on public land is strictly
controlled. Several special deer
hunts have been held in recent
years in Jackson County's Fleming
Park, however, because of an overly
large deer population. Call the state
telephone numbers above for more
information.

HUNTING SPORTS PLUS
710 Main St.
Blue Springs
816/228-8700
This group provides hunting access
to 200,000 acres of private land in
Kansas, Missouri, and contiguous
states. Game options include quail,
pheasant, prairie chicken, deer,
turkey, duck, and goose. (East Metro)

MID-AMERICA GAME BIRD
ASSOCIATION
11922 Grandview Rd.
Grandview
816/761-3636
Specializing in game birds including

duck, pheasant, quail, and goose, the Mid-America Game Bird Association opens some 200,000 acres in Kansas and Missouri to hunters. Arrangements may also be made to hunt deer and fish. Guides available. ♿ (East Metro)

Ice Skating

AMF ICE CHATEAU
8788 Metcalf Ave.
Overland Park
913/648-0129
Located indoors with its sister AMF West Bowling Center, this 85-by-185-foot rink is large enough to host regulation United States Figure Skating tests and competitions. The chateau is open Mon, Tue, Thu, Fri 10–5; Wed 10 a.m.–12:30 a.m., Sat–Sun 2–4 and 8–10:30. $5.50–$6; $2 skate rental. ♿ (Johnson County)

CROWN CENTER ICE TERRACE
2450 Grand Blvd.
Kansas City
816/274-8411
Between November and March, the Crown Center Ice Terrace is one of the most popular places in town. The free-form tent over the outdoor rink sets the stage for an enjoyable afternoon or evening of skating. Sun–Thu 10–9, Fri–Sat in Nov–Dec until 11. $5 adults, free seniors over 60, $4 children under 13. Skate rental $1.75 ♿ (Downtown)

Paintball

JAEGERS SUBSURFACE PAINTBALL
9300 NE Underground Dr.
Kansas City
816/452-6600
Quite possibly the world's only underground paintball field, Jaegers features 180,000 square feet of subterranean space at a year-round 56 degrees. Within the facility, players can choose from six to ten different games. Located east of I-435 and just north of the Missouri River. Tue–Fri 6–10:30, Sat 9 a.m.–10:30 p.m., Sun 10 a.m.–10:30 p.m. A three-hour session, including gun and paintballs, averages $25. ♿ (Northland)

Roller Skating

SKATE WORLD
I-35 and Shawnee Mission Pkwy.
Merriam
913/262-0711
This popular rink offers a variety of options for skaters of every skill level. Among the sessions are a Friday Teen Skate, a Saturday morning learn-to-skate session, and a Wednesday Retro Music Night, featuring music from recent decades. $2.50–$5. ♿ (Johnson County)

NORTHLAND ROLLADIUM SKATE CENTER
1020 S. Kent St.
Liberty
816/792-0590
North-of-the-river skate buffs enjoy this rink, with its selection of inexpensive packages, including Wednesday night's Cheap Skate and Friday's Super Session. Those new on wheels can try the beginners' class Saturday afternoon from 1 to 2. $1–$4.50. ♿ (Northland)

Running and Road Races

Running routes and regular runners abound in Kansas City. You'll even see fanatical folks jogging through the snow. Competitive road races range from the nationally ranked

Ten Places to Reflect on Nature

by Marty Kraft, environmental educator, director of the Heartland All Species Project, and former Kansas City Earth Day organizer

Finding a place to commune with nature requires traveling to two places. One is a geographic location, and the other is a receptive place in your mind. Here are some of the many spots to practice around Kansas City:

1. Walk by the spring at the **Cave Springs Interpretive Center**.

2. Feel the contrast between the surrounding mowed lawn and the grove just south of the tennis courts in **Loose Park**.

3. Drive along **Cliff Drive** and see the cliffs formed by the Missouri River; look out across the river valley.

4. See the river valley from bluff to bluff at the Missouri River, one block south of downtown **Parkville**.

5. Visit the **Maple Woods Nature Preserve**, the largest grove of sugar maples west of the Mississippi.

6. Hike along the hill south of the **Lake of the Woods** in Swope Park.

7. Stop by the beautiful wooded hillsides at **Roanoke Park** (38th Street and Roanoke).

8. See the native prairie grasses at the **Prairie Center** in Olathe.

9. Experience the beautiful rolling, wooded hills at **Wyandotte County Lake Park**.

10. Walk along the **Big Blue River** in Minor Park at Red Bridge, just west of Holmes.

Hospital Hill Half-Marathon to the 10,000-runner Michael Forbes Trolley Run to the Groundhog Run, a 10K threading through an underground system of limestone caves, the largest underground storage space in the country.

For information about competitive races and fun runs, call the Kansas City Track Club at 816/333-7223.

Sailing/Sailboarding

HERITAGE PARK
16050 Pflumm Rd.
Olathe
913/831-3355
This 1,160-acre park in south Johnson County sports a 45-acre lake, the only waters within the Johnson County Parks & Recreation Department that offer sailboarding rentals.

The lake is on the north end of the park, accessible from either 159th Street or Pflumm Road. Boardsailors can cruise by Black Bob Island—more of an islet, actually—that can be rented for private parties. Rentals from $12/hour–$60/day. (Johnson County)

LAKE JACOMO
East of I-435 on Woods Chapel Rd.
Lee's Summit
816/795-8888

Fleming Park's largest lake offers 970 acres for sailors. The limited-horsepower regulations on pontoon and fishing boats keep the waters calm. The lake has a full-service marina, boat rentals, concessions, tackle, bait, dock fishing, and boat ramps. Dolphin Sr. sailboats rent for $10/hour, $25/four hours, and $45/day. Although sailboard rentals are no longer available on the lake, Jacomo—especially near the dam—is a favorite with local boardsailors. Permit required. (East Metro)

LONGVIEW LAKE
South of I-470 on Raytown Rd.
Kansas City
816/795-8200

Winds can get gusty at this 930-acre lake, making it a prime spot for wind-surfing. Board rentals are not available, but those with their own equipment have plenty of open area for tacking, jibing, and long runs. The boat ramp at Longview Marina, near the dam, makes a good launch site. The marina also sells the required one-day permit ($15). Personal flotation devices are required, and board-sailing is limited to Mon–Thu. (East Metro)

SHAWNEE MISSION PARK
7900 Renner Rd.

Hospital Hill Half-Marathon

Lenexa–Shawnee
913/888-4713

Johnson County's largest park features a 150-acre lake that's a good spot for beginning boat sailors. Besides sailing classes, organized through Johnson County's Parks & Recreation Department, the park's boathouse rents Sunfish sailboats from late spring through early fall. $36/half-day, $72/full day. (Johnson County)

Skiing

FLEMING PARK
Off Woods Chapel Rd.
816/229-8980

During January and February, the Jackson County Parks & Recreation Department holds cross-country ski classes at Fleming Park (weather permitting). Rentals available. Call for details. (East Metro)

LANDAHL PARK RESERVE
East Truman Rd.
Independence

816/795-8200

Landahl Reserve is popular with cross-country skiers because of the many trails that wind through the hilly, 1,397-acre reserve. Look for trailheads at the Truman Road and Argo Road shelters. The reserve is two miles west of Highway 7 on Truman Road. (East Metro)

SNOW CREEK
1 Snow Creek Dr.
Weston
816/640-2200

Hoping to capitalize on local ski fanatics, Snow Creek opened in 1985 and now includes nine intermediate trails, two triple chairlifts, and two beginner areas served by three rope tows. Snow Creek can make its own snow and has lighted slopes for night skiing. A day lodge with a cafeteria and lounge provides après-ski relaxation. Lessons available. Open mid-Dec–mid-Mar, various hours. Adults $19–$29, depending on session, $39–$49 with ski rental; $15 children 7–12 all sessions, $30 with rental; children under 7 free, $15 with rental. & (Northland)

Swimming

ROELAND PARK AQUATIC CENTER
4830 Rosewood Dr.
Roeland Park
913/432-1377

Everyone who wants to escape the heat should head over to this two-pool facility, built next to the Roeland Park Dome. One end of the large pool has a diving well for one- and three-meter diving, along with 50-meter swim lanes. The other end, designed for wading and small kids, has a flat entry into the pool and play apparatus. Daily noon–8. Nonresidents: $4 adults, $3 children. & (Johnson County)

YMCA OF GREATER KANSAS CITY
3100 Broadway Blvd.
Kansas City
816/561-9622

Of the 10 YMCAs in Greater Kansas City, seven have swimming pools, and five offer indoor or indoor and outdoor pools. Hours and rates vary. A one-day pass for nonmembers generally $5–$10. & (all zones)

Tennis

EISENHOWER RECREATION CENTER
2901 N. 72nd St.
Kansas City, Kansas
913/299-1118

Four lighted courts are available at this city-run outdoor facility. Nearby baseball fields, playground equipment, and a paved walking track expand the exercise options. 8 a.m.–11 p.m. Free. & (Kansas City, Kansas)

HAPPY ROCK PARK
7600 NE Antioch Rd.

TRIVIA

On summer Sunday afternoons, the Jacomo Sailing Club (816/454-7639) stages a variety of sailing regattas near the Lake Jacomo marina. In addition, the Johnson County Sailing Society (913/268-5683, Nick Hockman) sponsors Sunday summer races and social events at Shawnee Mission Park.

Gladstone
816/437-2450

Four lighted courts are complemented by soccer fields, basketball courts, a playground, and a picnic shelter. 6 a.m.–11 p.m. Free unless reserved for city tournament. ♿ (Northland)

INDIAN CREEK RECREATION CENTER
7401 W. 103rd St.
Overland Park
913/341-4350

These eight courts have no lighting. A playground, picnic shelter, and paved fitness trail are nearby. A tennis pro gives lessons during summer months. Daily 8 a.m.–8 p.m. $1/player per hour or $2/court if reserved in advance. ♿ (Johnson County)

PLAZA TENNIS CENTER
4747 J.C. Nichols Pkwy.
Kansas City
816/561-5120

These 14 lighted courts on the Country Club Plaza are open Mon–Thu 8 a.m.–10 p.m., Fri–Sun 8–8. Regular courts $4–$8, two practice backboards free. ♿ (Plaza/Westport)

SANTA FE PARK
2800 Santa Fe Rd.
Independence
816/325-7360

This popular Independence park includes eight courts, four lighted, plus three baseball diamonds, a concession stand, playground equipment, a small shelter house, and three picnic areas. Daily 7 a.m.–11 p.m. Free. ♿ (East Metro)

Convention and Visitors Bureau of Greater Kansas City

11

PERFORMING ARTS

What shall we see tonight? The options are nearly endless when it comes to Kansas City's performing arts. Whether it's a rousing rendition of Beethoven's Fifth, a spirited "Dance of the Sugar Plum Fairy," or a stirring choral ensemble singing Handel's Messiah, you can find it in this town. Kansas City has a major symphony, many smaller musical orchestras, several dance companies, traveling arts series, and enough live theater to make it one of the best drama-oriented towns in the country. What do you want to see? How will you ever decide?

THEATER

AMERICAN HEARTLAND THEATRE
2450 Grand Blvd., Suite 314
Kansas City
816/842-9999

The American Heartland Theatre presents Broadway-style comedies, musicals, mysteries, and dramas throughout the year, using local theatrical talent and visiting headliners. Set on Crown Center's Level 3, the theater is a well-appointed facility with a stage that extends into the audience. Seats rise sharply from the stage, giving all an unobstructed view. There's a full-service bar in the lobby at intermission, and the

American Heartland allows you to take your drink into the performance. Performances slated for 1999 include Swingtime Canteen, Forbidden Broadway, Steel Magnolias, Murder Among Friends, and Red Rock Diner. & (Downtown)

HEART OF AMERICA SHAKESPEARE FESTIVAL
4800 Main St., Suite 302
Kansas City
816/531-7728

The annual Heart of America Shakespeare Festival has been a fortuitous addition to Kansas City's theater scene, bringing thousands to Southmoreland Park each summer to enjoy

TRIVIA

With 12 professional acting companies, Kansas City ranks third in the nation for professional theaters per capita. Nearly a dozen community theater companies also provide entertainment for drama fans.

the Bard for free. In the hilly esplanade opposite the Nelson-Atkins Museum of Art, the equity company presents high-quality performances that have included *Romeo and Juliet*, *A Midsummer Night's Dream*, and *The Tempest*. In 1998, the festival ran two plays on alternate nights for the first time—*Love's Labour's Lost* and *Measure for Measure*—a sure sign of popular acclaim. Fans bring blankets and picnics early to be sure they get close to the stage. Southmoreland Park is at 47th Street and Oak, east of the Country Club Plaza. ♿ (Plaza/Westport)

MARTIN CITY MELODRAMA & VAUDEVILLE COMPANY
13340 Holmes Rd.

American Heartland Theatre

Convention and Visitors Bureau of Greater Kansas City

Kansas City
816/942-7576

Not content to present mere melodrama, the Martin City Melodrama & Vaudeville Company adapts old standards to its highly wacky purposes. Productions in the past have included *Ivanhoe*, or *Ivanrake*; *Jezebel*, or *Gone With the Men*; and *The Invisible Man*, or *No Guts, No Glory!* The evening's entertainment—held out south in a wood-frame theater building—also includes a rousing vaudeville revue. ♿ (South Kansas City)

MISSOURI REPERTORY THEATRE
4949 Cherry St.
Kansas City
816/235-2700

The Missouri Repertory Theatre has entertained Kansas Citians ever since one muggy night in June 1964, when the theater troupe staged Emlyn Williams' *The Corn is Green* in an old playhouse on the UMKC campus. Now the professional company presents five plays each season, between September and May, and *A Christmas Carol* every December. Its intimate facility is still on the university grounds. Plays slated for 1999 include *The Last Night at Ballyhoo*, *The Miracle Worker*, *Laughter on the 23rd Floor*, and *WMKS: Where Music Kills Sorrow*. ♿ (Plaza/Westport)

QUALITY HILL PLAYHOUSE
303 W. 10th St.
Kansas City

816/235-2700

This small theater specializes in off-Broadway dramas, comedies, and musicals in a season that lasts all year. The playhouse is an intimate setting that makes the theater company's productions especially memorable. Recent plays have included *Romance, Romance,* a musical comedy that looks at the lives of two couples, one in Victorian England, the other in the Hamptons in the 1980s; *Kindertransport,* a drama based on the true stories of children who escaped to England from Nazi Germany; and *New York, New York,* featuring show tunes and cabaret songs from the Big Apple. ♿ (Downtown)

STARLIGHT THEATRE
Swope Park
4600 Starlight Rd.
Kansas City
816/363-7827

When it opened nearly 50 years ago, the Starlight Theatre symbolized the revival of legitimate theater in Kansas City. Today it's one of only two professional, self-producing outdoor theaters in America. The theater, set in the midst of 1,700-acre Swope Park, has concentrated largely on Broadway shows and national concert attractions during its summertime season. Recent productions have included *Crazy for You; Fiddler on the Roof,* starring Theodore Bikel; and *Peter Pan,* with Cathy Rigby in the title role. ♿ (South Kansas City)

THEATER LEAGUE
301 W. 13th St.
Kansas City
816/421-7500

Set in downtown's sumptuous Music Hall, the Theater League sponsors professional touring companies that focus on big-production musicals, both new plays and revivals. Recent shows have included *Rent, Sunset Boulevard,* and *Big.* ♿ (Downtown)

THEATRE IN THE PARK
7799 Renner Rd.
Lenexa
913/464-9420

Thereby Hangs a Tale

In 1991, Marilyn Strauss decided she would launch an annual outdoor Shakespeare Festival. The native Kansas Citian had just returned from a long career in New York and wanted to add a major dramatic event to her town's annual offerings. Strauss persuaded companies to donate time and cash, and even lured actor Kevin Kline for fund-raising readings. Finally, in 1993, the first performance of the Heart of America Shakespeare Festival opened in Southmoreland Park. The Tempest *was a huge success. Strauss has since moved to Reno, Nevada, but she returns each year for the Festival.*

A Haunted Theater?

Although it's a tradition that seems to have started years earlier, the Missouri Repertory Theatre's annual production of Charles Dickens' A Christmas Carol *was launched in 1981. The professional acting company had moved to its new Helen F. Spencer Theatre on the UMKC campus only two years before, and the facility was perfect for a holiday extravaganza. The company took full advantage of the new theater's state-of-the-art facilities, using lighting, sound, trap doors, and special effects to portray the play's rich imagery.*

Ironically, some believe the apparitions who visit Scrooge each year aren't the only ghosts to haunt the Mo Rep. In 1957, a former Broadway actress died of a heart attack in the lobby of the now-demolished University Playhouse, the company's previous location. Unexplained events and unusual noises on the Spencer stage lead many to believe the actress' ghost still performs for the Kansas City troupe.

Every summer, Shawnee Mission Park hosts a variety of outdoor musicals in its amphitheater. All locally cast and directed, the plays often include full-scale Broadway-style productions. Recent performances have included *Cinderella*, *42nd Street*, and *Big River*. Performances begin after dark, at about 8:30 p.m. ♿ (Johnson County)

UNICORN THEATRE
3820 Main St.
Kansas City
816/531-7529
The Unicorn has made a name for itself throughout the region for producing daring plays. Set in an intimate Midtown theater, the small Equity company specializes in adventurous off-Broadway productions

and original work. Recent plays have included Paula Vogel's *How I Learned to Drive*, which won a 1998 Pulitzer Prize; *Having Our Say–The Delany Sisters' First 100 Years*, adapted by Emily Mann from the best-selling autobiography by Sadie and Bessie Delany; and *As Bees in Honey Drown*, a recent off-Broadway hit by Douglas Carter Beane. ♿ (Plaza/Westport)

MUSIC AND OPERA

FRIENDS OF CHAMBER MUSIC
4643 Wyandotte St., Suite 201
Kansas City
816/561-9999
During its concert season, the Friends of Chamber Music imports

a variety of established and new chamber music artists from around the globe to play at downtown Kansas City's Folly Theater. Running from fall to spring, the Friends' series have included such recent guests as the Muir String Quartet, the Orpheus Chamber Orchestra, and the St. Lawrence String Quartet, as well as pianist Mia Chung and Trio Fontenay. & (Downtown)

KANSAS CITY CHAMBER ORCHESTRA
11 E. 40th St.
Kansas City
816/960-1324

During its five-concert season, the Kansas City Chamber Orchestra provides first-rate small-ensemble music at the Unity Temple on the Plaza and the Old Mission United Methodist Church at Shawnee Mission Parkway and Mission Road. Recent series include "Mozart Mania" and "Baroque by Candlelight," featuring pieces by Handel, Scarlatti, and Telemann. During the holidays, the orchestra teams with the Kansas City Chorale and Friends of Chamber Music for a non-series performance. & (Plaza/Westport)

KANSAS CITY CHORALE
201 Westport Rd.
Kansas City
816/931-7669

The Kansas City Chorale is a 24-voice professional choir that was the first American ensemble to be recorded by Nimbus Records of Great Britain. The Chorale has released five CDs that are available worldwide on this label. The Chorale maintains a local subscription series and appears throughout the Midwest, dedicating itself to performing music from diverse historical periods. Composers range from Bach to Bernstein. & (Plaza/Westport)

KANSAS CITY SYMPHONY
1020 Central St., Suite 300
Kansas City
816/471-0400

After the 1997–98 season, longtime Kansas City Symphony Maestro Bill McGlaughlin handed off his baton to Anne Manson, who takes over in the 1999–2000 season. At 37, Manson, a renowned conductor in Europe, will be one of the youngest musical directors in the world. Who knows what changes she'll make; she wants to raise the orchestra's playing standards, broaden its repertory, find a better concert hall, and combine her Kansas City job with a guest-conducting career concentrated in Europe. Previously, the Symphony played 12 concerts in its annual Classical Series between

TRIVIA

After four years of studying outdoor theaters—and another six years of securing funds and building the complex—organizers finally opened the Starlight Theatre in 1950. Its debut production was Kansas City's Centennial Pageant, *Thrills of a Century*, starring Gloria Swanson. Since then, the amphitheater has hosted actors such as Carol Burnett, Richard Harris, and Carol Channing, as well as musical performers including the Beach Boys, Elton John, and Bette Midler.

Kansas City Symphony

September and May. In addition, a seven-concert NightLights Pops Series teamed the orchestra with major jazz, country, and pop artists. ♿ (Downtown)

LYRIC OPERA OF KANSAS CITY
1029 Central St.
Kansas City
816/471-7344

In summer 1998, Ward Holmquist was named artistic director of the Lyric Opera, signaling some new directions for the company. One will be performances in languages other than English—a first for the Lyric— and the installation of projected text-translation monitors. The oldest performing arts organization in Kansas City, the Lyric Opera stages five operas each season in its 1,660-seat Lyric Theatre. Recent productions have included *La Traviata*, *Billy Budd*, and *Die Fledermaus*. ♿ (Downtown)

RLDS TEMPLE AND AUDITORIUM
River St. and Walnut Ave.
Independence
816/833-1000

The world headquarters of the Reor-

ganized Church of Jesus Christ of Latter-Day Saints features two outstanding organs that are frequently shared with the community. During the summer, staff organists give free concerts Sunday at 3 p.m. The rest of the year, the RLDS invites musicians to stage concerts on the auditorium's 110-rank, 6,000-pipe organ and on the temple's 102-rank pipe organ. Recent concerts have included Brahms' *Requiem*, the Durufle and Faure *Requiems*, and the annual performance of Handel's *Messiah*. ♿ (East Metro)

UMKC CONSERVATORY OF MUSIC
4949 Cherry St.
Kansas City
816/235-2700

The acclaimed Conservatory of Music at the University of Missouri–Kansas City holds more than 350 concerts annually, both by students and professionals. The Conservatory offers graduate programs in orchestral and solo instruments as well as voice, and many students perform regularly for the public at White Recital Hall in the Center for Performing Arts. Recent concerts have in-

Kansas City Symphony (vertical caption, left margin)

PERFORMING ARTS **185**

cluded soprano Roberta Gumbel and Penny Thompson Kruse and Patricia Higdon, violin and piano, with Steven Kruse, viola, and Nina Gordon, violin-cello. ♿ (Plaza/Westport)

WILLIAM JEWELL COLLEGE FINE ARTS PROGRAM
William Jewell College
500 College Hill
Liberty
816/781-8250
Not solely an educational institution, William Jewell College also sponsors a nationally recognized arts series that features nearly two dozen productions a year. Major performers, from vocal groups to orchestras to dance companies and theater troupes, travel to Kansas City as part of the program, playing primarily at downtown's Music Hall or Folly Theater. Performances set for 1999 include the Academy of St. Martin-in-the-Fields, the Russian National

Ballet, and the St. Louis Symphony. ♿ (Downtown)

DANCE

CITY IN MOTION DANCE THEATER
700 W. Pennway
Kansas City
816/472-7828
The founders of this experimental dance company renovated an old brick church near downtown, then put together a company that performs an annual series. Local choreographers and dancers are spotlighted here; concerts are energetic and fun. ♿ (Downtown)

KANSAS CITY FRIENDS OF ALVIN AILEY
201 Wyandotte St.
Kansas City
816/471-6003
Kansas City is the second home of

Ten Classical Favorites Played by the Kansas City Symphony
by Tiberius Klausner, concertmaster of the Kansas City Symphony

1. Beethoven's Symphony No. 5
2. Brahms' Symphony No. 1
3. Elgar's *The Enigma Variations*
4. Mahler's Symphony No. 1
5. Mendelssohn's Symphony No. 4 (*"Italian"*)
6. Mozart's Symphony No. 41 (*"Jupiter"*)
7. Mussorgsky's *Pictures at an Exhibition*
8. Schumann's Symphony No. 4
9. Shostakovich's Symphony No. 5
10. Verdi's *Requiem*

the Alvin Ailey American Dance Theatre. Each fall, the Kansas City Friends of Alvin Ailey host the New York–based company in a two-week residency. The lively dance troupe holds public performances at the Midland Theatre and conducts in-school programs throughout the area. ♿ (Downtown)

STATE BALLET OF MISSOURI
706 W. 42nd St.
Kansas City
816/931-2232

The only fully professional ballet company in Missouri, the State Ballet of Missouri performs classical and contemporary works during its season each year. The Ballet's artistic direc-

tor, William Whitener—who's worked with the Joffrey Ballet and Twyla Tharp—has added a new perspective to performances at the Midland Theatre and Lyric Theatre. Recent concerts include *The Prodigal Son*, *Offenbach in the Underworld*, and *Giselle*. ♿ (Downtown)

CONCERT VENUES

FLAMINGO HILTON CASINO
1800 E. Front St.
Kansas City
816/855-7777

Among its many draws, the Flamingo now stages concerts for those who'd rather rock than gamble. Groups that

The Folly Theater, p. 188

Convention and Visitors Bureau of Greater Kansas City

have appeared at the Kansas City casino include the Turtles, Atlanta Rhythm Section, and the Mamas & the Papas, among others. While acts may not be at the top of the charts currently, tickets average about $10. (Downtown)

FOLLY THEATER
12th and Central Sts.
Kansas City
816/474-4444
The Folly was not the first theater built in Kansas City, but it happens to be the oldest one still standing downtown. Now this painstakingly restored neo-Palladian burlesque house features a variety of theater and concerts on stage. Placed on the National Register of Historic Places, the Folly is home to the Folly Jazz series, the Friends of Chamber Music series, the William Jewell Fine Arts Program, and many other events. & (Downtown)

TRIVIA

The Folly Theater was erected at the turn of the century as one of more than 10 legitimate theaters in town. Like the others, it regressed from vaudeville to burlesque over the years. It remained standing even after theater's "golden era" ended in the 1920s. In the early Eighties, when interest in theater and historic preservation resurged, the Folly underwent a $4-million renovation.

GEM THEATER CULTURAL AND PERFORMING ARTS CENTER
1615 E. 18th St.
Kansas City
816/842-1414
Originally opened as a movie theater in 1912, the Gem has been thoroughly modernized with the latest in lighting, sound, and acoustical design. Smack-dab in the heart of the historic 18th & Vine District, the Gem now hosts a variety of musical performances, theater productions, and multimedia events, from the smash-hit musical *Ms. Holiday's Blues* to an annual 18th & Vine Gala, hosted by the likes of Harry Belafonte and Danny Glover and drawing talent such as Ray Charles, George Benson, and Oleta Adams. & (Downtown)

JOHNSON COUNTY COMMUNITY COLLEGE
12345 College Blvd.
Overland Park
913/469-4445
The college's 1,400-seat Yardley Hall provides a welcoming venue for arts groups such as the symphony and chamber music ensembles, but JCCC holds its own performing-arts series, too. Performers have included notables such as violinist Nadja Salerno-Sonnenberg, the St. Petersburg State Symphony Orchestra, and the Vienna Boys Choir. & (Johnson County)

KEMPER ARENA
1800 Genessee St.
Kansas City
816/421-6460
Although it's primarily a sporting venue—hosting everything from basketball finals to the American Royal Barbecue & Rodeo—the 16,300-seat Kemper also offers concerts and other events. Set west of downtown in an area known as the

It Don't Mean a Thing … If It Ain't Got That Swing

For all practical purposes, Count Basie invented Kansas City jazz. The distinctive swing music he and his band refined at the Reno Club in the mid-'30s is the style most often associated with this city. It was that sound—uncomplicated, economical, vibrant—that caught producer John Hammond's ear and catapulted Basie to international fame. Count Basie's music influenced many other bands and many other jazz artists, but the pianist and bandleader was modest about his accomplishments. "I never did call it Kansas City jazz," he said. "I just called it swing." Basie died in Hollywood in 1984. His legacy lives on in the 18th & Vine Historic District, including the newly refurbished Gem Theater.

West Bottoms, Kemper has recently been visited by Eric Clapton, bluesman extraordinaire and onetime member of the legendary Yardbirds and Cream; the rhythm and blues sounds of Boyz II Men; and the Ice Capades. ♿ (Downtown)

MIDLAND THEATRE
1228 Main St.
Kansas City
816/471-8600
In 1927, Loew's spent $4 million to build this elegantly ornate facility as a movie theater, marking a new day for moving pictures. Now, several performing arts groups hold their events in the 2,800-seat venue, including the Friends of Alvin Ailey and the State Ballet of Missouri. This stunning building is listed on the National Register. ♿ (Downtown)

MUSIC HALL
1310 Wyandotte St.
Kansas City
816/274-2900
Located within Municipal Auditorium, this art deco masterpiece hosts a variety of fine arts programs. Originally opened in 1936—in the midst of the Depression—the Music Hall was recently restored. Anyone who appreciates architecture should notice the rotunda above the grand staircase; the building's light fixtures were the inspiration for the new *Sky Stations* atop Bartle Hall's pylons next door. ♿ (Downtown)

SANDSTONE AMPHITHEATRE
633 N. 130th St.
Bonner Springs
913/721-3400
Located west of town near Bonner Springs, Sandstone is a natural amphitheater with 6,700 permanent seats. Terraced lawns add space for another 11,000 fans. From April through October, top recording acts

perform under the stars. Recent concerts have included Rod Stewart, the Lilith Fair, and Van Halen. Don't even think of trying to sneak in food or alcohol—coolers are not allowed, and meticulous guards check backpacks, bags, and purses. ♿ (Kansas City, Kansas)

STATION CASINO
I-435 and Birmingham Rd.
Kansas City

816/414-7000
Since it opened in 1997, Station Casino has become a magnet for entertainment of all varieties, including concerts featuring groups such Tower of Power, the Average White Band, and the British Rock Symphony and Choir, with Roger Daltry of The Who. The 1,200-seat venue also stages country stars, comedians, and professional boxers. (Northland)

12

NIGHTLIFE

Kansas City's nightlife scene buzzes—and it's little wonder. This is, after all, the place where cattlemen and other early Westerners enjoyed bustling gambling halls, ornate saloons, and fine restaurants. Later on, jazz and blues greats such as Charlie "Yardbird" Parker, Count Basie, and Joe Turner jammed their ways through numberless late-night sessions here. Today Kansas City has no less to offer. From hole-in-the-wall pubs where you can swill $1 bottles of beer to sophisticated cabarets serving vodka martinis, from two-step taverns to rock 'n' roll-eramas—the metro area gives night owls multiple ways to wind up or unwind in style.

DANCE CLUBS

ADOLFO'S DISCOTHEQUE
1111 Grand Blvd.
Kansas City
816/221-7650
A mix of 1970s and 1980s disco and funk music keeps traffic flowing on the dance floor of this new nightlife palace near downtown. Overhead, a mirror ball casts its light on the dance floor, and a generous bar set behind the columns in the former bank space provides a mellow refrain to the dancing. Twenty-somethings are well represented at Adolfo's, but so are graying Boomers looking in on the

singles scene. There's a dress code on weekends. (Downtown)

BLAYNEY'S
415 Westport Rd.
Kansas City
816/561-3747
Blayney's loves its live music, and its clientele appreciates the club's eclectic approach. Each night, the Westport tavern features a different musical style, from reggae to rock to rhythm and blues. Blayney's even spotlights jazz and blues in its intimate location. Bands have included the Nace Brothers, Jhamm, and the 39th Street Blues Band, as well as the

Roland Allen Blues Jam and K.C. Brass and Electric. (Plaza/Westport)

KIKI'S BON TON MAISON
1515 Westport Rd.
Kansas City
816/931-9417
Get ready for a Cajun party at Kiki's, where the house band is the Bon Ton Soul Accordion Band. This Louisiana-style restaurant was opened by Richard and Kiki Lucente back in 1987 so that Kiki could cook and Richard could play his wild Cajun numbers. It's been a rollicking good time ever since. Prepare to dance up a storm. The restaurant is open daily for lunch and dinner; music Wed and Sat. (Plaza/ Westport)

THE LEVEE
16 W. 43rd St.
Kansas City
816/561-2821
The Levee's a fun neighborhood bar whose regular band, Hothouse, plays highly danceable tunes, ranging from Sixties and Seventies favorites to more recent rock 'n' roll. Set in a wood-frame building northeast of the Country Club Plaza, the Levee also books guest artists like Boko Maru, The Bidets, and Camp Harlow. The outdoor deck is popular in warm weather. (Plaza/ Westport)

MUSIC CLUBS

Jazz

THE BLUE ROOM
1600 E. 18th St.
Kansas City
816/474-2929
The 18th & Vine area was the birthplace of Kansas City jazz, so the revitalization of the area—with museums, theaters, and shops—has been a historic event. Operating inside the Jazz Museum, the Blue Room provides a venue to experience more than artists from the past. Here, jazz musicians such as the Ervin Brown Quintet, Eddie Sanders & his K.C. Originals, and the Sam Johnson Jr. Company entertain the crowds who gather for an uptown musical encounter. Glass tables encase ticket stubs, band photos, and Count Basie's original 1936 Musician's Union card, making the historic connections even more apparent. (Downtown)

CLUB 427
427 Main St.
Kansas City
816/421-2582
Open since July 1995, Club 427 has quickly become one of the city's best jazz venues. The upscale club—which also serves a delicious menu of fish, pasta, and salads—has provided a winning showcase for local jazz talent such as Steve Miller, Karrin Allyson, and the Pat Morrissey Trio in its two-level setting. This cabaret provides one of the classiest jazz settings to be found west of the Mississippi. (Downtown)

CLUB MARDI GRAS
1600 E. 19th St.
Kansas City
816/842-8463
One of the notorious music haunts in the historic 18th & Vine District, Club Mardi Gras still contributes an irresistible locale for upcoming jazz and blues talent to play together. Some of the musicians at Club Mardi Gras include King Alex & the Untouchables, the Mac Lace Band, and the Tim Perryman Quintet. (Downtown)

Ten Best Jazz Venues in the Kansas City Area

by Vanessa Barnard, longtime president of the Jazz Ambassadors, a local nonprofit organization dedicated to the support of jazz

1. **Club 427**. This stylish addition to Kansas City's jazz scene boasts top entertainment with wonderful acoustics, great food, and a New York–like atmosphere in the historic River Market area.

2. **The Phoenix Piano Bar & Grill**. This hot spot for the after-work downtown crowd features music continuing into the night and good bar-type food. The place to see and be seen.

3. **Club Mardi Gras**. On the corner of 19th and Vine in the original jazz district, this club has been the home of such jazz greats as Charlie Parker and Count Basie. The history (and the ghosts) live on.

4. **Jardine's**. In addition to the best late-night jam session on Friday and Saturday nights (until 3), this place features fabulous food and smokin' music.

5. **Mutual Musicians Foundation**. Here, the best late-late-night jam session in the historic jazz district is open to the public on Saturday nights. It begins around midnight and lasts until . . . . Come ready to party until sunrise and hear the best Kansas City has to offer.

6. **Jazz-A Louisiana Kitchen**. Spicy Cajun food mixed with some of the hottest bands in town deliver a winning combination. Live music Wednesday through Sunday. Prepare to eat, drink, and dance in a fantastic and fun New Orleans setting.

7. **The Kansas City Blues & Jazz Festival**, Penn Valley Park. Held the third weekend in July, this is simply the best. Featuring three days of locals and the biggest names in national blues and jazz, it's one of the finest festivals in the country.

8. **18th & Vine Jazz Heritage Festival**. Held the third weekend of August, this weekend-long festival offers some of the best local and national talent free of charge to the public.

9. **The Club at Plaza III**. A restaurant upstairs and intimate jazz club downstairs (food also served in the club), this place boasts wonderful steaks, romantic atmosphere, and some of the greatest talent in jazz.

10. **Annual Jazz Lovers' Pub Crawl**. Held each year in June, Kansas City crawls to approximately 20 clubs around town. Transportation is provided by bus, and a one-time admission fee allows access to all spots. Sponsored by the Kansas City Jazz Ambassadors, it's designed to kick off the summer jazz season and is one of the year's best events.

TIP

For information on who's playing around town, call the 24-hour Kansas City Jazz Ambassadors' Hotline, 816/753-5277.

THE CLUB AT PLAZA III
4749 Pennsylvania St.
Kansas City
816/753-0000

Beneath the venerable Plaza III steakhouse lurks a jammin' spot for jazz geniuses. Previously called the City Light Jazz Club, this spot attracts national acts and local artists. Performers have included everyone from saxophonist Bobby Watson and pianist Henry Butler to vocalist Queen Bey and ensemble David Basse & the City Light Orchestra. (Plaza/Westport)

IVY'S RESTAURANT & JAZZ CLUB
240 NE Barry Rd.
Kansas City
816/436-3320

Ivy's is the place for live jazz in the Northland. Although located in a strip mall surrounded by a dry cleaner's, a beauty supply store, and a chiropractor's office, owners Sam and Carol Cross have designed the restaurant and the club for the purpose at hand. This hopping spot offers live jazz on Thursday, Friday, and Saturday, featuring talent that includes Angela Hagenbach, Dave Stephens, and Russ Long. Reservations are recommended. (Northland)

JARDINE'S RESTAURANT & JAZZ CLUB
4536 Main St.
Kansas City
816/561-6480

Jardine's has emerged as a hot jazz spot in Kansas City, where noted local musicians and vocalists such as Ida McBeth, Mike Metheny, and Lisa Henry perform regularly. At Jardine's you can hear live jazz as many as seven nights a week, plus sit in on several weekly jams. Drummer Tommy Ruskin hosts a jam every Saturday afternoon from 3 to 6. No cover, an eclectic menu, and a cozy jazz-club ambiance. (Plaza/Westport)

JOHN'S FOOD & DRINK
928 Wyandotte St.
Kansas City
816/474-5668

As long as the weather's nice—from March through October—this downtown establishment offers live music on John's Big Deck, otherwise known as the roof. It makes for an amiable live-music venue, and features some get-down blues musicians, such as Dan Bliss, Groove Agency, and Fast Johnny. Lunch and dinner daily; live music Mon–Sat. (Downtown)

LIQUID LOUNGE
333 Southwest Blvd.
Kansas City
816/421-6888

Neon greets you outside and in at the Liquid Lounge. A true happy-hour club in an old brick storefront near downtown, the lounge provides live music several nights a week, featuring bands such as the Wax Tadpoles, Soul Bandit, Easy Money,

Phoenix Piano Bar & Grill

and Dave Stephens Swing Quartet. On Friday and Saturday, alternating bands play jazz, blues, funk, and swing. (Downtown)

MUTUAL MUSICIAN'S FOUNDATION
1823 Highland Ave.
Kansas City
816/471-5212

Set in the historic 18th & Vine District, the Mutual Musicians Foundation is a living shrine to jazz. Designated a National Historic Landmark in 1982, the foundation was where Charlie Parker, Jay McShann, and other jazz legends got started. These days, the foundation packs in fans for weekend after-hours jazz jams. Music starts around midnight and can go until dawn, depending upon who shows up to play. The foundation can also arrange pub crawls for people who want to hear authentic jazz in locales throughout the Kansas City area. (Downtown)

PHOENIX PIANO BAR & GRILL
302 W. 8th St.
Kansas City
816/472-0001

The cozy Phoenix is a relaxing neighborhood pub with big-name musical talent. The affable Tim Whitmer—now a co-owner of the joint—and his K.C. Express often hold the stage, but the Phoenix hosts other talented musicians, too. The Max Groove Band, Dave Stephens' Martini Bash, and the Toni Oliver Quartet play here, and other entertaining jam sessions take place as well. Local entertainers often head to the Phoenix for their own record-release parties. (Downtown)

Blues

BB'S LAWNSIDE BAR-B-Q
1205 E. 85th St.
Kansas City
816/822-7427

One of Kansas City's unique barbecue

joints sits in a ramshackle roadhouse on the south side of town. There, blues lover Lindsay Shannon and his wife, Jo, opened BB's Lawnside Bar-B-Q, a restaurant that combines their passionate interests in blues and barbecue. A founder of the Kansas City Blues Society, Shannon owns more than 5,000 recordings and presents a weekly blues radio show. Wednesday through Saturday nights at BB's, blues artists such as Bill Laursen, Little Hatch, and the Lonnie Ray Blues Band keep the music alive. (South Kansas City)

BLUE NOTE CAFÉ
9617 W. 87th St.
Overland Park
913/642-6625
Out on West 87th Street, the Blue Note Café occupies a strip mall next door to the Johnson County Central Library. Among this restaurant's neighbors are a tanning salon, a veterinary center, and a karate school. But indoors, the mellow ambiance transports patrons to the world of music. Here, you can listen to jazz and blues on weekends, from Camp Harlow to Old Guys with Real Jobs. (Johnson County)

GRAND EMPORIUM
3832 Main St.
Kansas City
816/531-1504
The Grand Emporium has gained a national reputation among blues cognoscenti—and rightfully so. This loud, smoky club has hosted the likes of John Lee Hooker, Koko Taylor, and B.B. King. But the Grand Emporium's excursions into jazz, alternative rock, and world music have been successful, too. Featuring nightly performances, this place has hosted everyone from DDJ a.k.a. Doo Daddy Jemson to Indigo Swing. (Plaza/Westport)

Top Ten Song Requests in Kansas City
by Tim Whitmer, popular Kansas City jazz pianist and bandleader who plays regularly at The Phoenix and other area venues.

1. "Kansas City"
2. "What a Wonderful World"
3. "Route 66"
4. "Let the Good Times Roll"
5. "Georgia"
6. "When the Saints Go Marching In"
7. "In the Mood"
8. "All of Me"
9. "Unforgettable"
10. "St. Louis Blues"

Club 427, p. 192

HARLING'S UPSTAIRS
3941 Main St.
Kansas City
816/531-0303
Originally a blues venue, Harling's Upstairs also strays into alternative and world music, especially of the Irish variety. Every Saturday afternoon a blues jam session heats up the joint. Harling's hosts artists such as Eddie Delahunt, Mama Ray & Rich Van Sant Band, and Ceili's Muse. (Plaza/Westport)

QUINCY'S
I-70 and Blue Ridge Cut-off
Kansas City
816/737-4719
Located in the Adam's Mark Hotel, near the Truman Sports Complex, Quincy's attracts an impressive roster of talented artists. A small club frequented both by residents and visitors, Quincy's schedule includes popular blues crooner Ida McBeth, the get-down-and-have-fun Scamps, and the rocking group Retro. (East Metro)

THE ROXY
7230 W. 75th St.
Overland Park
913/236-6211
On Sunday, The Roxy features an open blues jam with the BWB band that many consider to be one of the best groups of its kind. Guest performers at The Roxy have included Albert Flasher, Charlie & the Stingrays, and No Parking. A dance floor and three pool tables add to the scene. (Johnson County)

Rock

ATLANTIS AND THE CAVE
3954 Central St.
Kansas City
816/753-0112
Young party animals head to this two-bars-in-one complex. Atlantis offers Top 40 dance music and, with 160-plus video screens, the largest light and video show in the region. The Cave features live bands in an underground, cave-like atmosphere. (Plaza/Westport)

DAVEY'S UPTOWN RAMBLERS CLUB
3402 Main
Kansas City
816/753-1909

They say this unobtrusive joint was once the hangout of corrupt politicians who gathered in the back room to hammer out deals. These days, though, the club hosts a wide mix of groups, including the Alejandro Escavado Orchestra, Bindlestiffs, Puddle of Mudd, Reverb Brothers, and In a Sick Way. Live music every night but Sunday. (Plaza/Westport)

THE HURRICANE
4048 Broadway Blvd.
Kansas City
816/753-0884

One of the most popular places in town, The Hurricane features everything from alternative rock bands to solo acoustic guitarists. Popular artists have included the likes of Go Kart, Art Dodge, Carribe, Creme De La Femme, and Julia Surrendered. Music five to six nights a week; open nightly until 3. (Plaza/Westport)

NIENER'S BAR & GRILL
815 N. Noland Rd.
Independence
816/461-6955

A popular spot for local rock bands as well as their traveling peers, Niener's attracts groups such as Spinning Grin, Full Power, and Euphoria. The Independence club also hosts frequent open jam sessions, where musicians gather to collaborate on classic and new rock songs. (East Metro)

ROADHOUSE RUBY'S SOUTH
11950 Strang Line Rd.
Olathe
913/829-8200

Roadhouse Ruby's was a rock 'n' roll staple when it opened in Olathe, quickly becoming one of the hottest night spots in the area. Live music ranges from Vixen to Night Ranger, but Ruby's also features dancing to DJ-spun tunes. Ruby's Gourmet Truckstop offers lunch and dinner specials and prime rib on Sat. Roadhouse Ruby's North is at 5502 NE Antioch Rd., Kansas City; 816/455-1600. Call for schedules. (Johnson County)

That's Entertainment

Nightlife varies in venues all over town. If you compare Johnson County to Midtown, however, you'll note some general differences: Johnson County clubs and nightspots attract a mostly white, suburban crowd. Mixed with the young set are couples, many of whom have left the kids home with a babysitter. Midtown hangouts appeal to a younger, multicultural group, often single, who head to the bars and bistros to drink, dance, and discourse. The Plaza generally caters to a somewhat older, upscale, and professional crowd.

Country and Western

THE BEAUMONT CLUB
4050 Pennsylvania St.
Kansas City
816/561-2668
Music at this Westport club tends to be recorded, but that doesn't stop the two-steppers who fill the largest wooden dance floor in the city. A mechanical bull ride and lots of special events, from boxing matches to dance contests, keep Beaumonters busy. (Plaza/Westport)

ORLANDO'S NITE CLUB
126 S. Clairborne Rd.
Olathe
913/393-2582
Louie Orlando opened the club that bears his name in 1997, after stints at country bars in south Kansas City and Lawrence. He launched his newest effort in an old country bar that dates to the 1800s—then added some decidedly modern touches for the suburban crowd. Fun at Orlando's includes line-dance lessons on Saturday night. (Johnson County)

PUBS AND BARS

CHARLIE HOOPER'S BROOKSIDE BAR & GRILLE
12 W. 63rd St.
Kansas City
816/361-8841
If you want any European imported beer, you'll find it at Hooper's. A convivial neighborhood bar in Brookside, Hooper's features 35 different kinds of beer on tap and another 140 bottled varieties, as well as other drinks and a grill menu. (South Kansas City)

COACH'S BAR & GRILL
414 W. 103rd St.

Kansas City
816/941-2286
Coach's is the kind of relaxed and informal place that just makes you want to hang out. A sports bar first—with some 16 TV sets and two big screens—this amiable neighborhood spot also attracts a considerable crowd with its impressively varied menu. A small patio on the east side overlooks Indian Creek, making Coach's a pleasant place to while away a summer afternoon or evening. (South Kansas City)

KELLY'S WESTPORT INN
500 Westport Rd.
Kansas City
816/753-9193
Set at the corner of Westport Road and Pennsylvania, this long narrow tavern occupies the oldest building in Kansas City. Here, a new drawing, sign, or handbill tacked over the old is considered a major change in decor. Once the site of an outfitter serving the Santa Fe Trail, Kelly's is famous for its flowing booze, no-frills atmosphere, and extremely devoted crowds. In the back, Joe's Pizza Buy the Slice adds a tasty dining option

TRIVIA

Who appears regularly in Kansas City area dinner theaters? Frequent performers include Don Knotts of *The Andy Griffith Show*, Jamie Farr from *M*A*S*H*, Marion Ross of *Happy Days*, and Elinor Donahue from *Father Knows Best*.

J.C. Nichols Fountain on the Plaza, p. 94

to this drinking stalwart. (Plaza/ Westport)

NORTH KANSAS CITY BAR & GRILL
1613 Swift Ave.
North Kansas City
816/221-5255
The North Kansas City Bar & Grill is the epitome of the neighborhood pub, supplying juicy burgers, a pool table, juke box, and video games to its diverse and loyal crowd. The motto: "If you're not here to have fun, you'd better go somewhere else." (Northland)

O'DOWD'S LITTLE DUBLIN
4742 Pennsylvania St.
Kansas City
816/561-2700
This authentic Irish ale house and pub comes complete with its own outdoor beer garden and ballad singing on Monday, Wednesday, and Sunday. Besides its varieties of Irish spirits, O'Dowd's serves food specialties saluting the Emerald Isle, such as Corned Beef and Cabbage, Old Style Dublin Fish & Chips, and Molly Mal-

one Seafood Boxty. Closed Mon. (Plaza/Westport)

THE PEANUT
5000 Main St.
Kansas City
816/753-9499
A Kansas City institution, the Peanut hovers between friendly neighborhood bar and classic dive. You can see all sorts here, from suits relaxing after work to the pierced crowd of nearby UMKC. An unpretentious hangout, the Peanut also serves food. (Plaza/Westport)

THE QUAFF
1010 Broadway Blvd.
Kansas City
816/471-1918
Downtown workers gather here after a hard day to belly up to the long bar and order a burger. The Quaff is also near Quality Hill, a renewed residential area for urban pioneers, and a number of loft developments that attract those who long for life near the heart of the big city. (Downtown)

THE VELVET DOG
400 E. 31st St.
Kansas City
816/753-9990
How many different martinis are there? At the swanky, Forties-style Velvet Dog, you'll find at least 16 versions of James Bond's favorite concoction. The club attracts an after-work, Midtown yuppie crowd eager to try a new cocktail and the Dog's eclectic Italian fare. (Plaza/Westport)

Drinks with a View
CLASSIC CUP CAFÉ
ON THE PLAZA
301 W. 47th St.
Kansas City
816/753-1840
The Classic Cup surrounded its southern deck with a high wooden fence, then filled the space with umbrella-topped tables. The expanse attracts a see-and-be-seen sort of crowd. Café tables lining the north sidewalk are reminiscent of Paris. (Plaza/Westport)

SKIES
2345 McGee St.
Kansas City
816/435-4199
The panorama from this revolving restaurant atop the Hyatt Regency Crown Center ranges from the bright lights of downtown to the more distant sparkles of the Plaza. Skies' lounge is a popular spot for before-dinner drinks but also attracts an after-work crowd that can't resist the view. (Downtown)

COFFEEHOUSES

BROADWAY CAFÉ
4106 Broadway Blvd.

Kansas City
816/531-2432
Owned and operated by young entrepreneur Sara Honan, the Broadway Café was one of the first coffeehouses in the area, and it boasts an ardently loyal following as a result. Its sidewalk is a favorite hangout during warm weather months. (Plaza/Westport)

EAST 51ST STREET
COFFEE HOUSE
318 E. 51st St.
Kansas City
816/756-3121
This coffeehouse is near the UMKC campus, offering delicious pastries with its java. In addition, the spot hosts a weekly songwriters' circle and one-person local acts. The bar offers beer on tap and wine as well. (Plaza/Westport)

MILDRED'S COFFEEHOUSE
7921 Santa Fe Dr.
Overland Park
913/341-0301
Besides coffee, Mildred's features live music on Friday, occasional poetry readings, and art show openings once a month. Owned by Kathleen Kraushaar, a.k.a. Mildred, this funky coffee house adds a decidedly fun and refreshing flavor to downtown Overland Park. (Johnson County)

THE SUPREME BEAN
1615 W. 39th St.
Kansas City
816/960-6652
This cleverly named coffee house—once located in the basement of a church—offers live folk and acoustic music most weekends, along with salads, sandwiches, and heavenly java. (Plaza/Westport)

WESTPORT COFFEE HOUSE
4010 Pennsylvania St.
Kansas City
816/756-3222

In addition to a tasty bean and brew, the Westport features open jazz and blues jams, classical guitar lunches, and performances from groups like the Midtown Jazz Quartet. Downstairs, the Westport Coffee House Theatre also stages various dramatic productions during the year. (Plaza/Westport)

COMEDY CLUBS

KANSAS CITY COMEDYSPORTZ
512 Delaware St.
Kansas City
816/842-2744

Like the popular British TV show *Whose Line is it Anyway?* Kansas City ComedySportz relies on audience participation for its improvisational theater. Quick-thinking, athletically minded comedy teams must deliver their on-the-spot humor within a set time, then the audience acts as judges. ComedyCourtz sets the show in a courtroom. (Downtown)

STANFORD'S COMEDY CLUB
504 Westport Rd.

Kansas City
816/756-1450

Kansas City's first comedy club has returned to its original location, above the restaurant with the same name. The club brings in a variety of touring acts, from John Wesley Austin to Howard Morgan, and also holds an open-mike night every Monday. (Plaza/Westport)

DINNER THEATERS

MARDI GRAS MURDERS
8821 State Line Rd.
Kansas City
816/452-1144

The entertaining Mardi Gras Murders holds forth during its season at the Colony Steak House and Lobster Pot, whose turf 'n' specialties have become legendary. Recent productions have included *All in the Momma's Family* and *Almost Untouchables*. (South Kansas City)

NEW THEATRE RESTAURANT
9229 Foster St.
Overland Park
913/649-7469

The only year-round Equity theater in Kansas, New Theatre Restaurant has been noted by the *Wall Street*

The song "Kansas City" was penned by Jerry Leiber and Mike Stoller, the songwriting team behind hits such as "Hound Dog," "Stand by Me," "Love Potion No. 9," and "Yakety Yak." The blue-eyed soul duo actually recorded "Kansas City" themselves in 1952, with Texas bluesman Little Willie Littlefield. The song has been covered numerous times since then, by singers such as Little Richard, the Beatles, James Brown, and Peggy Lee. The version that hit *Billboard*'s No. 1 spot was recorded by Wilbert Harrison in 1959.

TRIVIA

Journal as "the best in their business." The building, erected especially for the theater, includes a revolving stage, a state-of-the-art sound system, and a buffet created by an on-site chef and staff of 15. Some of the most memorable performances at this enjoyable venue have included *George Washington Slept Here,* starring Jamie Farr; *On Golden Pond,* with Don Knotts; and *Teahouse of the August Moon,* with Gary Sandy. (Johnson County)

MOVIE HOUSES OF NOTE

With more than 2,000 screens in 22 states, the District of Columbia, Portugal, and Japan, Kansas City—

Ten Favorite Places to See a Movie in Kansas City
by Patti Broyles Watkins, director of the Film Commission of Kansas City, Missouri

1. **IMAX at the Kansas City Zoo**. A great venue right in the zoo, in an architecturally splendid setting.

2. **Nelson-Atkins Museum of Art Auditorium**. A place to see experimental film series in an attractive atmosphere that's free with museum admission.

3. **Plaza Theatre**. A beautiful old theater. I like to sit in the balcony for first-run movies.

4. **Independence 20**. Always a great selection and wonderful high-backed seats with adjustable armrests.

5. **Tivoli**. A small independent-film venue in an intimate setting; like watching with a group of friends.

6. **Fine Arts Theatre**. The theater always shows smaller art films that might not make it to Kansas City otherwise.

7. **Tivoli Manor Square**. Showcases a variety of independent films. Both Tivoli theaters are in Westport, which offers great places to eat and drink, for a total movie experience.

8. **Westglen**. Terrific screens, seats, and sound system. Great for pictures with special effects, such as *Apollo 13* or *Waterworld.*

9. **Englewood**. Usually shows old movie classics on the big screen. Wooden benches.

10. **Film festivals**. These include Film Fest Kansas City and the Kan Film Festival; the Tivoli also has several featured series.

As a young man, Kansas City native Walt Disney rented a tiny studio above a café on 31st Street, where he experimented with animation. His Laugh-O-Gram Films made very little money; and his stenographer typed menus for the diner below the office in exchange for free lunches for the staff. Disney left Kansas City in 1923; his first Mickey Mouse film debuted six years later.

based AMC Theatres has become the world's second-largest movie chain. CEO Stan Durwood has tried several new movie-watching ideas on his friends and neighbors in the Midwest, giving the area first crack at a variety of theatrical innovations. Notable theaters in the area are listed below.

ENGLEWOOD THEATER
10917 E. Winner Rd.
Independence
816/252-2463
The historic Englewood shows movie classics, from *His Girl Friday* to *How the West Was Won*. (East Metro)

FINE ARTS THEATRE
5909 Johnson Dr.
Mission
913/262-4466
An intimate neighborhood theater, the Fine Arts showcases art and independent films. You can rent videos in the front corner of the lobby. (Johnson County)

SPRINT IMAX THEATRE
Kansas City Zoo, Swope Park
6700 Zoo Dr.
Kansas City
816/871-4629
The screen at this IMAX theater is 50 by 80 feet, about 10 times the size of a standard movie screen. The first IMAX located at a zoo, the Sprint IMAX has shown *Everest* and *The Living Sea*, among other specially filmed works. (South Kansas City)

TIVOLI THEATRE
425 Westport Rd.
Kansas City
816/756-1030
A tiny art house in Westport, the Tivoli has often been the only theater in town showing daring or foreign films. Lines form for favorably reviewed flicks. (Plaza/Westport)

WARD PARKWAY
8600 Ward Pkwy.
Kansas City
816/333-2046
In the 1960s, hometown cinema company AMC Theatres decided to install two screens in the neighborhood Ward Parkway Shopping Center. It was a way for the company to maximize its movie-renting dollar—but it was also the first multiplex in the nation. Now Ward Parkway features 22 different screens on two levels of the center, while larger and larger multiplexes spring up across the country. (South Kansas City)

Lawrence Convention and Visitors Bureau

13

DAY TRIPS FROM KANSAS CITY

Day Trip: Lawrence, Kansas

Distance from Kansas City: 35 miles or about 45 minutes by car
Kansas Citians have a soft spot in their hearts for Lawrence because so
many of them graduated from the highly regarded **University of Kansas**
there. But there's more to it than that: The college town has a decidedly
hip atmosphere that's downright magnetic.

Since it's a college town, start at the university, which perches atop
Mount Oread. Founded in 1866, KU boasts an enrollment of more than
25,000 students; the institution has been recognized by such publications
as *U.S. News & World Report* and *Barron's* for providing a high-quality education at a relatively low cost. Moreover, the picturesque campus was
noted as one of the nation's most beautiful by architect Thomas Gaines in
his book *The Campus as a Work of Art.*

The **Spencer Museum of Art** at KU features 11 well-stocked galleries
and is best known for its Asian art, seventeenth- and eighteenth-century
European paintings, and nineteenth- and twentieth-century American
paintings. Indeed, the Spencer is considered one of most comprehensive
university art collections in the United States (Mississippi Street; Tue–Sat
10–5, Thu until 9, Sun noon–5, closed Mon; free). **Lied Center**, also on the
KU campus, is a $14.3-million multipurpose facility that provides a state-
of-the-art setting for concerts, plays, and other performances. You can
view the building Mon–Fri 9–5; check local newspapers for events ranging
from the Tokyo String Quartet to *Tap Dogs* to The Who's *Tommy.*

Such artistic endeavors are only partly why Lawrence was included
in author John Villani's *The 100 Best Small Art Towns in America* (Santa

KANSAS CITY REGION

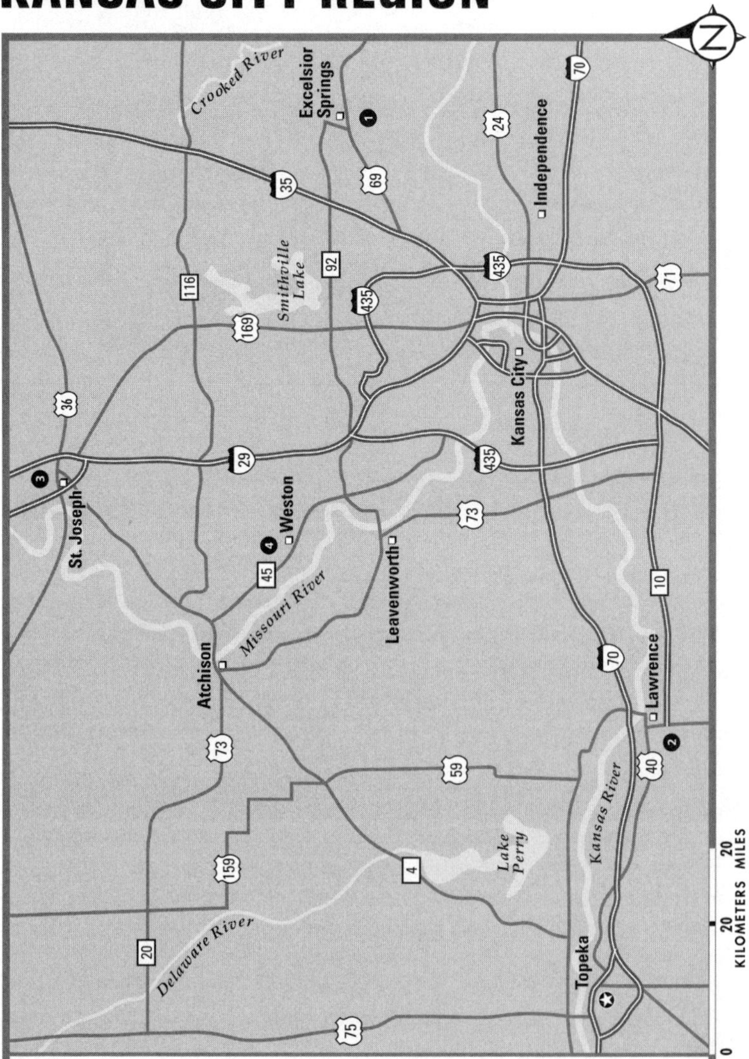

N

Crooked River

Excelsior Springs

1

24

Independence

70

35

69

Smithville Lake

92

435

435

71

116

169

Kansas City

36

29

Weston

4

73

45

Leavenworth

St. Joseph

3

Missouri River

10

Atchison

70

Lawrence

73

59

40

2

159

4

Lake Perry

Kansas River

20

Delaware River

Topeka

75

20   20
KILOMETERS   MILES

0

Day Trips

1 Excelsior Springs, Missouri
2 Lawrence, Kansas
3 St. Joseph, Missouri
4 Weston, Missouri

Haskell Indian Nations University

The University of Kansas isn't the only institution of higher learning in Lawrence. Haskell Indian Nations University (south of downtown on 23rd Street) is the only intertribal university for Native Americans in the United States. Opened in 1884 as an elementary school, the school now offers two-year programs in liberal arts, science, and business, as well as a bachelor's degree in elementary education. The 320-acre campus is a National Landmark and contains 12 sites listed in the National Register. Campus walking maps are available from the Visitors Information Center across the Kansas River from downtown Lawrence.

Fe, New Mexico: John Muir Publications, 1998). The town also features venues such as the **Lawrence Arts Center**, housed in the 1904 Carnegie Library building at the corner of 9th and Vermont (Mon–Fri 9–5, Sat 9–3, closed Sun). The Lawrence Art Guild, the annual Indian Art Show, and Roy's Gallery—among other places—also provide ample opportunities to experience art.

Actually, Lawrence's downtown is a work of art. A classic main-street setting, Massachusetts Street between the Kansas River and South Park affords prime strolling opportunities. Antiques shops, funky clothing boutiques, and bookstores sit tooth-by-jowl with popular hangouts like the **Eldridge Hotel**, which still welcomes guests in its turn-of-the-century rooms; **Teller's**, an elegant restaurant in a restored bank building; and the **Free State Brewery**, one of the first brew pubs in the Midwest, and certainly among the most beloved.

Outdoorsy types will want to try the hiking, biking, and *volkswalk* trails along the **Kansas or "Kaw" River** in Lawrence. Trails snake along a 10-mile stretch on one side of the riverfront and, opposite, along the levee. Other trails wind through town, but remember that Lawrence's hills may leave you puffing. You can get a map showing walkways and bike paths at the **Visitors Information Center** in the historic Union Pacific Depot (across the river from downtown) or at the Parks and Recreation office at 6 E. 6th Street.

Three miles southwest of Lawrence, **Clinton Lake** lures those who want to boat, swim, fish, hike, or camp within its 7,000 acres. The marina at **Clinton State Park** offers complete facilities for boating and fishing, including rentals and licenses (go west on 23rd Street, then follow the signs).

Shoppers will appreciate Lawrence's two factory outlet malls. The older mall, **Lawrence Riverfront Factory Outlets**, just north of downtown on the banks of the Kansas River, features some 50 stores, including Bass, Mikasa, and J. Crew. The newer option, **Tanger Factory Outlet Center**, is just south of I-70. Its stores include Adolfo II, Liz Claiborne, and Reebok.

Getting there: You can drive to Lawrence on I-70 or take I-435 in Kansas City, then continue west on Highway 10. I-70 becomes a toll road at Bonner Springs, so expect to pay a few dollars if you take that route.

Day Trip: Excelsior Springs, Missouri

Distance from Kansas City: 25 miles or about 30 minutes by car

Some folks might say that Excelsior Springs is a Kansas City suburb; certainly enough people commute the 25 miles to work downtown. But this charming burg looks more like it was plucked out of the 1940s and dropped intact into the Heartland. Soaring elm and oak trees cover the steep hills that surround the town; quaint storefronts line the narrow streets.

In the 1940s, people such as Franklin Roosevelt and Harry Truman used to venture to **Excelsior Springs** for its healing waters. **Siloam Springs**, which bubbles up from under the mountain of the same name, is the only natural source of iron-manganese water in the United States. In all, five specific mineral waters are found here, more than in any other location in North America or Europe.

Although the mineral waters had long been revered by American Indians for their medicinal qualities, Excelsior Springs' town fathers discovered them shortly after they incorporated their city in 1880. In 1888, the Elms Hotel opened its doors and quickly became the place for healthful soaking. Truman was lapping up the Elms' healing powers himself the night he was elected president in 1948.

Over the years, however, Truman's favorite spa had fallen into disrepair. In mid-1996, a new owner set about renovating the historic hotel and, when it reopened two years later—after an $8-million overhaul—the five-story hotel had become a stunningly elegant property. Now called the **Elms Resort and Spa**, this lodging boasts an attentive staff trained by former Ritz-Carlton executives, as well as 153 freshly refurbished rooms, 22 of them in the Elms Club on the top level. Guests enter with a key, and a

TIP

Golfers will want to try the Excelsior Springs Golf Club, an old English-style club built in 1915, which makes it one of the oldest courses in the region. Set on Excelsior Springs' eastern boundary—next to the Municipal Airport in Ray County—the 18-hole course offers a full-service pro shop and a clubhouse that was built around an original 1825 log cabin. For more information, call 816/637-3731.

concierge sees to their needs. Food and beverage buffets are available all day, encompassing continental breakfast, luncheon hors d'oeuvres, afternoon tea, social hour cocktails and appetizers, and after-dinner cordials with petit fours. Appropriately, the Elms offers spa services such as Swiss and Vichy showers; mud, aloe, and seaweed algae wraps; and a variety of massages. A new fine-dining restaurant, a family restaurant, a smoking lounge, and a bistro off the new, bell-shaped pool complete the amenities (Regent and Elms Blvd.; 816/630-2141).

Excelsior Springs also sprouted a plush new inn in 1996, after Bruce and Anne Libowitz purchased and refurbished a 1915 brick mansion set between two crescent ponds on 22.5 acres. There, at the **Inn at Crescent Lake**, the couple offers eight rooms with private baths in peaceful surroundings that include a pool, tennis courts, walking trails, and fishing in the summer. A corporate executive and an attorney, the Libowitzes met at the French Culinary Institute in New York, where each was launching a new career in cuisine. Their delectable three-course dinners are available each night for an additional $35 (1261 St. Louis Ave.; 816/ 630-6745).

Healing waters have long been popular in Excelsior Springs. Witness, for example, the historic **Hall of Waters**, built in 1937 to be the finest and most complete health resort in America. Inside you'll find a swimming pool, water-bottling facility, and the world's longest water bar. You can still get a massage, salt rub, or hot mineral water bath and steam in the cavernous art deco building now on the National Historic Register (201 E. Broadway; Mon–Fri 8–5; free admission to the building, fees for spa services).

Four miles north of Excelsior Springs on Highway 69, you'll come to **Watkins Mill State Park**, one of the most scenic state parks in Missouri. Within this 1,000-acre area are walking and biking trails, fishing, swimming, camping, picnic shelters, and the 100-acre Williams Creek Lake. The park also includes **Watkins Woolen Mill State Historic Site**, the country's only nineteenth-century textile factory with its original machinery still intact. Built by Waltus Watkins in 1861, the three-story mill and factory spun wool into yarn, then turned it into cloth and blankets. Watkins opened at the right time: He did a booming business during the Civil War. Next door, you can visit Watkins' elegant home, built in 1850, as well as the Mt. Vernon Church

(1871) and Franklin School (1856). Tours Mon–Sat 10–4; winter, Sun 11–4; summer, Sun noon–6.

Getting there: *Go north on I-35; take Highway 69 and exit at Excelsior Springs.*

Day Trip: Weston, Missouri

Distance from Kansas City: 40 miles or about 45 minutes by car

Back in 1837, Weston's first settlers discovered that the rich black soil bordering the Missouri River was perfect for growing the hemp and tobacco from their native Virginia, Kentucky, and Tennessee. By 1853, Weston was the second largest port in Missouri; steamboats plied the waters, carrying the town's two big moneymakers to market. Today you can still see evidence of Weston's booming days. More than 100 antebellum buildings and homes have been preserved within a 22-block area in and around downtown Weston, now designated a National Historic District.

But Weston wasn't frozen in time. The downtown area has become a haven for artists, antiques dealers, retailers, and restaurateurs, who've filled the four-block stretch with plentiful places to prowl. The **Missouri Bluffs Boutique and Gallery**, for example, features an eclectic mix of apparel and accessories. Nearby, the **Avalon Cafe** is set in an antebellum home once called White Lace. **O'Malley's Pub** serves its Irish libations in the limestone cellars of the old Weston Brewing Company, which is once again producing suds, and in its restaurant, serving meals that range from a Celtic breakfast to an 1842-style supper. **Pirtle's Winery** has a tasting room and shop in a cavernous 1867 German church. The **McCormick Country Store**, an outlet for **McCormick Distilling Co.**, pays tribute to Weston resident Benjamin J. Holladay, who learned that the natural limestone spring water flowing through the area was the secret to creating fine whiskey. Up on a slight hill, visitors flock to the cozy, fine-dining experience set in an 1845 home called **The Vineyards**.

For those who want to learn more about Weston's past, the **Weston Historical Museum** displays artifacts and photos from Weston's glory days

T I P

At least five charming bed-and-breakfast options await Weston visitors, which makes the Missouri River town a popular weekend getaway for Kansas Citians. The Inn at Weston Landing (Short and Welt Streets) offers four rooms in an 1842 building that was once the Weston Royal Brewing Company. The Hatchery dates from 1845 and has four rooms with private baths (618 Short Street).

Midwest Living magazine named Weston one of the best towns in the Midwest in which to hunt for quality antiques. Start your search on Main Street at Tobacco Road Antiques, Bo Jingles, or the Painted Lady. The Old Brewery Antiques Mall (500 Welt Street) is one block east of Main, behind City Hall.

in the mid-nineteenth century (601 Main St.; Tue–Sat 1–4; Sun 1:30–5; free). The **Herbert Bonnell Museum** depicts life in the late 1800s, including a farmhouse, outbuildings, and tools (May–Oct weekends 1–5; free).

One of the best antebellum homes open to the public once belonged to Colonel James A. Price and his wife, Russella Warner Price. Russella was the great-granddaughter of Daniel Boone, while husband James was Robert E. Lee's cousin. Built in 1857, the home was occupied until the couple's last descendant passed away in 1991; the **Price-Loyles House** still contains nearly everything the family owned through five generations (718 Spring St.; Fri and Sat 10–5; tours available other times).

One mile south of Weston on Highway 45, **Weston Bend State Park** comprises 1,133 acres of wooded hillsides, walking and biking trails, camping, and picnic areas. Adjacent to the Missouri River, these native lands are where the Sac, Fox, and Kansa Indians once hunted game. The old Leavenworth Road at the rear of the park provides panoramic views of the Missouri.

Weston is filled with romantic bed-and-breakfast inns for those who want to spend a night there, including the **Inn at Weston Landing** (Short St. at Welt, 816/640-5788), **Benner House** (645 Main St., 816/640-2616), **The Hatchery** (618 Short St., 816/640-5700), and the **Lemon Tree** (407 Washington St., 816/386-5367).

Getting there: *Take I-29 north, then go west on Highway 45.*

Day Trip: St. Joseph, Missouri

Distance from Kansas City: 60 miles or about 1 hour by car
St. Joseph dates from 1826, when Joseph Robidoux established an Indian trading post on these bluffs overlooking the Missouri River. The town grew into a major trade center; in 1843, the Frenchman incorporated the town and named it after his patron saint. You can see where the town's founder lived by visiting the restored homes at the **Robidoux Row Museum** (3rd and Poulin; May–Sept Tue–Fri 10–4, Oct–Apr noon–4, weekends 1–4).

St. Joseph's ties are surely with the West: The town outfitted thousands of forty-niners when gold was discovered in California. But St. Joseph's most famous link westward came just prior to the Civil War, when

Robidoux Row Museum, p. 211

the Pony Express was born. Indeed, history buffs will want to check out St. Joseph's **Pony Express National Memorial**, the birthplace of the famous delivery service and one of 13 museums within the city. The memorial honors the company's founders and the hardy riders (led by Johnny Fry and his pony, Sylph) who saddled up and lit out for Sacramento—nearly 2,000 miles west—on April 3, 1860 (914 Penn St; Mon–Sat 9–5, Sun 1–5, open an hour later June–Sept).

Coincidentally, that same date 22 years later marks the central event of another St. Joseph landmark. It was April 3, 1882, when Bob Ford gunned down his fellow gang member, the infamous Jesse James, in what's now known as the **Jesse James Home Museum** (12th and Penn Sts.; Mon–Sat 10–4, Sun 1–4, one hour later June–Aug). Other museums also capture pieces of St. Joseph's past. An internationally famous Native American collection appears at the **St. Joseph Museum** (1100 Charles; Mon–Sat 9–5, Sun 1–5); and the **Knea-Von Black Archive** features two floors of local and national black history exhibits, from a simulated underground railroad to a 1920s kitchen (1901 Messanie; by appointment, 816/233-6211).

St. Joseph also offers wonders of the art world, thanks to 12 women

TRIVIA

The Kemper name in St. Joseph's Albrecht-Kemper Museum and in Kansas City's Kemper Museum of Contemporary of Art indeed refers to the same family. Along with his family's foundations, R. Crosby Kemper, head of Kansas City's United Missouri Bank, is a huge arts patron who has directed millions to the arts in both communities.

Like Kansas Citians, St. Joseph residents approved riverboat gambling several years ago. And in the same fashion as its neighbors downriver, the St. Jo Frontier Casino doesn't actually ply the Missouri. Instead, gamblers stand nearly solid-ground steady before the blackjack, craps, video poker, and slot machines on board. Open daily; "cruise" times vary.

with a passion for art who founded the St. Joseph Art League in 1913. Today the **Albrecht-Kemper Museum of Art**, boasting a new 21,000-square-foot wing, houses one of the Midwest's most diverse collections of eighteenth-, nineteenth-, and twentieth-century American art. Visitors can see colonial portraiture, Albert Bierstadt's rugged landscapes, and the paintings of George Caleb Bingham (2818 Frederick; Tue–Sat 10–4, Sun 1–4).

Shoppers head to St. Joe for the plethora of antiques stores, including the **Robidoux Landing Antique Mall** (720 Felix) and the **Penn Street Square** (122 Penn). **Howard's Church Artisan's Studios & Gallery** was an 1880 church where Jesse James once attended services; the renovated house of worship now provides a venue for the area's fine artists to create, display, and sell their work (12th and Penn). And the **Stetson Hat Factory Outlet** (3601 S. Leonard Rd.) lets shoppers buy its famous headgear at direct-from-the-manufacturer prices.

Getting there: *Take I-29 north, then follow signs to downtown.*

EMERGENCY PHONE NUMBERS

Police/ Ambulance/Fire, 911
Poison Control Center
   Missouri, 816/234-3430
   Kansas, 913/588-6633
Crime Stoppers of Kansas City
   816/474-8477
Mental Health Crisis Line
   800/955-8339

HOSPITALS AND EMERGENCY MEDICAL CENTERS

Ask a Nurse
Emergency Medical Advice
913/676-7777

Children's Mercy Hospital
2401 Gillham Rd., Kansas City
816/234-3400

Independence Regional
Health Center
1509 W. Truman Rd., Independence
816/836-8100

Liberty Hospital
2525 Glenn W. Hendren Dr., Liberty
816/781-7200

Shawnee Mission Medical Center
9100 W. 74th St., Overland Park
913/676-2000

St. Luke's Hospital
4401 Wornall Rd., Kansas City
816/932-6200

University of Kansas Medical Center
3901 Rainbow Blvd., Kansas City, KS
913/588-5000

RECORDED INFORMATION

Kansa City Star Information
816/889-7817

Road Conditions
800/585-7623

Time and Temperature
816/844-1212

POST OFFICES

Kansas City Post Office
315 W. Pershing
Kansas City, MO 64108
816/374-9180

Shawnee Mission Post Office
6029 Broadmoor
Mission, KS 66202
913/831-5350

VISITOR INFORMATION

Brochures, maps, and other materials are available from the Downtown Information Center in the City Center Square (1100 Main St., Suite 2550) and from the Plaza Visitor Information Center at the Clock Tower (222 W. 47th St., across from FAO Schwarz). For recorded information on events and activities, call 816/691-3800.

Greater Kansas City
Convention & Visitors Bureau
816/221-5242

Kansas City, Kansas
Convention & Visitors Bureau
913/321-5800

Metropolitan Transportation
Services, Inc. (MTSI)
816/471-6050

Overland Park
Convention & Visitors Bureau
913/491-0123

Kansas City Internet Addresses
http://www.kansascity.com
http://www.experiencekc.com

CAR RENTAL

Avis
800/831-2847

Budget Car & Truck Rental
800/527-0700

Enterprise Rent-A-Car
800/325-8007

Hertz
800/654-3131

Thrifty
800/367-2277

DISABLED ACCESS INFORMATION

Governor's Committee on Disability
816/373-0353

Johnson County Accessibility
913/894-8811

MULTICULTURAL RESOURCES

Black Chamber of Commerce of
Greater Kansas City
816/474-9901

Hispanic Chamber of Commerce of
Greater Kansas City
816/472-6767

Jewish Federation of Greater
Kansas City
913/327-8100

Women's Chamber of Commerce of
Greater Kansas City
913/262-5190

OTHER COMMUNITY ORGANIZATIONS

Gay/Lesbian Information
816/737-0700

Mid-America Arts Alliance
816/421-1388

SeniorLink
816/753-4474

BABYSITTING/CHILDCARE

Most major hotels can arrange for reputable babysitting services in your hotel room. In addition, the following companies provide child care at your location:

A-1 Tiny Tots Pre-School & Sitter
Service
816/254-4433

TLC Caregivers
816/444-6400

CITY MEDIA

General Newspapers
Kansas City Star, 816/234-4141
    (www.kcstar.com)
Kansas City Kansan, 913/371-4300
Sun Newspapers, 913/381-1010

Business News
College Boulevard News
    913/381-5755
Johnson County Business Times
    913/649-8778

Kansas City Business Journal
816/421-5900
(www.amcity.com/kansascity)

Entertainment/
Alternative News
Pitch Weekly, 816/561-6061
(www.pitch.com)

Ethnic News
Dos Mundos (Latino), 816/221-4747
Kansas City Call (African
American), 816/371-5400
Kansas City Globe (African
American), 816/531-5253
Kansas City Jewish Chronicle
913/648-4620

Magazines
Ingram's, 816/842-9994
Kansas City Magazine, 816/421-4111

Radio Stations
WDAF 610 AM, country
KMBZ 980 AM, news, talk, sports
KPHN 1190 AM, CNN news, talk
KFEZ 1340 AM, adult standards
KPRT 1590 AM, gospel
KCMW 90.9 FM, public affairs,
jazz, classical
KCMO 94.9 FM, oldies
KXTR 96.5 FM, classical
KUDL 98.1 FM, adult comtemporary
KPRS 103.3 FM, adult urban
contemporary
KBEQ 104.3 FM, country
KCIY 106.5, smooth jazz
KNRX 107.3 FM, new rock

Television Stations
ABC, Channel 9 (KMBC)
CBS, Channel 5 (KCTV)
FOX, Channel 4 (WDAF)
NBC, Channel 41 (KSHB)
PBS, Channel 19 (KCPT)
UPN, Channel 29 (KCWB)
WB, Channel 62 (KSMO)

BOOKSELLERS

Anderson's Bookshop
5429 Antioch Center Mall
Kansas City
816/454-7677

B. Dalton Booksellers
11391 W. 95th St., Overland Park
913/888-1416
5600 E. Bannister Rd., Kansas City
816/966-0014
400 NW Barry Rd., Kansas City
816/436-5250
2020 Independence Center,
Independence
816/795-8210
8600 Ward Pkwy., Kansas City
816/333-2047
3925 W. 69th Terr., Prairie Village
913/362-6772

Barnes & Noble Booksellers
420 W. 47th St., Kansas City
816/753-1313
4751 W. 117th St., Leawood
913/491-4535
19120 E. 39th St., Independence
816/795-9878
8121 NW Roanridge, Kansas City
816/741-8330

Bookshop at Brookside
116 W. 63rd St., Kansas City
816/444-8187

Bookshoppe at Town Pavilion
1111 Main St., Kansas City
816/472-6657

Borders Books & Music
9108 Metcalf Ave., Overland Park
913/642-3642
12055 Metcalf Ave., Overland Park
913/663-2356

Brentano's Bookstore
4715 Johnson Dr., Mission
913/384-5236

The Complete Traveler
7321 W. 80th St., Overland Park
913/648-1560

Foozles
20320 W. 151st St., Olathe
913/393-2063

Global Connections
4201A Noland Rd., Independence
816/373-2452

Kansas Union Bookstore
University of Kansas
Kansas Union, Level 2, Lawrence
913/864-4640

Last Chapter Bookshoppes
11128 Antioch, Overland Park
913/339-6616
12024 W. 63rd St., Shawnee
913/631-3184

Rainy Day Books
2706 W. 53rd St., Fairway
913/384-3126

Raven Bookstore
8 E. 7th St., Lawrence
913/749-3300

Reading Reptile Books and Toys for Young Mammals
4120 Pennsylvania St., Kansas City
816/753-0441

Waldenbooks
5600 E. Bannister Rd., Kansas City
816/761-6755
9641 Metcalf Ave., Overland Park
913/642-2755
2450 Grand Ave., Kansas City
816/474-8774
1042 Independence Center
Independence
816/795-8077
11689 W. 95th St., Overland Park
913/888-3367
400 NW Barry Rd., Kansas City
816/436-5566
8600 Ward Pkwy., Kansas City
816/523-4580
4200 Blue Ridge Blvd., Kansas City
816/737-2584

Waldenbooks & More
7311 Quivira, Shawnee
913/962-1428

INDEX

You'll Feel like a Local When You Travel with Guides from John Muir Publications

CiTY·SMART™ GUIDEBOOKS

Pick one for your favorite city: *Albuquerque, Anchorage, Austin, Calgary, Charlotte, Chicago, Cincinnati, Cleveland, Denver, Indianapolis, Kansas City, Memphis, Milwaukee, Minneapolis/St. Paul, Nashville, Pittsburgh, Portland, Richmond, Salt Lake City, San Antonio, St. Louis, Tampa/St. Petersburg, Tucson*

Guides for kids 6 to 10 years old about what to do, where to go, and how to have fun in: *Atlanta, Austin, Boston, Chicago, Cleveland, Denver, Indianapolis, Kansas City, Miami, Milwaukee, Minneapolis/St. Paul, Nashville, Portland, San Francisco, Seattle, Washington D.C.*

TRAVEL✦SMART®

Trip planners with select recommendations to: *Alaska, American Southwest, Carolinas, Colorado, Deep South, Eastern Canada, Florida Gulf Coast, Hawaii, Illinois/Indiana, Kentucky/Tennessee, Maryland/Delaware, Michigan, Minnesota/Wisconsin, Montana/Wyoming/Idaho, New England, New Mexico, New York State, Northern California, Ohio, Pacific Northwest, Pennsylvania/New Jersey, South Florida and the Keys, Southern California, Texas, Utah, Virginias, Western Canada*

Rick Steves' GUIDES

See *Europe Through the Back Door* and take along guides to: *France, Belgium & the Netherlands; Germany, Austria & Switzerland; Great Britain & Ireland; Italy; Russia & the Baltics; Scandinavia; Spain & Portugal; London; Paris;* or the *Best of Europe*

ADVENTURES IN NATURE

Plan your next adventure in: *Alaska, Belize, Caribbean, Costa Rica, Guatemala, Honduras, Mexico*

JMP travel guides are available at your favorite bookstores. For a FREE catalog or to place a mail order, call: 800-888-7504.

John Muir Publications P.O. Box 613 ✦ Santa Fe, NM 87504

ABOUT THE AUTHORS

Michael J. Flynn and Linda Kephart Flynn are a Kansas City–based writing and editing team whose work has appeared in publications such as *Hemispheres*, *Endless Vacation*, *Modern Bride*, *EXPO*, and the *San Francisco Chronicle*. Both Flynns are contributing editors at *Telecommute*, a national magazine for teleworkers, and have been co-editors of *Kansas City Bride & Groom* and *Vanguard Discoveries*, a Kansas City–based in-flight magazine. Michael was born and raised in the Kansas City area and met Linda, an Arizona native, when they were editors at  *Discover Hawaii* magazine in Honolulu. They now live and work in a three-story, 87-year-old house just south of the Country Club Plaza.

JOHN MUIR PUBLICATIONS and its City•Smart Guidebook authors are dedicated to building community awareness within City•Smart cities. We are proud to work with LIFT (Literacy Investment For Tomorrow) as we publish this guide to Kansas City .

LIFT (Literacy Investment For Tomorrow) is a private, not-for-profit 501(c)(3) organization serving Missouri's Literacy Resource Center. Established in 1988, LIFT develops and promotes resources to increase the literacy skills of Missourians so that all individuals can reach their personal and economic potential. LIFT maintains offices in Kansas City and St. Louis to do the following:

- provide training, technical assistance, accessible resources, and computer technology to adult and early childhood educators
- establish effective collaborations among literacy providers and supporting agencies
- advocate for literacy programs among policy makers, business leaders, and the general public

For more information, please contact:
LIFT-Missouri
1740 W. 92 St.
Kansas City, MO 64114
phone: 816/363-7648
literacy line: 800/729-4443

LIFT-MISSOURI